KU-205-848

Approaches to Social Enquiry

Advancing Knowledge

Second Edition

Norman Blaikie

polity

Copyright © Norman Blaikie 2007

The right of Norman Blaikie to be identified as Author of this Work has been asserted in accordance with the UK Copyright, Designs and Patents Act 1988.

First published in 2007 by Polity Press

Polity Press
65 Bridge Street
Cambridge CB2 1UR, UK

Polity Press
350 Main Street
Malden, MA 02148, USA

All rights reserved. Except for the quotation of short passages for the purpose of criticism and review, no part of this publication may be reproduced, stored in a retrieval system, or transmitted, in any form or by any means, electronic, mechanical, photocopying, recording or otherwise, without the prior permission of the publisher.

ISBN-10: 0-7456-3448-6
ISBN-13: 978-07456-3448-7
ISBN-10: 0-7456-3449-4 (pb)
ISBN-13: 978-07456-3449-4 (pb)

A catalogue record for this book is available from the British Library.

Typeset in 10 on 12 pt Sabon
by Servis Filmsetting Ltd, Manchester
Printed and bound in India by Replika Press Pvt Ltd.

The publisher has used its best endeavours to ensure that the URLs for external websites referred to in this book are correct and active at the time of going to press. However, the publisher has no responsibility for the websites and can make no guarantee that a site will remain live or that the content is or will remain appropriate.

Every effort has been made to trace all copyright holders, but if any have been inadvertently overlooked the publishers will be pleased to include any necessary credits in any subsequent reprint or edition.

For further information on Polity, visit our website: www.polity.co.uk

Approaches to Social Enquiry

LIVERPOOL JMU LIBRARY

3 1111 01162 8714

For Catherine

Contents

Figures, Tables and Boxes

Preface to the First Edition

While this book is primarily a textbook for students of social science, it is also intended for both novice and experienced social researchers. The issues covered lie at the heart of the social science enterprise and must be addressed if progress is to be made beyond the present uncertain state.

In addition to reflecting on my own research experience, the book has emerged from nearly twenty-five years of teaching courses in philosophy of science and social science, methodology of social research, and quantitative and qualitative research methods, at both undergraduate and postgraduate levels, to students from many disciplines. I came to the conclusion very early on that an understanding of ontological and epistemological assumptions, of logical and methodological issues, was important if students were to avoid perpetuating the mindless and sometimes sophisticated empiricism that frequently passed for social research.

While the theoretical and methodological issues have changed during this period, the fundamental philosophical questions have remained. The growing recognition of paradigmatic pluralism has made the need to address these issues more urgent. However, this task is doubly difficult for both students and their lecturers; not only are the issues complex, with a variety of positions adopted and advocated, but there is also a vast literature that needs to be covered to deal with them. Few texts, if any, come anywhere near resolving these difficulties.

The issues involved in these questions are likely to challenge taken-for-granted beliefs and assumptions, to require students to examine critically both their ideas about research and the core elements of their worldview. In my experience, they have found this process to be, simultaneously, both disturbing and stimulating. With very few exceptions, students have told me that the effort and discomfort has been well worthwhile. Most have found the experience to be of vital importance to their intellectual development; and it has had a significant and lasting benefit for their capacity to undertake useful research and for their understanding of social science in general. I hope this book will make the task more manageable.

While the book spans a wide range of positions in philosophy, social theory and methodology, it is necessarily selective in the writers discussed. I have chosen to review and critique a range of approaches to social enquiry rather than advocate a specific approach, but I suspect my own preferences will be in evidence. Readers are encouraged to evaluate these approaches, and their accompanying research strategies, and to choose an approach which suits their purpose, prejudices and personality.

I am indebted to the many students who have travelled this path with me over the years. They have provided me with the need to grapple with these issues, they have forced me to reflect on my own position, they have taught me a great deal, and they have confirmed that the task is necessary and worthwhile.

Norman Blaikie

Preface to the Second Edition

It is now fourteen years since the first edition of *Approaches to Social Enquiry* was published. As a consequence of persistent demand for it over this period, and further developments in the field, a revision is required. In using the first edition in a number of courses, and with a wide variety of students, I found that the material was easier to digest if presented in a different order. The first edition began with reviews, and then critiques, of both classical and contemporary approaches to social enquiry and then outlined and discussed four logics of enquiry – research strategies – that are associated with these approaches. It concluded with a discussion of methodological issues and choices.

The revised structure reverses this sequence. It begins with a discussion of the major choices and dilemmas in social enquiry (chapters 1 and 2) and then elaborates the four research strategies (chapter 3). This is followed by a discussion of the classical and contemporary approaches to social enquiry (chapters 4 and 5) – now called research paradigms. The final chapter reviews the research paradigms in terms of their ontological and epistemological assumptions, critiques each paradigm, and returns to the methodological dilemmas introduced in chapter 2.

The original theme – the relationship between the logics of enquiry in the natural and social sciences – has been supplemented with another more basic one that was only implicit in the first edition – how knowledge can be advanced in the social sciences. This change also supports the restructuring of the original content, most of which has been retained, and requires the addition of some new sections. These include a review of fundamental choices and dilemmas in social research, a discussion of postmodernism and social research, and the inclusion of phenomenology, ethnomethodology and complexity theory. At the same time, the section on feminist social enquiry has been revised and expanded. In the course of the revision, the material has been made more accessible, many more headings have been inserted, new summaries have been added at the ends of sections in the later chapters, and there is now a point summary at the end of each chapter. Empirical examples have been included where appropriate.

The process of restructuring the original content has been like dismantling a house and rearranging the parts in a new configuration. At the same time, some additions have been made, the initial deficiencies rectified, and more modern fittings and finishes added. On first inspection, the house may not be recognizable, but closer examination will show that most of the original components are still there.

The new structure has allowed me to follow some pedagogical principles that should make the material easier to grasp and digest. Key ideas are first introduced in a simplified form and are then revisited, perhaps more than once, in greater detail and depth, and in different contexts. In the final chapter, ideas that have been dealt with sequentially earlier are compared and evaluated. As the book presents the reader with a developmental process, the chapters are best read in sequence.

Since the first edition was published, I have taught many more courses, in both Australia and Malaysia, using it as a text. Along the way, I wrote *Designing Social Research* as a companion text. I am indebted to Ong Beng Kok, for the way his enthusiasm for the first edition stimulated me to undertake this revision; to Erica Hallebone, for encouraging her students to read the first edition, as well as *Designing Social Research*, and for her helpful comments on a draft of parts of this edition; to Ray Pawson and Malcolm Williams for assistance with one of the empirical examples; and to the invaluable and generous comments that two anonymous reviewers provided on various drafts; and to the University of Auckland for full use of library facilities.

Norman Blaikie

Introduction

For the past fifty years, the social sciences have been plagued by theoretical and methodological controversies. The demise of structural functionalism in American social theory, and the emergence of new philosophies of science and social science, have been followed by a period of dispute between a variety of theoretical perspectives and approaches to social enquiry. The issues and dilemmas that have been exposed by these contemporary controversies are not new; their ingredients can be traced back to philosophical traditions that were established in the nineteenth century, traditions that have their roots in antiquity. What *is* new is that social scientists can no longer ignore these issues as being the pastime of philosophers. Social enquiry has lost its innocence. Social researchers must now face up to, and deal with, a range of choices and dilemmas that lead to the use of fundamentally different research strategies and have the possibility of producing different research outcomes.

The social sciences are now characterized by a diversity of approaches to social enquiry, and there is an extensive literature on their strengths and weaknesses. The task of coming to grips with this literature, from the philosophy of science and social science, and from social theory and methodology, is a daunting one for students of social science and novice researchers. A common solution to this problem is to adopt one theoretical perspective or paradigm uncritically. Another is to combine, perhaps unwittingly and unreflectively, components of various approaches. While it may have been possible to sustain such behaviour in the past, it is no longer defensible. More sophisticated solutions are required.

This second edition, like the first, spans a wide range of positions in philosophy, social theory and methodology, and provides a comprehensive and critical review of alternative approaches to social enquiry that social researchers are likely to encounter. It also outlines four major research strategies that are associated with these approaches, either singly or in combination. A vast range of literature is reviewed to provide the reader with a basis for evaluating the relative strengths and weaknesses of these approaches and research strategies for particular research projects, and to facilitate the making of informed and defensible methodological choices.

The structure of this second edition is designed to complement and dovetail with my *Designing Social Research* (2000). The common starting point is a research problem that needs to be translated into one or more research questions. This is followed by a choice from amongst the four research strategies in terms of which one or ones are regarded as providing the best way of answering the research question(s). This decision is likely to be influenced by the research paradigm or paradigms with which a researcher prefers to work, or which is/are regarded more pragmatically as providing appropriate ontological and epistemological assumptions. However, there is no necessary association between the research strategies and paradigms. Whereas some research strategies fit closely with certain research paradigms, for others the association is much looser. And if more than one research strategy is required to answer a set of research questions, it may be necessary to work with more than one research paradigm. It is the elaboration of these paradigms particularly that extends the focus of *Designing Social Research*.

To conclude this Introduction, some of the central and, perhaps, less familiar concepts are elaborated. The fields of scholarly endeavour covered in this book carry a baggage of diverse concepts that have varied and multiple uses. Writers in these fields not only use different concepts to refer to the same basic ideas, but when they use the same concepts, they are also inclined to give them different meanings. It has therefore been necessary to adopt a consistent vocabulary. Where possible, I have endeavoured to follow dominant traditions in the literature. However, some concepts are different from those used by other writers, and I have had to invent or adapt some new ones as well. Therefore, the reader needs to be alert to these differences in the usage and meaning of concepts and categories, and not confuse the ones used here with those of other writers. To help with this task, a brief discussion of the key concepts used in this book, as well as less familiar concepts or meanings of concepts, is included. As the significance of these concepts may not be evident at this point in the book, it may be necessary to refer back to this section later.

Five key concepts are used: research question, research strategy, research paradigm, ontology and epistemology. There are three types of research questions, four types of research strategies, ten types of research paradigms, six ontological assumptions and six epistemological assumptions.

Research Questions. The formal expressions of intellectual puzzles. The vehicles through which a research problem is made researchable. The choice of one or more research questions gives research focus and direction, delimits its boundaries, makes the research project manageable, and anticipates a successful outcome. In short, a research project is built on the foundation of its research questions.

There are three main types of research questions: 'what', 'why' and 'how'. 'What' questions seek descriptions, 'why' questions seek understanding or explanations, and 'how' questions are concerned with intervention and problem solving. (See chapter 1.)

Research Strategies. Logics of enquiry: processes required to answer research questions, to solve intellectual puzzles, to generate new knowledge. Each research strategy specifies a starting point, a series of steps and an end point.

There are four major research strategies: the *inductive, deductive, retroductive* and *abductive*. The research strategies are based on particular styles of reasoning. The notions of *inductive* and *deductive* reasoning are probably familiar, the former involving the movement from specific statements to general statements, and the latter movement from general statements to specific ones. In the context of social research, this means either generalizing from specific instances or cases, or testing general ideas against specific instances or cases (see pp. 56–82).

Retroductive and *abductive* reasoning are less familiar. Both concepts were used by Charles Peirce (1934), although the basic ideas can be traced back to Aristotle. However, I have adopted Roy Bhaskar's (1979) usage of 'retroduction' to refer to the use of reason and imagination to create a picture or model of the structures or mechanisms that are responsible for producing observed phenomena. The task is then to try to establish their existence. This logic involves moving back from observations to the creation of a possible explanation (see pp. 82–9). Abductive logic is also a creative process in which social scientific concepts and theories of social life are derived from social actors' everyday conceptualizations and understandings. While this idea is evident in a number of social scientific traditions, my view of abduction draws heavily on the work of Alfred Schütz (see pp. 88–104).

One way of distinguishing these logics of enquiry is to see *induction* and *deduction* as involving linear processes, the former being bottom up and the latter top down, and *retroduction* and *abduction* as involving much more complex processes that can be thought of as a rising spiral involving numerous iterations. These four research strategies are introduced in chapter 1 and elaborated in chapter 3.

This use of the concept 'research strategy' should not be confused with another common usage, which refers to methods of data gathering and/or analysis, such as survey research, participant observation, case studies and grounded theory. The choice of such methods has only a secondary role to play in answering research questions or advancing knowledge; they are subservient to the choice of a logic of enquiry.

Research Paradigms. Broad philosophical and theoretical traditions within which attempts to understand the social world are conducted. They provide different ways of making connections between ideas about the social world, the social experiences of people and the social world within which social life occurs. Research paradigms are also referred to as perspectives or theoretical perspectives, and I referred to them in the first edition as 'approaches to social enquiry' (see Blaikie 1993). This change implies that the title of the book now encompasses both research strategies and research paradigms. Ten research paradigms are elaborated and reviewed in chapters 4–6.

Differences between research paradigms can be traced to their particular ways of looking at the world as well as their ideas about how it can be understood, i.e. to their ontological and epistemological assumptions.

Ontological Assumptions. Ways of answering the question: 'What is the nature of social reality?' These assumptions are concerned with what exists, what it looks like, what units make it up, and how these units interact with each other. Six different types of ontological assumptions are discussed in chapter 1.

Epistemological Assumptions. Ways of answering the question: 'How can social reality be known?' Epistemology is concerned with the nature and scope of human knowledge, with what kinds of knowledge are possible, and with criteria for judging the adequacy of knowledge and for distinguishing between scientific and non-scientific knowledge. Six different types of epistemological assumptions are discussed in chapter 1.

In chapter 2, three preliminary views of the relationship between the natural and social sciences are discussed: *naturalism, negativism* and *historicism*. The concept *naturalism* has two main meanings. In this context, it refers to the view that the methods or, more particularly, the logics of enquiry used in the *natural* sciences can be used in the social sciences. The other usage of naturalism is concerned with the conduct of research in natural settings, where social life occurs naturally, as against contrived or experimental situations.

The use of *negativism* here may be my invention; it expresses the opposite view to naturalism, i.e. that natural scientific logics should not or cannot be used in the social sciences. In its extreme form, *negativism* identifies the view that a science of social life is impossible.

Naturalism is an element of one of the research paradigms known as Positivism. However, *negativism* entails different views from those expounded in Positivism; it is not an alternative paradigm to it. *Historicism* identifies a third position in which one natural scientific logic, of projecting future trends or states of affair from historical trends or patterns, is regarded as being appropriate in the social sciences. This logic has not been included with the four used in this book, as it is generally considered to be unscientific. There is no logic that makes it possible to predict future events with any certainty, as the conditions that produced historical trends may not apply in the future. Of course, it is worth noting that this logic is used extensively in some fields, such as economics, but with limited efficacy.

1

Major Choices in Social Enquiry

Introduction

Over the past century, a range of approaches to social enquiry have emerged, and a wide variety of research methods for collecting and analysing data have been developed, to advance knowledge of social life. Approaches to social enquiry are concerned with both the logics used to develop new knowledge – with the steps and procedures that this involves – and with philosophical and theoretical ideas and assumptions about what constitutes social reality and how knowledge of it can be produced. Research methods, on the other hand, are techniques that are used, within a particular approach, to generate and analyse data to describe or explain characteristics, patterns and processes in social life.

As very little attention is given in the social scientific literature to the logics available for generating new knowledge, this book concentrates on them and their philosophical and theoretical foundations. It does not deal with research methods *per se*.

Before a researcher can undertake social enquiry, a number of choices have to be made. These include:

- the research problem to be investigated;
- the research question or questions to be answered;
- the research strategy or strategies to be used to answer these questions;
- the posture to be adopted by the researcher towards the researched; and
- the research paradigm containing assumptions about reality and how it can be studied.

The first two of these choices depend mainly on the nature of the research being undertaken, and on practical considerations, but the last three are heavily influenced by theoretical and methodological commitments.

The choice of research strategy and posture poses a number of dilemmas for the social researcher. A dilemma is a choice for which there is no straightforward answer. That is, the appropriateness of each alternative has been both advocated and contested, with the result that the choice becomes more a matter of weighing up strengths and weaknesses in relation to a particular research problem.

However, researchers deal with these dilemmas in different ways, depending on their ideas about the nature of science and scientific knowledge, on the way they view the social world, and on the views and commitments of the social scientific community or communities to which they belong. In other words, these choices are more ideological than practical in nature (see Blaikie 2000 for a more detailed discussion of these choices). The remainder of the chapter deals with the range of these choices, while chapter 2 deals with some of the major dilemmas.

Research Problem

All social enquiry needs to address a research problem. The statement of the problem provides both a signpost for what will be studied and a set of boundary markers to delimit the territory to be covered. It points to what the research is about and where it will be conducted. Here is an example.

Some degree of long-term unemployment is a characteristic of modern capitalist societies, particularly when there are downturns in the economic cycle, new technologies replace certain categories of occupations, and companies relocate manufacturing to low-wage economies. Of course, at any time, some members of a population may choose a lifestyle that does not involve being in regular paid employment, and others may have a disability that prevents them from undertaking normal work. They are not the concern of this study. Rather, it is those who want to work, but who have been unable to find suitable employment for an extended period; that is the focus of this study. As most people need to earn a living through work in order both to survive and to have a satisfactory lifestyle, this situation is regarded as both a personal and a social problem.

Research on this problem could be given the following title:

The nature, causes and consequences of long-term unemployment.

Selecting a research problem is the first and most fundamental choice. However, to be researchable, a research problem has to be translated into one or more research questions.

Research Questions

Research Questions (RQs) are the foundations of all research; they make a research problem researchable.

Types of research questions

RQs are of three main types: 'what' questions, 'why' questions and 'how' questions.

- **What** questions require a descriptive answer; they are directed towards discovering and describing the characteristics of, and patterns in, some social phenomenon.

- **Why** questions ask for either the causes of, or the reasons for, the existence of characteristics and regularities in a particular phenomenon. They seek an understanding or explanation of the relationships between events, or within social activities and processes.
- **How** questions are concerned with bringing about change, with intervention and practical outcomes.

Examples

Here are examples of the three types of questions that could be used to address the research problem on long-term unemployment.

1 What kinds of people experience long-term unemployment?
2 What is it like to be unemployed for an extended period?
3 Why are these people unemployed?
4 How could they be re-employed?

Answering RQ 1 is the first stage of the research. The answer would provide a description of the characteristics of long-term unemployed people and, perhaps, patterns of association amongst these characteristics. RQ 2 explores the consequences of long-term unemployment on the unemployed person. We want to know what it is like for them, and how they cope with it. RQ 3 brings us to the crux of the problem. This is what welfare workers and policy makers want to know. While unemployed people will usually have some idea of why they are unemployed, answers to this RQ could also provide them with a bigger picture that could help them to regain employment. The final RQ seeks solutions to the problem. It is one thing to describe and explain unemployment; it is another to be able to reduce its level.

These RQs may look innocent enough, as their wording is straightforward. However, as we shall see, finding satisfactory answers can be rather complex. This research problem, and its RQs, will be used throughout the book to illustrate the philosophical, theoretical and methodological discussions.

Research questions in sequence

It is important to note that the three types of research questions form a sequence: 'what' questions normally precede 'why' questions, and 'why' questions normally precede 'how' questions. In other words, we need to know what is going on before we can explain it, and we need to know why something happens the way it does before we can be confident about introducing interventions to change it. The sequence also represents a hierarchy of difficulty; 'what' questions are generally easier to answer than 'why' questions, and 'how' questions can be the most challenging of the three.

It is not necessary for every research project to address all three types of RQs. Some may deal with only one or more 'what' questions. Others will take the next step and seek answers to 'why' questions. The pursuit of answers to 'how' questions is confined to applied research projects. Where limited or no research has been conducted on a topic, the first step will normally be to answer appropriate 'what' questions, before proceeding to 'why' or 'how' questions. However, in areas where adequate description of the problem is already available, a researcher may be able to proceed directly to answering one or more related 'why' questions. Similarly, if answers to both 'what' and 'why' questions exist already, the research may simply pose one or more 'how' questions. Therefore, whether a researcher sets out with all three types of RQs will depend on the nature of the research problem and the state of knowledge in the field. Nevertheless, the sequence implicit in answering these three types of questions remains.[1]

Research Strategies

The major task in designing a piece of social research is to work out how to answer the RQ(s). This involves much more than deciding which methods will be used to collect and analyse data. What is required is a procedure, a logic, for generating new knowledge. Research Strategies (RSs) are such logics; they provide a starting point and a set of steps by means of which 'what' and 'why' questions can be answered.

Following the choice of a research problem and RQs, the choice of a RS, or a combination of them, is the most important decision that a researcher must make. These RSs will be elaborated in detail in chapter 3. However, in order to discuss other choices, they need to be introduced here.

There are four distinct RSs: the Inductive, Deductive, Retroductive and Abductive. Each one provides a distinctly different way of answering RQs (see table 1.1).

Table 1.1   The logics of the four research strategies

	Inductive	*Deductive*	*Retroductive*	*Abductive*
Aim:	To establish universal generalizations to be used as pattern explanations	To test theories, to eliminate false ones and corroborate the survivor	To discover underlying mechanisms to explain observed regularities	To describe and understand social life in terms of social actors' motives and understanding
Start:	Accumulate observations or data	Identify a regularity to be explained	Document and model a regularity	Discover everyday lay concepts, meanings and motives
	Produce generalizations	Construct a theory and deduce hypotheses	Construct a hypothetical model of a mechanism	Produce a technical account from lay accounts
Finish:	Use these 'laws' as patterns to explain further observations	Test the hypotheses by matching them with data	Find the real mechanism by observation and/or experiment	Develop a theory and test it iteratively

Inductive research strategy

The Inductive RS starts with the collection of data, followed by data analysis, and then proceeds to derive generalizations using so-called inductive logic. The aim is to describe the characteristics of people and social situations, and then to determine the nature of the patterns of the relationships, or networks of relationships, between these characteristics. Once generalizations about characteristics and/or patterns have been established, some writers claim that they can be used to explain the occurrence of specific events by locating them within the established pattern. This RS is useful for answering 'what' questions, but is very limited in its capacity to answer 'why' questions satisfactorily.

Deductive research strategy

The Deductive RS adopts a very different starting point and works in the reverse order to the Inductive RS. It begins with a pattern, or regularity, that has already been discovered and established, and which begs an explanation. The researcher has to find or formulate a possible explanation, a theoretical argument for the existence of the regularity in the social phenomenon under consideration. The task is to test that theory by deducing one or more hypotheses from it, and then collect appropriate data. Should the data match the theory, some support is provided for its use, particularly if further tests produce similar results. However, if the data do not match the theory, then the theory must be either modified or rejected. Further testing of other candidate theories can then be undertaken. According to this RS, knowledge of the social world is advanced by means of trial and error processes. It is only appropriate for answering 'why' questions.

Retroductive research strategy

The Retroductive RS also starts with an observed regularity, but seeks a different type of explanation. This is achieved by locating the real underlying structure(s) or mechanism(s) that is (are) responsible for producing an observed regularity. To discover a previously unknown structure or mechanism, the researcher has first to construct a hypothetical model of it, and then proceed to try to establish its existence by observation and experiment. This may require the use of indirect methods, as the structure or mechanism may not be directly observable. The search is for evidence of the consequences of its existence. Should it exist, certain events can be expected to occur. Retroduction is a process of working back from data, to an explanation, by the use of creative imagination and analogy. This RS provides an alternative way of answering 'why' questions.

As we shall see in chapter 3, the Retroductive RS comes in two versions. One version locates explanations in social structures that are external to social actors, while the other version focuses on cognitive mechanisms and socially constructed rules for behaviour. To put this in another way, the former adopts a structuralist view of social life, and the latter a social constructionist view.

Abductive research strategy

The Abductive RS has a very different logic to the other three. The starting point is the social world of the social actors being investigated. The aim is to discover their constructions of reality, their ways of conceptualizing and giving meaning to their social world, their tacit knowledge. The main access a researcher has to these constructions is through the knowledge that social actors use in the production, reproduction and interpretation of the phenomenon under investigation. Their reality, the way they have constructed and interpreted their activities together, is embedded in their everyday language. Hence, the researcher has to enter their world in order to discover the motives and reasons that accompany social activities. The task is then to redescribe these actions and motives, and the situations in which they occur, in the technical language of social scientific discourse. Individual motives and actions have to be abstracted into typical motives for typical actions in typical situations. These social scientific typifications provide an *understanding* of the activities, and may then become ingredients in more systematic explanatory accounts. This RS can be used to answer both 'what' and 'why' questions.

While the RSs have been constructed so that their logics of enquiry are incompatible, it is possible that they can be combined in practice, such as being used in sequence, or one incorporated in part of another. We shall return to this in chapter 3.

Each RS has a philosophical ancestry and foundation, and includes ontological assumptions about the nature of reality and epistemological assumptions about how that reality can be known. The RSs are elaborated in chapter 3, and the RPs, with which they are associated, are discussed in chapters 4 and 5.

Basic difference: working top down or bottom up

One of the basic differences between the RSs is the way they answer 'why' RQs. One possibility is to apply existing theory or ideas to the problem, or to invent a new theory, and then test its/their relevance in that context (the Deductive RS). This choice between theory testing and theory construction may be influenced by the state of knowledge on a research problem. Alternatively, it is possible to postulate one or more explanatory mechanisms and try to establish their existence (the Retroductive RS). In these RSs, knowledge is advanced by working 'top down': that is, by trying out the researcher's ideas – concepts, theories or mechanisms – on the research situation in the hope that they represent the way reality works.

The alternative is to work 'bottom up': that is, by deriving concepts and theory from the situation. In using the Abductive RSs, and in the initial stages of the social constructionist version of the Retroductive RS, the researcher works 'bottom up'.

The early advocates of the Inductive RS claimed it to be a 'bottom up' procedure, but, as we shall see, it turns out to be 'top down'.

Researcher's Stance

In addition to the basic choices of research problem, RQ(s) and RS(s), three other choices are discussed here. They have to do with the relationship between the researcher and the researched, with the stance that the researcher adopts regarding the type of involvement she or he has with the research participants.

Outsider or insider

In trying to generate new knowledge, social researchers have to choose both the kind of relationship they wish to have with the people they are researching and the kind of role they will take. The choice has to be made somewhere between two extreme positions. The first requires the researcher to stand back from the social phenomenon being investigated, and to use methods that allow him or her to observe the phenomenon as an *outsider*. The second requires the researcher to be thoroughly immersed in the social situation and to use these *insider* and personal experiences as a basis for understanding what is going on.

The choice is between either maintaining a 'professional' distance from the research participants or becoming thoroughly immersed in their social world. In the former, the researcher remains aloof and separate, while in the latter, the researcher is engaged in close relationships with the research participants, even to the point of becoming an accepted member of that group or community. The researcher allows him or herself not only to be influenced by those researched, but may also have an influence on them.

Expert or learner

The social researcher has to choose between another two extremes: between being an *expert* or a *learner*. In the former role, the researcher approaches the problem armed with relevant existing knowledge in the form of concepts and theory, and/or previous research findings. These social scientific concepts and ideas influence the way the research problem and RQ(s) are formulated, and the ways in which answers are sought. On the other hand, in the role of learner, the researcher aims to set aside existing social scientific knowledge and to help the research participants reveal how they conceptualize and understand that part of their social world of interest to the researcher. In this case, the answers to the RQs emerge from this learning process, rather than from a body of social scientific knowledge.

Normally, these two choices concerning the relationship between the researcher and the researched will coincide as 'outside expert' or 'inside learner'. Of course, there is a range of intermediate positions between these two extremes. This choice has a bearing on how objectivity is viewed in social research, and is a matter to which we will return in chapter 2.

On, for or with people

Running parallel to the two choices just discussed is another that concerns the social researcher's relationship with the research participants. Research can be done *on* people, *for* people or *with* people. In the first case, the researcher is the expert, and the researched are merely subjects or respondents; the research may be undertaken primarily for the benefit of the researcher, e.g. to satisfy curiosity. While the results may have some benefit for the research participants, or 'society' more generally, this is not the primary purpose. In the second case, the researcher is still the expert, but acts as a consultant; the researcher does the research for a client group, to provide them with the knowledge they need. The client(s) and the researched can coincide, or they may be different. In the third case, the clients are in charge of the research, and the researcher is a facilitator; she or he assists them in conducting their own research on *their* situation, usually to solve some problem, to evaluate some programme, or to bring about some change.

These three relationships between the researcher and the researched do not exhaust all possibilities (see Blaikie 2000: 52–6 for an elaboration). There is one position that could be added here to the combinations of 'outside expert' and 'inside learner', to signal other possibilities. It is associated particularly with Critical Theory and feminist research (see chapter 5), where the researcher is committed to the emancipation of oppressed groups. This may consist in helping them to understand better their oppressed situation, as well as finding their way out of it. In such cases, the researcher is a *reflective partner*, or a *conscientizer*.

It is clear that researchers are faced with a number of choices in the way they relate to research participants. While the type of relationship adopted may be influenced by the nature of the research topic, invariably, experienced researchers have strong commitments regarding it. They can give methodological and ideological reasons for their choice, and these are likely to have a bearing on their choice of RS. This is because it is easier to put these commitments into practice in some RSs than in others. For example, it is easy to be an outside expert when working with the Deductive RS and an inside learner when working with the Abductive RS. The reverse is not the case.

Research Paradigms

Research strategies are located within the broader frameworks of theoretical or philosophical perspectives, commonly referred to as *paradigms*. We shall review ten different Research Paradigms (RPs)[2] in some detail in chapters 4 and 5, and review and critique them in chapter 6. However, in the meantime, we need to discuss the two distinguishing characteristics that form their core and on which they differ: namely, the assumptions made about the nature of the social reality that is investigated (ontological assumptions) and a related set of assumptions about the way in which knowledge of this reality can be obtained (epistemological assumptions).

The fundamental methodological problem that faces all social researchers is what kinds of connections are possible between ideas, social experience and social reality. Ideas refer to the ways of conceptualizing and making sense of experience and reality – such as concepts, theories, knowledge and other interpretations. Social experience refers to individual conduct, social relationships and cultural practices in everyday life, and to the everyday interpretations and meanings associated with these. Social reality refers to the material and socially constructed world within which everyday life occurs, which can have an impact on people's lives, in terms of both providing opportunities and imposing restrictions (Ramazanoğlu and Holland 2002: 9).

The various RPs present different ways of making connections between ideas, social experience and social reality. To a large extent, this is expressed in the ontological and epistemological assumptions they adopt: that is, their particular way of looking at the world, as well as their ideas on how it can be understood.

It will become evident as we go along that it is difficult to discuss ontological and epistemological assumptions separately (see Crotty 1998: 10; Williams and May 1996: 69). Assertions about what constitute social phenomena have implications for the way in which it is possible to gain knowledge of them. And the reverse is also true. They are discussed separately at this stage, in order that their characteristics and the range of alternatives can be highlighted.

Ontological assumptions

Ontology is a branch of philosophy that is concerned with the nature of what exists. In the social sciences, ontologies answer the question: 'What is the nature of social reality?' Each RP embodies a view of the world that is underpinned by ontological assumptions. In their domain of interest, RPs implicitly or explicitly make different claims about what kinds of things do or can exist, the conditions of their existence, and the ways in which they are related.

Theories about the nature of social reality are frequently reduced to two opposed, mutually exclusive categories: *idealist* and *realist*. An *idealist* theory assumes that what we regard as the external world is just appearances and has no independent existence apart from our thoughts. In a *realist* theory, both natural and social phenomena are assumed to have an existence that is independent of the activities of the human observer.

The idealist/realist distinction has a long history in philosophy. More recently, the contrast is made between *relativist* and *realist* ontologies. However, as these dichotomies are now too crude for understanding the variety of ontological assumptions used in the social sciences, to be useful in understanding the nature of social enquiry, it is necessary to elaborate them.

The set of categories discussed here has been derived from a variety of sources, particularly the work of Bhaskar (1978, 1979, 1986) and his exponents, such as Collier (1994). The categories are not intended either to be exhaustive or to cover all subtle variations in the literature. The titles of the categories are not universal; the literature abounds not only with alternative categories, but also with different categorizations. My set of categories has been developed to help understand the range of commonly used RPs in the social sciences, and their accompanying RSs, to be discussed in later chapters.[3] The categories are: *shallow realist, conceptual realist, cautious realist, depth realist, idealist* and *subtle realist* (see fig. 1.1). What they all have in common is that they assert the existence of some kind of reality. The pertinent questions are: 'What is the nature of this reality?' and 'Where do we look for it?'

To the extent that researchers adopt ontological assumptions, they are most likely to do so implicitly and may not be able to articulate the assumptions they use. Ontological assumptions are embedded in the theoretical ideas that are used to guide research and in the RSs and methods that are adopted.

Shallow realist

The *shallow realist* ontology entails an unproblematic belief in an external reality, consisting of things and/or events and/or states of affairs, which are controlled by natural or social laws. This external reality consists of nothing more than objects or events that can be observed. This view is also referred to as *naïve realist, empirical realist* or *actualist* (Bhaskar 1979; Collier 1994: 7–11). It assumes that what we can observe is what exists, and is all that exists: 'What you see is what is there.'

This ontology asserts that there are patterns or sequences in these observable events, and that the challenge for science is to discover and describe them. They are referred to as empirical regularities, and descriptions of them are known as universal generalizations. The latter achieve the status of scientific laws when they have been observed across time and space, without exception: e.g. the temperatures at which pure water changes from liquid to either a solid or a gas.

This *shallow realist* ontology implies that there is nothing behind observed events that has a hand in their production. It is assumed that the world is made up of 'observable atomistic objects, events and regularities among them, as if objects had no structure or powers, and in particular, no unobservable qualities' (Sayer 2000: 11). Only that which can be observed, i.e. experienced by human senses, can be regarded as real and, therefore, as worthy of the attention of science. Human activity is understood as observable behaviour taking place in observable, material circumstances. Social reality is viewed as a complex of relations between events, and the causes of human behaviour are regarded as being external to the individual.

A *shallow* or *naïve realist* ontology 'assumes not only that the phenomena we study are independent of us, but that we can have direct contact with them, contact which provides knowledge whose validity is certain' (Hammersley 1992: 50). We shall come back to this in the discussion of the epistemology of *empiricism* later in this chapter.

This version of realist ontology is often associated with the doctrine of *naturalism*, which claims that because there is little difference between the behaviour of inanimate objects and that of human beings, the logic of enquiry appropriate to the natural sciences can also be used in the social sciences (see Introduction).

Conceptual realist

This ontology offers an alternative to *shallow realist* ontology by appealing to reason rather than experience. While reality is seen to have an existence independent of human minds, it is argued that it can be known only by the use of the innate human capacity of thought and reason. Any rational, thinking person should be able to discover it for themselves. It is for these reasons that this ontology is also referred to as *objective* conceptual realism (Bhaskar 1986: 8).

This type of reality is not the property of any individual; nor is it the construction of a social community. Rather, it is like a collective mind, or a collective consciousness. It exists in the realm of ideas, but is above and beyond the ideas of any individual; it is general, but not material. It is not directly observable, being a structure of ideas, separate from individual thoughts, but shared by a collective of human beings. '[S]ociety is a real and general phenomenon; it is a thing-in-itself which stands "outside" of, and is independent of, all those elements that make it up, such as individuals, their consciousness, and their circumstances' (Johnson et al. 1984: 149). The ultimate criterion of validity or truth is the absence of logical contradiction (Johnson et al. 1984: 151).

The *conceptual realist* ontology can be regarded as an odd version of realist ontology (a non-material yet independent reality), but could just as easily be regarded as an idealist or non-realist ontology. However, while 'non-realists may in the end turn out to be realists about something, they have a characteristic position, in that they deny that there is anything knowable that is independent of mind' (Collier 1994: 12).

It is worth noting that the cognitive process by which an idea is regarded as referring to something real is known as reification. *Reification* occurs when human beings believe that the social forms they have created are natural, universal and absolute. They forget that they are the producers and treat the products of human activity as being facts of nature or the result of divine will (Berger and Luckmann 1967: 89). For example, the notion of 'society', which may be regarded as referring to a reality that has an independent existence, is, according to this view, nothing more than a conceptual or theoretical tool.

Cautious realist

This ontology shares the view of the *shallow realist* ontology, that there is an independent external reality, but claims that it is impossible for humans to perceive it accurately because of the imperfections of the human senses and the fact that the act of observing is an interpretive process (see the discussion in chapter 4 on the theory dependence of observations). This ontology is called 'cautious' *realist* because researchers 'need to be critical about their work precisely because of these human frailties. But, although one can never be sure that ultimate reality has been uncovered, there can be no doubt that reality is "out there." Realism remains the central concept' (Guba 1990b: 20).

Depth realist

In the *depth realist* ontology, reality is seen to consist of three levels or domains: the empirical, the actual and the real (Bhaskar 1978). The *empirical* domain is the world that we experience through the use of our senses; the *actual* domain includes events whether or not anyone is there to observe them; and the *real* domain consists of the processes that generate events. It is implied that the empirical domain is superficial, as it is concerned only with what can be experienced; that the real domain is substantial, as it refers to the structures and powers of objects; and that the actual domain 'refers to what happens if and when those powers are activated, to what they do and what eventuates when they do' (Sayer 2000: 12). In the real domain of reality, the ultimate objects of scientific enquiry are considered to exist and act independently of scientists and their activity. As in the *shallow realist* and *cautious realist* ontologies, it is assumed that there is a reality 'out there' that exists whether or not it is being observed.

Seeing reality as consisting of these three domains, ranging from what can be observed to an underlying domain of causal structures and mechanisms, suggests the idea of ontological depth, of the stratification of reality that is independent of our knowledge of it (Bhaskar 1979: 16; 1986: 63). It is for this reason that this ontology is called *depth realist*. The aim of a science based on this ontology is to explain observable phenomena with reference to underlying structures and mechanisms.

Structures are regarded differently in the natural and the social sciences. Social structures do not exist independently of the activities they influence or social actors' conceptions of what they are doing in these activities. They are also less enduring than natural structures (Bhaskar 1989: 78).

When used by social scientists, this ontology takes two forms. Social reality is viewed either as social arrangements that are the products of material but unobservable structures of relations (Bhaskar 1979) or as a socially constructed world in which social episodes are the products of the cognitive resources that social actors bring to them (Harré 1977). This means that these two traditions seek explanations for observed phenomena in different places.

Idealist

In the *idealist* ontology, the external world consists of representations that are creations of individual minds. Whatever is regarded as being real is real only because we think it is real; it is simply an idea that has taken on the impression of being real. Reality is what human beings make or construct; it is the activities of creative subjects that constitute the world of objects. In other words, these subjective ideas refer to something that is regarded by the believers as real. This view of reality is different from both the *shallow realist* external world and the world of reason associated with *conceptual realism*.

The variety included within the category of *idealist* ontology can be identified in the following subcategories. At one extreme are the *atheistic idealists* who deny the existence or at least the relevance of an external world. In a way, this category represents the ideal-typical form of *idealist* ontology. At the other extreme are *perspective idealists* who regard constructions of reality as just different ways of perceiving and making sense of an external world. While the assumption that there is an external world runs counter to pure *idealist* ontology, the status of perspective-based realities is still in the realm of ideas.

Between these two extremes are a variety of other views. They include views that accept that the existence of an external world places both constraints and opportunities on the reality-constructing activities of social actors, but regard social constructions as having a high level of autonomy from it. They could be called *constrained idealists*. Others, such as *agnostic idealists*, neither affirm nor deny the existence of a world 'out there' (Gergen 1994). They have no interest in what might exist beyond the way in which social actors constitute their world as they talk it, write it and argue it (Potter 1996: 98).

The *idealist* position claims that there are fundamental differences between natural and social phenomena; that humans, unlike things in nature, have culture and live in a world of their shared interpretations. Social action is not mere behaviour but, instead, involves a process of meaning-giving. It is the meanings and interpretations created and maintained by social actors that constitute social reality for them. Social reality consists of the shared interpretations that social actors produce and reproduce as they go about their everyday lives.

Subtle realist

This ontology shares a major feature of the *shallow realist* and *cautious realist* ontologies, a belief in the existence of an external social reality. It has emerged as an attempt to overcome some of the deficiencies of both the *shallow realist* and the *idealist* ontologies. However, while having some elements in common with *depth realism*, *subtle realism* does not take on board the idea of ontological depth. It has been suggested by Hammersley (1992) as being appropriate for ethnographic research to deal with the incompatible positions of realism and relativistic idealism that have come to dominate such research. Ethnographers tend to adopt one or the other; they either believe in an independent, knowable reality, or they accept the idea of multiple and incommensurate, socially constructed realities. In the former, reality is seen to exist independently of the activities of scientists, as in both *shallow* and *depth realist* ontologies, and, in the latter, reality is seen to be a product of the interpretations of social actors, and the changes that result from putting these interpretations into practice over time.

> This subtle realism retains from naïve realism the idea that research investigates independent, knowable phenomena. But it breaks with it in denying that we have direct access to those phenomena, in accepting that we must always rely on cultural assumptions, and in denying that our aim is to reproduce social phenomena in some way that is uniquely appropriate to them. Obversely, subtle realism . . . [recognizes] that all knowledge is based on assumptions and purposes and is a human construction, but it rejects [the] . . . abandonment of the regulative idea of independent and knowable phenomena. Perhaps most important of all, subtle realism is distinct . . . in its rejection of the notion that knowledge must be defined as beliefs whose validity is known with certainty. (Hammersley 1992: 52)

Before leaving our discussion of ontology, it is important to note that it is one thing to examine how philosophers and social scientists view social reality, and quite another to discern lay views of the world. Lay people who are unfamiliar with philosophical views are unlikely to hold sophisticated ontologies of the kind discussed here. They are most likely to have some kind of *shallow* or *naïve realist* view about the status of the social world. While an expert may hold some kind of idealist ontology, social actors may be staunch realists. Such experts have solved this inconsistency by claiming that the lay view of the social world is a consequence of reification; that is, what is really a social construction is regarded as having an independent existence. Idealists could also make the same accusation against other experts who hold realist ontologies.

Epistemological assumptions

An *epistemology* is a theory of knowledge, 'a theory or science of the method or grounds of knowledge'. It is a theory of how human beings come to have knowledge of the world around them (however this is regarded), of how we know what we know. An epistemology provides a philosophical grounding for establishing what kinds of knowledge are possible – what can be known – and criteria for deciding how knowledge can be judged as being both adequate and legitimate (Crotty 1998: 8). In the social sciences, epistemologies offer answers to the question: 'How can social reality be known?' They make claims about which scientific procedures produce reliable social scientific knowledge.

In the sixteenth and seventeenth centuries, two alternatives to religious faith and revelation were offered as the foundations of knowledge: reason and experience (Benton 1977: 20). Reason, or rationalism, was concerned with being able to distinguish between what is true and what is false. Early rationalists, such as Descartes, believed that all humans have this capacity, in particular, to subject everything that is normally taken for granted to a process of systematic doubt. It was assumed that this critical process would reveal the truth. However, the problem was to be able to be certain about such judgements.

An alternative to the use of reason was to base knowledge of the world on human experience. 'Seeing' with one's own eyes was regarded as the ultimate way of establishing what the world looks like and how it works. In other words, only when evidence can be produced from the use of the human senses can knowledge of the world be regarded as certain.

Another way of thinking about epistemology is in terms of the relationship between researchers and the 'things' of which they wish to have knowledge. As we have discovered already, these 'things' or objects can be regarded very differently, fundamentally as either real or ideal, as having an independent existence or simply as being ideas. Researchers or observers give meaning to these 'things' in three basic ways. *Objectivism* views 'things' as having intrinsic meaning. The researcher's role is to discover the meaning that already resides in them. For example, a tree is a tree regardless of who observes it or whether it is observed at all; its meaning is independent of human consciousness and is simply waiting to be discovered. The thing takes precedence over the observer. Hence, all observers should discover the same meaning, the same truth about such things. The reverse is the case in *subjectivism*. Things make no contribution to their meaning; the observer imposes it. As there is no interplay between the observer and the thing, the thing plays no part in the meaning that the observer gives to it. Hence, things may be given quite different meanings by different observers. What one observer calls a tree, another might call a shelter. *Constructionism* rejects both of these views. On the one hand, meaning is not discovered; it is constructed. Rather than the meaning residing in 'things', the observer plays an active role in its creation. On the other hand, this creative process is constrained by the nature of the things themselves; their meaning is the result of the observer's engagement with them and, we need to add, the understandings of it that already exist (Crotty 1998: 8–9).

The first two of these epistemologies are commonly referred to as *empiricism*, and *rationalism*, respectively, and represent attempts of philosophers in the sixteenth and seventeenth centuries to replace the authority of tradition, divine revelation and faith with a rational or scientific foundation for knowledge. From these early beginnings in the physical sciences, a number of other epistemologies have emerged, of which *constructionism* is one. The types of epistemologies reviewed here include these three – *empiricism, rationalism* and *constructionism* – as well as three others – *falsificationism, neo-realism* and *conventionalism*.

Again, the range of theories of knowledge presented here is but one attempt to capture the diversity of epistemologies that have held some sway over the past fifty years or so. Variations within categories, and combinations of them, can be found in the literature.

Empiricism

Empiricism is most clearly associated with the *shallow realist* ontology, although it can be seen to have some affinities with the form of representation associated with *idealism* (Williams and May 1996: 42, 70, 80). It is based on the key idea that knowledge is produced by the use of the human senses, that knowledge comes from 'observing' the world around us. It is assumed that, by observing this external world objectively,[4] we can correctly represent it in scientific concepts and theories. It is claimed that knowledge has a sure and certain foundation in the evidence produced by the scientifically trained researcher properly applying reliable methods and procedures. These methods are supposed to allow the researcher to be a neutral observer, to have undistorted contact with reality; knowledge is a matter of accurate representation. 'The scientist is thus viewed as a *subject* who is attempting to understand an *object* and is trying to be objective by eliminating the bias that could lead to inaccuracy' (Doyal and Harris 1986: 2).

Crude empiricism is the popular view of scientific research amongst people without philosophical training. It is also implicit in the views of science commonly presented in the media (Doyal and Harris 1986: 2).

This epistemology is sometimes regarded as being *representationalist* and *foundationalist* because it claims that there are certain final, ultimate criteria that can determine when knowledge is a true representation of this – assumed to exist – external world. Knowledge is said to be true when it reflects or mirrors what is 'out there' by the direct, unmediated contact with it by an observer. Language is assumed to provide a 'pictorial description or conceptual representation of an external reality' (Schwandt 2000: 196).

A central tenet of *empiricism* is that, apart from analytic statements that are true by definition, anything we claim to know about the world is true only if it can be put to the test of experience. Any scientific idea that cannot be confirmed by observation is meaningless and has no role in science. Metaphysical ideas, those that have no observable manifestations, must be left out of scientific accounts of the world. Such accounts can only be derived from and verified by observations made by means of the human senses.

Explanations are achieved by generalizing from observed regularities between events. These 'constant conjunctions' are all that are needed to explain or predict an event. This is known as the 'pattern model' of explanation. The occurrence of an event, such as a juvenile crime, can be explained if the event that precedes it has already been established as a regularity, such as, 'juvenile delinquents come from broken homes'. Similarly, it can be predicted that juveniles who come from broken homes will become delinquents. Of course, such universal generalizations as this cannot be established in the social sciences to the same extent as they can in the natural sciences. However, this is the form of explanations advocated in *empiricism*.

In spite of the weaknesses that this epistemology contains, it is important to remember that empiricism was once part of a great liberating movement that rejected the authority of tradition, 'of established laws and customs, ancient texts, and so on, in favour of turning to "the great book of the world", and judging for oneself' (Collier 1994: 71).

Rationalism

The second epistemology, *rationalism*, is associated with the *conceptual realist* ontology. This ontology leads to an epistemology in which the direct examination of the structure of thought itself, a structure of 'mind' that is shared by all human beings, is the only path to knowledge of the real world (Johnson et al. 1984: 200).

> [W]hile the empiricists, for example, 'look at' the world in order to know it, on the grounds that what they can see or might see is all that exists, rationalists 'think' about the world in order to know it, on the grounds that behind the world that can be 'seen' or is given to the senses, there lies a world of thought; a structure that is innate, universal, and shared. (Johnson et al. 1984: 150–1)

> Because rationalists believe that social reality is made up of ideas – that is to say, has the same character as our own thoughts – and because they also believe that the empirical world of objects is a reflection of (to be explained by) this ideal reality, they conclude that the *direct* examination of thought is the only route to knowledge of the real world. (Johnson et al. 1984: 150)

The epistemology of *rationalism* looks for evidence of this unobservable reality, either in the consequences it has on people's lives or in thought processes and structures of the mind itself. The ideas that make up this kind of reality are assumed to determine both the consciousness of individuals and, therefore, their behaviour.

Until quite recently, *empiricism* and *rationalism* were regarded as being exhaustive and mutually exclusive epistemologies in the philosophy of the natural sciences. Their exponents produced their new conceptions of knowledge in defence of the claims of science as a (or the) source of genuine knowledge. Whereas rationalists used logic and mathematics as the standards whereby to judge knowledge claims, empiricists relied on observation and experiments.

Unlike *empiricism, rationalism* is now mainly of historical interest. While it was initially opposed to *empiricism*, social scientists are now more interested in the differences between *empiricism* and *constructionism*. As philosophies of both the natural and the social sciences have developed, other epistemologies have emerged. Three of these – *falsificationism, neo-realism* and *conventionalism* – were initially seen to apply to the natural sciences, but have also been used in the social sciences.

Falsificationism

Falsificationism is the epistemology associated with the *cautious realist* ontology and what has come to be known as the 'hypothetico-deductive method'. It was developed in the 1930s by Karl Popper (1959) to deal with deficiencies in the epistemology of *empiricism*.

According to Popper (1961), the logic of the social sciences, like that of the natural sciences, consists in trying out tentative solutions to research problems; solutions in the form of a theory are proposed and then criticized. A theory that is not open to criticism must be excluded as unscientific. The ultimate criticism is to attempt to refute the proposed theory by collecting appropriate data, by making appropriate measurements. If the theory is refuted, either it can be modified or another presented and tested. However, if the theory withstands the testing, it can be accepted temporarily, although it needs to be subjected to further criticism and testing. Hence, according to Popper, the method of science is one of tentative attempts to solve problems, by making conjectures that are controlled by severe criticism. The so-called objectivity of science lies in the objectivity of the critical method.

Popper argued that while science is a search for truths about the world or universe, it is never possible to establish whether these theories are true. All that can be done is to eliminate false theories by this process of conjecture and refutation, by proposing a theory and then trying to falsify it. Some theories will be rejected, and some tentatively accepted (corroborated). This allows us to get as near to the truth as possible, but we never know when we have produced a true theory.

Falsificationism is based on the idea that theories are invented to account for observations, not derived from them, as is the case in *empiricism*. Rather than scientists waiting for nature to reveal its regularities, they must impose regularities on the world. Although observations will usually precede the development of a theory, their role at this stage of research is to establish what it is that needs to be explained. However, the primary role of observation, or data collection, is in the testing of theories, in attempts to reject false theories, not in theory development.

Neo-realism

The epistemology of *neo-realism* is associated with the *depth realist* ontology. *Neo-realism* rejects *empiricism*'s pattern model of explanation: that explanation can be achieved by establishing regularities, or constant conjunctions, within phenomena or between events. According to *neo-realism*, establishing such regularities is only the beginning of the process. What is then required is to locate the structures or mechanisms that have produced the pattern or relationship. Mechanisms are nothing more than the tendencies or powers of things to act in a particular way. The capacity of a thing to exercise its powers, or the likelihood that it will, depends on whether or not the circumstances are favourable.

It may be necessary to postulate entities and processes that have never been observed in order to get beyond surface appearances to the nature and essences of things. In *neo-realism*, 'a scientific theory is a description of structures and mechanisms which causally generate the observable phenomena, a description which enables us to explain them' (Keat and Urry 1975: 5).

This view of causation allows for the possibility that competing or cancelling mechanisms may be operating when no event or change is observed; i.e. lack of movement may be due to opposing forces at work. Therefore, the independence of an event and its associated structures or mechanisms can be demonstrated.

Both *rationalism* and *neo-realism* entail the idea of an underlying reality, and both attribute causal powers to this reality. However, the former is a reality of shared, innate ideas, while the latter is an external, independent reality. Further, the causal powers of the underlying *conceptual realist* reality are seen to determine the behaviour of individuals, while the domain of the real in *neo-realism* is responsible for producing what happens in the empirical or surface domain. Hence, not only are the conceptions of reality very different; the influences on the inhabitants of this reality are to be found in different places.

Constructionism

Constructionism is associated with the *idealist* ontology. As we have already seen, *constructionism* provides an alternative to *empiricism* and *rationalism* by claiming that knowledge is neither discovered from an external reality nor produced by reason independently of such a reality. It is the outcome of people having to make sense of their encounters with the physical world and with other people.

This process of meaning-giving can be seen as either an individual or a social activity. Hence, *constructionism* has two branches: *constructivism* and *social constructionism*. The former, also known as radical constructivism, refers to the meaning-giving activity of the individual mind, to cognitive processes, while the latter refers to intersubjectively shared knowledge, meaning-giving that is social rather than individual (Schwandt 1994: 127). The focus of *social constructionism* is the collective generation and transmission of meaning (Crotty 1998: 58). As this book is about *social* enquiry, in all further discussion *constructionism* is intended to refer to *social constructionism*, not *constructivism*, as defined here.

The notion of *constructionism* can be applied to both social actors and social scientists. Social actors socially construct their reality. They conceptualize and interpret their own actions and experiences, the actions of others and social situations. From this same perspective, social scientists socially construct their knowledge of social actors' realities, their conceptions and interpretations of the actions of social actors and of social situations. As we shall see in chapter 3, it is the relationship between these two levels of construction with which the Abductive RS is concerned.

Constructionism, as practised by social scientists, rejects the claims of *empiricism*: namely, that the use of the human senses can produce a certain or true representation of an external world. Constructionist social scientists argue that because it is impossible for fallible human beings to observe an external world – if one exists at all – unencumbered by concepts, theories, background knowledge and past experiences, it is impossible to make true discoveries about the world. There can be no theory-free observation or knowledge. The activities involved in constructing knowledge occur against the background of shared interpretations, practices and language; they occur within our historical, cultural and gendered ways of being. In short, as all social enquiry reflects the standpoint of the researcher, and all observation is theory-laden, it is impossible to produce theory-free knowledge (Denzin and Lincoln 2000: 872).

Consequently, constructionists are *anti-foundationalists* or *non-foundationalists*, in that they argue that there are no permanent, unvarying criteria for establishing whether knowledge can be regarded as true, and there are no absolute truths. The only criteria available are those that can be agreed upon, through negotiation and argument, by a community of scientists, at a certain time, in a certain place, and under certain conditions. In this regard, constructionists hold some ideas of the epistemology of *conventionalism* (see next section).

While *constructionism* and *rationalism* share the view that social reality is a structure of ideas, they differ in the source of these ideas. For *rationalism*, the source lies in the universal innate structures of mind. For *constructionists*, the source is the product of the intersubjective, meaning-giving activity of human beings in their everyday lives. These ideas cannot be innate, because different cultures or communities are likely to have different constructions of social reality.

Conventionalism

Another epistemology to emerge out of dissatisfaction with *empiricism* is known as *conventionalism*. This epistemology is not explicitly adopted by any of the RSs or RPs that are reviewed in chapters 3–5, but it is the basis of some of the criticisms of the RPs discussed in chapter 6. It has been discussed mainly with reference to the natural sciences.

As an epistemology, *conventionalism* regards knowledge generation pragmatically. In order to overcome the problem of establishing the truth of scientific propositions, *conventionalism* argues that scientific theories are created by scientists as convenient tools to deal with the world. These tools are justified if they produce the desired results. Hence, there is no need to worry about whether they are true representations of the empirical world. Decisions about what are good theories, or which is the better of two competing theories, is a matter of judgement, not proof. It is not possible to rely on agreed facts to determine this, as theories are 'underdetermined' by data. In other words, theoretical claims go beyond what available data can determine. *Conventionalism* therefore undermines commonly held views on objectivity and rationality; science is viewed sociologically or psychologically, rather than logically. 'Conventionalists agree with empiricists on the origin of knowledge, but reject empiricism as a norm that allows us to justify all accepted judgements by appealing to experience, conceived as a sufficient criterion of their truth' (Kolakowski 1972: 158). The result is that whatever is regarded as reality is a consequence of the theory that is used; theories do not describe reality, they determine what is considered by the scientist to be real.

In summary, in *conventionalism*, as in *constructionism*, reality is regarded as a human creation. However, whereas in *constructionism* social reality is assumed to be produced by social actors as they conduct their everyday lives, in *conventionalism* reality is assumed to be an invention of the scientist. In both types of ontological assumptions, realities are regarded as serving particular purposes, either to cope with social life or to solve particular scientific or technical problems, and not as representing any absolute external reality. This clearly distinguishes these two epistemologies from *empiricism*, *falsificationism* and *neo-realism*.

The Status of Knowledge

Epistemologies can be distinguished in terms of the status of the knowledge that they claim to produce. Adherents of *empiricist* epistemology believe that it produces *absolute* knowledge. It is claimed that objective facts are arrived at by the direct observation of an external reality by the unencumbered use of the human senses. Such knowledge, it is argued, has a sure and certain foundation.

Rationalism is also seen by its adherents as producing *absolute* knowledge based on the innate human capacity to apply universally valid rational principles. 'For rationalism, knowledge-claims are valid to the extent that they conform to the deductive standards of proof already established in mathematics' (Benton 1977: 101).

In *falsificationism*, knowledge in the form of tested theories is always regarded as *tentative*. There is no way of knowing when a theory matches reality. All that can be done is to reject those theories that definitely do not match reality, in so far as the data we use allow us to do this. Theories that survive rigorous tests are all that can be relied on.

Neo-realism accepts that knowledge of structures and mechanisms is always *tentative*. Knowledge obtained of the domain of the empirical, and the models that are produced to discover structures and mechanisms, must be regarded as *tentative* (transitive) rather than absolute. This knowledge is constrained by the limitations of humans to be able to represent definitively both the surface and the hidden domains. This is due to the fact that our observations and measurements are always theory-dependent; we cannot eliminate the effects of language and culture, preconceptions and expectations, and scientific perspectives and theories, on the way we both see and interpret the world around us.

A *constructionist* epistemology is regarded as producing *relative* knowledge. This means that there is no one truth, but the possibility of a plurality of truths associated with different constructions of reality. This type of knowledge has no sure foundations. Whether each view of reality is granted equal status, or whether it is considered that 'rational' debates about their respective merits are appropriate, is a matter of considerable contention.

For *conventionalism*, the truth status of the theories used to understand and manipulate the world of objects and events is not important. Rather, it is what such theories allow us to do that matters. If a scientific perspective assumes that the earth is at the centre of the universe, and theories and measurements based on it allow us to successfully navigate the oceans using stellar observations, then the truth status of the theory is irrelevant. If it works, use it. Hence, *conventionalism* is a form of pragmatism.

Relationship between ontological and epistemological assumptions

Table 1.2 cross-tabulates the six ontological positions against the six epistemological positions. The question is: 'What combinations make logical sense, and what combinations occur in practice?' The answers are those shown in the table. The *subtle realist* ontology and the epistemology of *conventionalism* do not go together. They are alternatives to some of the others, and will be used in chapter 6 to deal with the criticisms that have been made of many of these assumptions.

Discussion of the ontological and epistemological assumptions of both the RSs and RPs must wait until after their elaboration in later chapters (chapter 3 for the former, and chapters 4 and 5 for the latter). The different types of assumptions have been reviewed here to set the scene for these later chapters. It is impossible to think about differences between the RSs and RPs without referring to differences in their ontological and epistemological assumptions.

It is important to note that it is not possible to establish by empirical enquiry which of the ontological and epistemological claims is the most appropriate. The proponents adopt a position partly as an act of faith in a particular view of the world. All that can be done is to debate their respective strengths and weaknesses. The important point is to be aware of the assumptions that are embedded in RSs and RPs, and the consequences that they have for research practice and outcomes.

It is possible to regard ontologies as being more relevant to life in general than to the conduct of research. For example, the categories could be used to understand how both research participants, and researchers in their non-professional lives, view the world. However, in the context of this book, they are presented as different sets of assumptions made by researchers *per se*. In addition to being embedded in the RSs and RPs that researchers employ, they can also influence the choice of research methods and how they are used to answer RQs.

Research Paradigms and Research Strategies

As we shall discover in later chapters, each RS, or logic of enquiry, is associated with one or more RPs. It is the overlap in their ontological and epistemological assumptions that creates an association between them. In order to review what has

Table 1.2 Combinations of ontological and epistemological categories

Ontology	Empiricism	Rationalism	Epistemology Falsificationism	Neo-realism	Constructionism	Conventionalism
Shallow realist	✓					
Conceptual realist		✓				
Cautious realist			✓			
Depth realist				✓		
Idealist					✓	
Subtle realist						

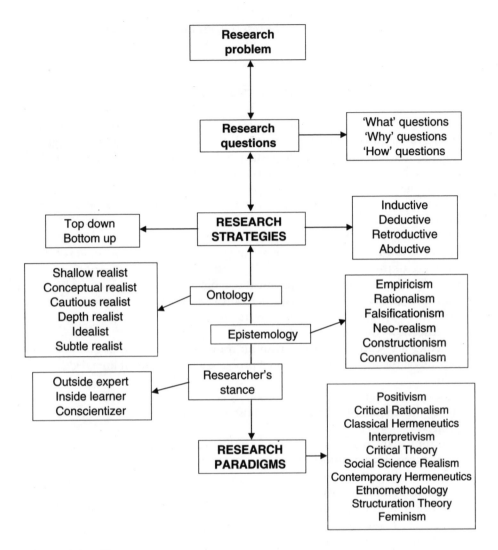

Figure 1.1   Choices

been discussed so far, and to anticipate what will be covered in later chapters, figure 1.1 summarizes the basic choices a social researcher has to make on any research project. The double-headed vertical arrows indicate that the decisions regarding the research problem, the RQs and the choice of RS and RP, are interrelated. While I have discussed them in a logical order, in practice, it is usually necessary to move back and forth between them before the decisions can be finalized.

The horizontal arrows indicate, for each area of decision, the basic categories between or amongst which choices need to be made. Of course, many more decisions are required in designing and conducting social research (in particular, see Blaikie 2000). The decisions regarding ontological and epistemological assumptions, and the posture the researcher adopts toward the people being researched, are located in the figure between RSs and RPs. Choices regarding all three are heavily influenced by the nature of the research problem and the way it is expressed in RQs.

Chapter Summary

- Social researchers need to make choices about the problem to be investigated, the research question(s) to be answered, the research strategy or strategies to answer these questions, and the posture to be adopted towards the researched.
- A research problem needs to be translated into one or more research questions that define the nature and scope of the research.
- There are three main types of research questions: 'what', 'why' and 'how' questions.
- 'What' questions require descriptive answers in the form of characteristics and/or patterns of association; 'why' questions seek causes or reasons for the existence of these characteristics and/or patterns; and 'how' questions are concerned with intervention and practical outcomes.
- Research questions form a sequence: answers to 'what' questions normally precede 'why' questions, and answers to both of these types of questions precede 'how' questions.
- Whether a researcher sets out with all three types of research questions will depend on the nature of the research problem and the state of knowledge in the field.
- Research strategies are logics of enquiry that are used to answer research questions, the choice of which is the most important decision in any research project.
- The four main research strategies – Inductive, Deductive, Retroductive and Abductive – provide different ways of answering the different types of research questions; they advance knowledge by solving intellectual puzzles and practical problems in different ways.
- The research strategies differ in their ontological assumptions, starting points, steps, use of concepts and theory, styles of explanation or understanding, and the status of their products.
- In selecting a research strategy, researchers are also choosing:

  - whether to work 'top down' or 'bottom up' in attempting to advance social knowledge; and
  - the type of posture they want to adopt towards the researched, to be an *outsider* or an *insider*, to be an *expert* or a *learner*, or to do research *on* people, *for* people or *with* people.

- Research strategies are located within theoretical and philosophical perspectives, or research paradigms.
- Research paradigms, and, therefore, research strategies, differ in their ontological assumptions – their view of the nature of social reality – and their epistemological assumptions – their view on how knowledge of this reality can be obtained.

- Six major ontologies and epistemologies have been presented: the *shallow realist, conceptual realist, cautious realist, depth realist, idealist* and *subtle realist* ontologies; and the epistemologies of *empiricism, rationalism, falsificationism, neo-realism, constructionism* and *conventionalism*.
- The status of knowledge of social reality that is produced on the basis of these epistemologies can be absolute (*empiricism* and *rationalism*), tentative (*falsificationism* and *neo-realism*), relative (*constructionism*) or pragmatic (*conventionalism*).
- Most of the ontological and epistemological positions are closely related in pairs: *shallow realist* with *empiricism*; *conceptual realist* with *rationalism*; *cautious realist* with *falsificationism*; *depth realist* with *neo-realism*; and *idealist* with *constructionism*.
- The *subtle realist* ontology and the epistemology of *conventionalism* have emerged as alternatives that can overcome the deficiencies of some of the others.

Further Reading

Bhaskar, R. 1979. *The Possibility of Naturalism.*
Blaikie, N. 2000. *Designing Social Research.*
Collier, A. 1994. *Critical Realism.*
Crotty, M. 1998. *The Foundations of Social Research.*
Guba, E. G. (ed.). 1990a. *The Paradigm Dialog.*
Hammersley, M. 1992. *What's Wrong with Ethnography?*
Keat, R. and J. Urry. 1982. *Social Theory as Science*, 2nd edn.
Lincoln, Y. S. and E. G. Guba. 2000. 'Paradigmatic controversies, contradictions, and emerging confluences'.
Schwandt, T. R. 1990. 'Paths to inquiry in the social disciplines'.
——2000. 'Three epistemological stances for qualitative inquiry'.
Williams, M. and T. May. 1996. *Introduction to the Philosophy of Social Research.*

2

Major Dilemmas in Social Enquiry

Introduction

Once a research problem has been identified, the formulation of RQs will be determined by what the researcher wants to achieve. In order to answer the RQs, a choice from amongst the RSs must be made. While the choice of RS(s) should be made on the basis of how best to answer the RQs, it is likely to be influenced by the RP to which a researcher is committed or which is regarded as providing the best orientation towards the research problem. The selection of a RP is more complex, being influenced by theoretical, philosophical, ideological and/or political considerations, as well as a researcher's past experiences, peer and audience expectations, and personal worldview.

The selection of a RP confronts a researcher with some very basic dilemmas. In order to make these more explicit, and to anticipate themes that will run through the following chapters, dilemmas are discussed here as a series of questions that a researcher needs to be able to answer. As each RP incorporates a position on these issues, it is important for researchers to be aware of what they are buying into when choosing both a RP and a RS.

The answers given to these questions here will be sufficient to set the scene for later discussions, and this will be done without getting into complex philosophical debates at this stage. We will come back to these and related questions in the following chapters, particularly chapter 6, where we will be in a position to consider more complex and detailed answers. However, before dealing with specific ontological and epistemological dilemmas, we need to examine a more general controversy that has a bearing on many of the questions to be discussed in this chapter.

Science and Social Science

This controversy can be expressed as a series of questions.

Are social *sciences* possible?

Can social sciences use the same methods and procedures as the natural sciences? What *are* the methods of the natural sciences?

Are social *sciences* possible?

The nature and status of social science as a science has been a matter of considerable debate. Unfortunately, there is no simple or straightforward answer to this question.

> [There] is a controversy which for more than half a century has split not only logicians and methodologists but also social scientists into two schools of thought. One of these holds that the methods of the natural sciences which have brought about such magnificent results are the only ones and that they alone, therefore, have to be applied in their entirety to the study of human affairs . . . The other school of thought feels that there is a basic difference in the structure of the social world and the world of nature. This feeling has led to the other extreme, namely the conclusion that the methods of the social sciences are *toto coelo* different from those of the natural sciences . . . It has been maintained that the social sciences are ideographic, characterized by individualizing conceptualizations and seeking singular assertory propositions, whereas the natural sciences are nomothetic, characterized by generalizing conceptualizations and seeking general apodictic propositions. The latter have to deal with constant relations of magnitude which can be measured and can perform experiments, whereas neither measurement nor experiment is practicable in the social sciences. In general, it is held that the natural sciences have to deal with material objects and processes, the social sciences, however, with psychological and intellectual ones and that, therefore, the method of the former consists in explaining, and that of the latter in understanding. (Schütz 1963a: 231–2)

While some progress has been made in achieving a better understanding of the nature of these schools of thought, and some proposals for alternative positions to bridge the differences have been offered, the issue of the extent to which social life can be studied in the same way as nature has identified it as 'the primal problem of the philosophy of the social sciences' (Bhaskar 1989: 66). (See also Keat and Urry 1975, 1982; Bhaskar 1979; Held and Thompson 1989.)

Can the social sciences use the same methods and procedures as the natural sciences?

There are four main ways of answering these questions. The two schools of thought identified by Schütz have been labelled here as *naturalism* and *negativism*. The former claims that the methods of the natural sciences can and should be applied in the social sciences, while the latter takes the opposite view. There is an intermediate position, known as *historicism*, which accepts that some of the methods of the natural sciences are inappropriate in the social sciences. These three positions have been debated for some time. The fourth and more contemporary position is *postmodernism*. It rejects the traditional ideas of science completely and advocates instead activities far removed from those that dominated the social sciences during the previous century.

The first three of these answers will be dealt with here. We will come back to the discussion of *postmodernism* in the concluding section of the chapter.

Naturalism

This doctrine maintains that just as there is a unity in nature, so there is also a unity in the methods and procedures used to investigate nature. In a more extreme version of *naturalism*, all phenomena are reduced to physical processes and properties, such as human emotions being reduced to physiological processes. It follows from this that only one set of methods is required for all the sciences.[1]

Naturalism argues that in spite of the differences in subject matter of the various scientific disciplines, both natural and social, the same methods can be used, although each science must elaborate them in a way appropriate to its objects of enquiry (Popper 1961; von Wright 1971; Kolakowski 1972).

It is important to note that the reference to 'methods' in these questions does not refer to the actual *techniques* of observation, data gathering or data analysis, but rather to the logic or strategy of enquiry, to the processes by which knowledge is generated and justified. The techniques of data gathering and analysis used in the various disciplines are related to the nature of their particular subject matters. While some techniques may be used in more than one discipline – e.g. particular statistical tests – the study of chemical structures is a very different activity from the study of social structures.

Back in 1843, the philosopher John Stuart Mill (1947) adopted this position as a way of rescuing the social (or moral) sciences from what he regarded as an unsatisfactory state. He believed that all scientific explanations have fundamentally the same logical structure.

A more recent philosopher, Karl Popper, adopted a similar position.

> I do not intend to assert that there are no differences whatever between the methods of the theoretical sciences of nature and of society; such differences clearly exist, even between the various natural sciences themselves, as well as between the various social sciences . . . But I agree with Comte and Mill – and many others . . . – that the methods in the two fields are fundamentally the same. (Popper 1961: 130–1)

Popper, as we shall see, had his particular view of *the* scientific method, and it is different from that advocated by Mill and the other early advocates of *naturalism*.

Hence, the question, 'Can the social sciences use the same methods and procedures as the natural sciences?', is answered in the affirmative. Not only is it acknowledged that social sciences are possible, but they should be seen as part of the spectrum of all sciences. Differences between the sciences in their subject matters are regarded as being irrelevant; for, after all, the natural sciences themselves deal with very different types of phenomena. If the social sciences are to flourish, it is argued, they should adopt the methods that have been so successful in the natural sciences.

Negativism

The proponents of *negativism* claim that the methods of the natural sciences cannot be applied in the social sciences. It is argued that, in contrast to natural phenomena, human beings have a component of 'free will' that undermines any attempts to explain and predict human activity. Arguments for this assertion come in various forms and have been usefully summarized by Popper (1961: 5–34), although they are not necessarily his views.[2]

1 While the so-called laws of nature are assumed to apply throughout space and time, the regularities in social life are time- and space-specific. Social uniformities cannot be generalized, because they change from one historical period to another and across cultures. Social uniformities are the result of human activity and can therefore be changed by human activity (Popper 1961: 7–8).

2 The use of the experimental method is based on the assumption that similar things will happen in similar circumstances. By artificially isolating and controlling the conditions, the influence of one factor on another can be demonstrated with a high level of confidence.[3] Social life, however, is much more complex than natural phenomena, and cannot usefully be isolated artificially. In social situations, similar conditions occur only within very limited time periods; history never really repeats itself. In large-scale social experiments, the experimental procedures may artificially eliminate the most important factors and may very well change what is being studied.

3 In the natural sciences (e.g. physics), nothing really new can happen; newness is merely a rearrangement of the elements. In the biological sciences, it is possible for organisms to lose the sense of novelty in experimental situations. The first application of the procedure changes the possible influence of later applications; organisms learn by experience. However, it is possible to dispose of organisms whose behaviour has been changed by experimental procedures. If societies or social groups are regarded as being like organisms, they too can learn by experience and achieve social newness, but they cannot be disposed of in the same way. This learning becomes part of a group's history.

4 The subject matter of the natural sciences, particularly physics, is much less complicated than the subject matter of the social sciences. Social life presupposes the existence of highly intelligent creatures that have both the capacity and the need for culture. Because they cannot rely on instincts to regulate their activities, they have to construct a social world to inhabit. Therefore, the social sciences face a dual complexity: the impossibility of artificial isolation and a subject matter that transcends the subject matters of the natural sciences. Even if social uniformities exist, these complexities may make it impossible to discover them.

5 Theories in the natural sciences are intended to make prediction possible. The form of this prediction is that if certain natural laws apply in a particular circumstance, and certain conditions are met, certain outcomes will follow. However, in the social sciences, a prediction may have an influence on the predicted event; knowledge of the outcome can change the way people behave, thus producing the possibility of either a self-fulfilling prophesy (Thomas 1928; Merton 1957) or a failed prediction.

6 It follows from the difficulties of making predictions in the social sciences that there is a complex interaction between the observer and the observed that may

threaten objectivity (Popper 1961: 16). Because the social scientist is a member of the category of phenomenon being studied, disinterested detachment may not be possible. Hence, it might be argued, objectivity and the search for truth are impossible in the social sciences; all social research will be contaminated by the values and interests of the researcher.

7 Whereas the natural sciences can work productively in an atomistic manner by regarding their phenomena as consisting of constellations of parts or elements or factors, a social group must be regarded as more than the mere sum of its members, or the sum of the personal relationships existing at any moment in time. Social groups have a culture and a history. In order to understand and explain social structures and processes, it is necessary to treat social groups holistically.

8 The natural sciences aim at causal explanations; the social sciences can aim only at an understanding of meaning and purpose. In proposing this distinction, Popper (1961: 20) has argued that, in fields such as physics, explanation is concerned with universal uniformities, expressed quantitatively and in mathematical formulae, while sociology must use qualitative notions and more intuitive understanding.

9 According to Popper, this use of quantitative analysis and mathematical formulae is not possible in the social sciences because the concepts found in social theories can be measured only qualitatively, or with a very low level of precision. This is not to deny that the social sciences may use certain statistical techniques in data analysis, but it is argued that it is not possible to formulate social laws in the precise mathematical terms possible in physics.

This litany of arguments was not made against social science in general, but is intended as an attack on *naturalism*. However, while the arguments are open to debate, they cannot be dismissed lightly. The extent to which they are seen to be a problem depends on the RP adopted. In varying ways, the RPs attempt to resolve those that are considered to be significant. In so far as *negativists* are prepared to accept that some form of social research is possible, they will limit it to purely descriptive research; explanation and prediction are considered to be impossible. According to this view, social research can produce descriptions of specific events in language that may have specific meanings, using singular statements that assert nothing beyond that event.

It can be argued that the problem of generalizing explanations throughout time and space is not confined to the social sciences. Comparisons that are made with positional astronomy, for example, neglect the fact that this area of the natural sciences is the exception rather than the rule. Predictions made in the natural sciences, even by means of well-known physical laws, occur only within certain artificial and idealized conditions, such as in a perfect vacuum. 'With the less exact sciences, such as meteorology, prediction is notoriously hazardous, while with living systems (not to say sub-atomic physics) we are seldom dealing with anything better than probabilities' (Richards 1983: 86–7). Whether these sciences will be able to improve their predictive capacity in the future is an open question. However, the influence of culture and history is regarded by the advocates of some RPs as making prediction impossible. But this does not rule out the possibility of social *science*; it just makes for a different kind of science.

On the problem of using experiments in the social sciences, Popper (1961: 93–7) has contended that the argument rests on a lack of understanding of the experimental method used in physics. Of course, without knowing a great deal about a particular phenomenon, it is difficult to describe what would constitute similar conditions and what kind and degree of similarity are relevant. Similarly, it may be difficult to establish what degree and type of experimental controls are necessary. These problems are present in both the natural and the social sciences and, according to Popper, can be resolved only by experimentation. While the physicist may be in a better position than the social scientist to cope with these problems, either because social phenomena are more complex than natural phenomena, or because physics has a longer history, Popper has argued that there is nothing fundamentally different between the two fields in their potential to conduct experiments.

It is worth noting, however, that many areas of the natural sciences – for example, astronomy – have developed without being able to use experimental manipulation, and in some areas of modern science, such as geology and evolutionary biology, there is little scope for it.

> Hence those areas of human social enquiry in which opportunities for controlled experiments are rare, cannot be disqualified from the ranks of science on this account alone. In any event there are some areas, notably social psychology, where experiments indistinguishable in design from those of the natural sciences are routinely performed, while economists make extensive use of idealized models which may be analysed mathematically in much the same way as in physics and physiology. Finally, the 'field investigations', in many social sciences, do not differ in any significant way from those in, say, botany or entomology. (Richards 1983: 86)

It has been argued that the possibility of social researchers allowing their values and prejudices to influence the research process – such as the choice of what is studied, how it is studied, what is regarded as acceptable evidence, how data are collected and how the results are interpreted – makes it difficult to achieve objectivity. Whether complete objectivity is possible, or even approachable, is a complex issue that will be taken up later. While such issues may appear to be less serious in the natural sciences, they are nevertheless present. Some of those who believe that value-free social science is not possible have suggested that social scientists should state their values and attitudes as fully and honestly as possible, to help others to be aware of possible influences and, hence, how the research results should be interpreted. However, while this may be desirable, it is difficult to establish the effects of a social scientist's values and attitudes on the research process and outcomes. Another radical solution has been to abandon the idea of a value-free or objective social science, to treat social phenomena as essentially subjective, and to maximize the subjective involvement of the researcher.

It is clear that there are some particular problems that make it difficult to model the social sciences on the natural sciences, but it is also clear that the natural sciences are not without their own problems. Whether the conclusion is that social science is not really possible will depend on how these difficulties are viewed, what responses are made and, more particularly, what kind of social science is considered to be appropriate.

Historicism

In part, *historicism* is a response to some of the problems raised by *negativism* about the possibility of social science. The central claim of *historicism* is that as there are fundamental differences between the natural and the social sciences, only some of the methods of the natural sciences can be applied in the social sciences. In particular, it is the issue of generalization that is considered to separate the two realms. According to *historicism*, historical and cultural relativity makes most of the methods of the natural sciences inapplicable in the social sciences (Popper 1961: 5–6).

In spite of this, *historicism* accepts that there are two common elements in the methods of the natural and the social sciences. Both methods are theoretical and empirical; they are concerned with explaining and predicting events through the use of theories, and they rely on observation both to identify these events and to accept or reject any theory. By observing the patterns or trends in the past, *historicism* claims that predictions can be made about future trends.

It is the success of fields such as positional astronomy, with its capacity to predict astronomical phenomena, such as eclipses and the paths of comets, which has encouraged *historicism* to argue that the social sciences can predict future events such as revolutions. It is acknowledged that social predictions may lack the detail and precision of natural science predictions, but their vagueness is compensated for by their scope and significance. *Historicism* is interested in large-scale forecasts, not short-term predictions (Popper 1961: 36–7).

Historicism aims to develop laws of historical development, laws that link up the successive historical periods, laws of process and change, rather than of uniformities. The experimental method is not appropriate for testing such laws. Observation of future events is the only way to establish the validity of such historical laws. Therefore, *historicism* claims that the discipline of sociology is theoretical history. 'Sociology thus becomes, to the historicist, an attempt to solve the old problem of foretelling the future; not so much the future of the individual as that of groups, and of the human race' (Popper 1961: 42). Thus, while *historicism* rejects the capacity of the social sciences to develop universal laws through the use of methods such as the experiment, it claims that through the establishment of laws of historical development it is possible to predict the future course of history.

Popper (1961) has attacked four of the arguments on which *historicism* is based: the holistic approach to social theories and social change, the character of historical laws, the variability of experimental conditions, and the relativity of generalizations. As the last two have been dealt with in the preceding section, only the first two will be discussed here.

As an alternative to *historicism*'s holistic approach to social theories and social change, Popper adopted what he called 'piecemeal engineering' to scientific investigation (1961: 67). This is a step-by-step process used to understand any phenomenon and to avoid unwanted consequences. It involves monitoring what has been achieved against what was expected. He argued that it is necessary to avoid conducting experiments or proposing social change of such complexity and scope that it is impossible to understand the processes that are occurring. Change may develop in unmanageable or undesirable directions. For this reason, Popper objected to 'utopian engineering' that attempts a complete reconstruction of a society in terms of a set of ideals. He preferred the process of learning by trial and error under conditions in which the errors are manageable.

Popper was critical of the central historicist doctrine regarding the claim that the task of social science is to develop laws of historical development, laws of evolution of society, which can be used to foretell its future. He argued that this claim is based on the false notion that evolutionary 'theories' include universal laws. Such propositions, he argued, are particular historical statements (Popper 1961: 108–9). While history may sometimes repeat itself in certain ways, this does not mean that any apparent repetition or cycle will continue to occur in the future (Popper 1961: 114). It is the case that social change may have certain trends or tendencies, but such trends are not universal laws. Trends may persist for hundreds of years, but may change at any time in the future (Popper 1961: 116). Popper objected to the kind of logic that is used to generalize from trends in the past to future states of affairs.

Popper's attack on *historicism* is an attack on Marx's claim that the revolutions throughout recorded history reveal a consistent trend in which oppressors are overthrown by the oppressed. Marx used this trend to predict the outcome of the class struggle, in which the bourgeoisie would be overthrown by the proletariat and, in this case, such struggles would cease, and a classless society would be created. In the process, Popper has provided arguments for a different view of science that will be discussed in the next chapter as Critical Rationalism.

What *are* the methods of the natural sciences?

In order to answer the question, 'Can the social sciences use the same methods and procedures as the natural sciences?', another question must also be answered: 'What *are* the methods of the natural sciences?' For the past fifty years or more, there has been as much if not more controversy over this second question than over the first one. Many philosophies of science have been proposed and debated, centring on issues such as the nature and importance of observation, when observation should occur in the process of developing scientific knowledge, the appropriate form of logic to be used in constructing theories, the role of theories themselves in this process, the structure of theories, and the extent to which scientists work with open minds or are constrained by the beliefs, values and orthodox practices of the community of scientists to which they belong.

Behind the question about the methods of the natural sciences lurks a common assumption that there is something called *the* scientific method. Some philosophers now tell us that the common-sense view of the scientific method, of scientists making careful observations and conducting experiments that lead to scientific 'discoveries', is not only logically unsatisfactory, but also does not reflect good scientific practice.

Therefore, it is no longer possible to provide one prescription for such a method. What has been regarded as *the* scientific method has been changing, at least over the past fifty years. Answers to the question about the methods of the natural sciences now fall into three main categories, identified in chapter 1 as the Inductive, Deductive and Retroductive RSs. The first proposes that scientific research begins with pure observations, and that generalizations or theories are produced from them. The second argues that scientific research begins with a tentative theory that is expected to explain some observed phenomenon, and observations are then made to test whether this theory can be accepted. The third proposes that, as observed regularities are produced by hidden structures and/or mechanisms, it is necessary to build models of these structures and mechanisms and then to look for evidence of their existence. In short, there is no consensus on what constitutes *the* scientific method; there are a number of contenders. (See the discussions of Research Strategies in chapters 1 and 3.)

This brings us back to the earlier question: 'Are social sciences possible?' What methods are appropriate for the social sciences if they are to be regarded as 'real' sciences? As we have seen, some writers have taken the view that social life does not lend itself to any kind of scientific investigation. Others have argued that the social sciences should follow the lead set by the natural sciences if they want to be recognized as sciences. And then there is the further position that the social sciences are a different kind of science.

The conclusion that must be drawn from this discussion is that it is not possible to answer the question about whether the methods and procedures used in the natural sciences are appropriate in the social sciences with a simple 'yes' or 'no'. After all, this question has been a matter of vigorous debate for more than a century, and was the central issue in the paradigmatic dispute in the social sciences in the 1970s.[4] As we have seen, more than one method or logic has been claimed to be appropriate in the natural sciences, and, as we shall discover, both 'yes' and 'no' answers have been qualified in various ways. A wide variety of answers to this question will be explored in subsequent chapters, and arguments encountered for the use of a particular logic or method in both the natural and the social sciences.

Major Dilemmas

In making choices about how to advance knowledge in the social sciences, researchers are faced with a number of serious dilemmas. Most of these are derived from the fact that it is necessary to adopt both ontological and epistemological assumptions when conducting social research.

Ontological dilemmas

This category of dilemmas arises from having to face alternative ontological assumptions in the choice of RSs and RPs. They are addressed here as two questions with which a social researcher needs to deal.

Is there only one social reality in any social situation?
Where do we look for answers to 'why' RQs?

Is there only one social reality in any social situation?

The *shallow realist* ontology, and its accompanying epistemology of *empiricism*, are usually associated with the view that, in any particular context, there is only one social reality; it is 'out there', objective and 'real'. On the other hand, the *idealist* ontology, and the epistemology of *constructionism*, allow for the possibility of multiple realities being present in any social context. Multiple realities are the consequence of different groups having inherited and/or created different ways of viewing and understanding their world. In extreme cases, these groups may be regarded as living in different worlds, even though they may occupy the same general geographical or social space. This contrast between insisting on a single reality and allowing for the possibility of multiple realities differentiates the RPs.

A variation of the *shallow realist* ontology claims that there is only one reality, but people have different views of it. It is a bit like asking people to report what happened at a motor accident, and getting different accounts from them. The questioner may be hoping to find out what actually happened, as courts of law do, thus assuming that, ultimately, there is only one correct version. Each observer's account would be seen as representing only a partial view of the event.

The situation is rather more complex in the *depth realist* ontology. Its stratified view of reality allows for the possibility that a single, independent and, perhaps, largely hidden 'real' domain of reality exists alongside multiple views or constructions of reality at the 'empirical' level.

When multiple realities are asserted, when different groups of people are seen to inhabit different social worlds, it makes no sense to talk about *the* social reality, or of people having different views of a single reality. Within a defined social space, groups or communities may live in and maintain, and defend the legitimacy of, different social realities. For example, in nations or regions where racism has been sanctioned, such as in the southern United States before the success of the civil rights movement in the 1960s, or, until more recently, in apartheid South Africa, groups with a belief in racial equality have existed. Those who adhered to the dominant racist ideology existed in a different world from those with egalitarian ideologies. They may have lived in the same country, but they saw and experienced the world differently. Members of the opposing groups believed in the rightness of their position, and defended their own views with arguments based on their particular values.

The same kinds of disputes can be found between advocates of different theoretical perspectives in the social sciences. Let us go back a few decades and observe the theoretical debates that raged in American sociology in the 1960s, between structural functionalists, conflict theorists and symbolic interactionists. The advocates of each theoretical perspective inhabited different theoretical worlds. They believed in the rightness of their own position and denied legitimacy to other positions. The inhabitants of each of these three theoretical worlds believed that they had the best way of understanding social activity and society. However, there was no neutral place or privileged position from which they could stand to conduct a rational, unprejudiced debate about the relative merits or legitimacy of their positions. Their ontological and epistemological commitments prevented this.

When the ontological assumptions of particular worldviews cannot be recon-
ciled, they are deemed to be incommensurable. It would be possible for an outsider, someone who is not committed to any of these positions, to evaluate their
respective claims. However, as this person will need to set up their own criteria to
make their judgements, they will adopt a position in doing so; they will hold
certain ontological assumptions that will influence their judgements. We will
return to this issue in the following chapter, and particularly in chapter 6.

The consequence of this discussion is that, as social researchers, we are faced
with a choice between alternatives that are a matter of ontological preference. Do
we assume that there is only one social reality, and conduct our research on that
basis? Or do we assume that there are likely to be multiple realities in any social
space, and that we will need to take this into account? If required to do so, we may
be able to mount a defence of the choice we make; but, ultimately, we are adopting a set of ontological assumptions.

Where do we look for answers to 'why' research questions?

In order to answer a 'why' RQ, we need to be able to locate something within the
social reality being investigated that can be shown to have an influence on what it
is we are trying to explain. For example, if our RQ seeks an explanation for low
levels of job satisfaction within an organization, then we need to know where to
look for the answer. Do we look for patterns of association between job satisfaction
and other factors in the situation, such as salary or wages, and/or levels of job autonomy and responsibility? Do we investigate the various social constructions of the
work situation held by the participants? Or do we try to identify the mechanisms
that link job satisfaction with, say, job autonomy – if they are associated? In the first
case, our ontological assumptions are probably *shallow realist*; in the second case
idealist, and in the third case *depth realist*. Hence, each approach to answering the
RQ assumes a different kind of reality and looks in different places for the answer.

The ontological assumptions with which we choose to work will usually be
derived from the RP to which we are committed or which we have adopted for
this particular research project. As a consequence, our choice of assumptions may
be rather incidental and implicit. We may simply follow the dominant tradition of
research in this field, having bought the ontological assumptions with the package,
with little or no consideration. Alternatively, we may have a strong commitment
to a particular ontology, be very aware of the assumptions involved, and have
chosen to look for a particular kind of answer to the RQ.

This issue of where to look for such answers overlaps with some of the epistemological dilemmas that we will now examine. Where we look for the answer to
a 'why' RQ blends into what we look for there, how we look for it, and what kind
of an answer we produce.

Epistemological dilemmas

This set of dilemmas is also expressed as a set of questions that a social researcher
needs to consider. In this case, the list is much longer.

Is it possible to observe directly a social reality that is assumed to exist independently of the social participants?

Is it possible to be objective in social enquiry?

And does the achievement of objectivity lead to true accounts of the world?

What use should social researchers make of the way in which research participants
conceptualize and understand their world?

What should the relationship be between everyday, lay language and social scientific, technical language?

Is it possible to observe directly a social reality that is assumed to exist independently of the social participants?

If social reality is assumed to have an existence that is independent of both social
participants and researchers, then we have the problem of how to study such a
reality. The issue here is the nature of the relationship between the human mind
and such an external world.

As we have already seen, the epistemology of *empiricism* accepts both the existence of an external world and the idea that humans have the capacity to observe
this world directly and objectively. In its pure form, *empiricism* argues that what
we see is what exists. If we need concepts to talk about this external reality, they
will be inherent in the reality itself. For example, if we observe a mountain, then
the idea 'mountain' will be contained in what we are observing. As observers, we
will not have to invent the concept.

A later school of thought, the *conceptual realist*, has argued that what we see
around us is determined by the concepts that we have available. Concepts allow
us to structure and organize the mass of sense impressions that impinge on us. We
can only see things because we already have ideas about them. We recognize an
object as a mountain because we already know to what types of objects the label
'mountain' applies.

What we see when we use technical concepts will be influenced by the theories within which the concepts are embedded. Hence, in our research, we take
with us a selection of theoretical concepts and ideas, and these allow us to
identify social objects, to make our observations, to classify objects, and to
measure their characteristics. Because we have to use concepts to 'see', our observations are already contaminated. Use different concepts, and we see different
things. This means that both the everyday language that we use within our
culture and the concepts in the RP that we choose to use determine what we see
as social reality.

There are two variations in this alternative school of thought. One says that
by selecting the correct concepts and ideas, through a trial-and-error process, we
can see the social world as it really is. However, it is not quite as simple as that,
as we can never be sure when this process has been completed. A bell doesn't
ring when we have finally got the correct match between our concepts and
reality. The other variation suggests that as reality is rather ill-defined, the very
act of using concepts means that the researcher is imposing some form on it. In
this case, the initial selection of concepts will have a large bearing on what is
eventually 'discovered'.

Is it possible to be objective in social enquiry? And does the achievement of objectivity lead to true accounts of the world?

The first question leads us directly into two further questions. They relate to an extensive body of contentious literature in the philosophy of social science. This literature has emerged in response to claims that the use of the scientific method is the ultimate way to acquire reliable knowledge and, thus, to establish truths about the world. It has been a commonly held view that the natural sciences are objective and the social sciences subjective. It is argued that because the natural sciences use detached, replicable observational procedures to investigate the world, as well as using logic to construct explanations, the knowledge they produce can be regarded as true and reliable. Social science knowledge is seen to lack these certainties. These views have been defended and challenged, and a variety of alternatives presented. It is too early in our journey to lay out these debates in detail.[5] Many positions will be encountered along the way: in chapter 4 (Classical Hermeneutics), chapter 5 (Contemporary Hermeneutics and Feminism), and in the section on 'Objectivity and truth' in chapter 6. All I will attempt here is a brief review of some of the major positions.

Just what 'objectivity' is has been a matter of considerable dispute. There are two senses in which the word is used. The first is concerned with the desire to produce true descriptions of the world as it is. The second has to do with modes of enquiry, with the use of non-arbitrary and non-subjective criteria for developing, accepting and rejecting hypotheses and theories (Longino 1990). It is commonly assumed that if objectivity is achieved in the second sense, it will also be achieved in the first sense.

> Objectivity is a characteristic ascribed variously to beliefs, individuals, theories, observations, and methods of inquiry. It is generally thought to involve the willingness to let our beliefs be determined by 'the facts' or by some impartial and nonarbitrary criteria rather than by our wishes as to how things ought to be. A specification of the precise nature of such involvement is a function of what it is said to be objective. (Longino 1990: 62)

Initially these debates centred on the idea that 'facts' and 'values' can and should be kept separate. Facts were regarded as true descriptions of some phenomenon, while values were regarded as either involving judgements – ascribing worth – or as prescribing and proscribing certain behaviour. It was assumed that, to be objective, science must be 'value-free'; that is, science is only about facts. The researcher's values must be kept out of all stages of scientific investigation by the use of neutral, detached procedures and attitudes.

Early responses to these claims raised doubts about the capacity of researchers to achieve this. One solution was to require researchers to declare their values, to enable the users of their research to judge whether and to what extent values had contaminated the results. While this position is still advocated (see, e.g., Seale 1999: 25–6), it is not completely satisfactory, as it is unusual for anyone to be fully aware of their values and assumptions, and difficult for observers to judge their influence, even if they can be exposed.

In time, it became accepted that values enter into research at various stages. At a fundamental level, in the very act of observing the world scientifically, a researcher must use technical concepts, whose meanings are impregnated with the theories and assumptions within which the concepts are located. In addition, a researcher's biography, culture, professional training and membership in a scientific community influence the ontological and epistemological assumptions adopted. This, in turn, influences what is seen, and how it is understood. In short, it was argued that as all observation is theory-laden, observation involves interpretation. Hence, there are no pure facts.

One solution to this was to accept that all knowledge is tentative and open to revision. Because researchers cannot rely on their observations to tell them how the social world works, a trial-and-error procedure is required. A researcher can theorize about how it works, and then proceed to test those ideas by making observations. The hope was that, over time, what is learnt from this critical testing process would get us somewhere near the truth. The problem here is that if all observation is interpretation, the testing of theories against reality is also a flawed process.

A further development of the view that observation is theory-laden was to argue that how a researcher views the world is not a matter of personal assumptions and values but, rather, a result of shared assumptions and interpretations. Knowledge is a view from somewhere, and that somewhere is the shared worldview of a scientific community. Scientists are socialized into such worldviews, which are maintained and defended by community members. Assumptions about what constitutes reality, and how it can be known, are the property of a scientific community, not just a matter of personal choice.

One line of argument to come out of this is that knowledge is socially constructed. The adoption of particular background assumptions and the use of acceptable research procedures produce certain kinds of knowledge that is sanctioned by such communities. What are regarded as facts about the social world are a matter of intersubjective agreement, not detached, value-free procedures. An outcome of the adoption of this position is that all knowledge is relative, not absolute. When different assumptions are adopted, and different procedures are used, different knowledge will be produced. This notion of relative knowledge can be pushed further by arguing that as there is no neutral position from which to judge the merits of knowledge claims, arguments about which knowledge is true cannot be settled; there are just different ways of describing and understanding the social world.

A conclusion that has been drawn from this position is that 'anything goes'. However, attempts have been made to retrieve the situation. While the theory dependence of observation and the socially constructed nature of knowledge are accepted, alternative conceptions of objectivity have been proposed. We shall examine just two.

Longino (1990) has argued that objectivity is a consequence of research being a social, not an individual, activity. Researchers depend on one another for ideas and methods; they are socialized into existing scientific communities; and they depend on society valuing their activities. The production of scientific knowledge emerges from the work of many individuals engaged in different kinds of activity.

Most importantly, what is accepted as knowledge is a matter of social negotiation. When science is a public activity, it is open to criticism by peers and the wider society. An aspect of this criticism is the exposure of the subjective preferences in background beliefs and assumptions. 'While the possibility of criticism does not totally eliminate subjective preference either from an individual's or from a community's practice of science, it does provide a means for checking its influence in the formation of "scientific knowledge"' (Longino 1990: 73). Hence, background beliefs and assumptions are subject to social controls, and may be modified or abandoned in the face of criticism. Criticism is transformative.

> Objectivity, therefore, turns out to be a matter of degree. A method of inquiry is objective to the degree that it permits transformative criticism. Its objectivity consists not just in the inclusion of intersubjective criticism but in the degree to which both its procedures and its results are responsive to the kinds of criticism described. (Longino 1990: 76)

Longino has proposed four criteria for achieving transformative critical discourse: (1) there must be recognized avenues for the criticism of evidence, of methods, and of assumptions and reasoning; (2) there must exist shared standards that critics can invoke; (3) the community as a whole must be responsive to such criticism; (4) intellectual authority must be shared equally among qualified practitioners (Longino 1990: 76).

By taking this approach to objectivity, we end up with knowledge that a community of scientists is prepared to accept, and which can be used as a basis for action. However, we have not arrived at ultimate truths. 'To say that a theory or hypothesis was accepted on the basis of objective methods does not entitle us to say it is true but rather that it reflects the critically achieved consensus of the scientific community. In the absence of some form of privileged access to transempirical (unobservable) phenomena it's not clear that we should hope for anything better' (Longino 1990: 79). Hence, achieving objectivity in this way does not guarantee truth.

It is possible to criticize Longino's approach, particularly with regard to the nature of scientific communities and the processes by which responses to criticism are made. Criticism is a dynamic process, which may not achieve a consensus, and even if consensus is achieved, it does not mean that the community view is true. When an individual researcher is faced with criticism, it is possible that the individual is right and not the community (Williams 2005: 117). In the social sciences the situation is complicated by the fact that there are competing communities, each of which champions a particular research paradigm and defends its own assumptions and beliefs. While criticism within a community may produce the kinds of outcomes that Longino hoped for, cross-community criticism is another matter. Nevertheless, she has moved our attention away from individual solutions to the problem of objectivity, and has highlighted the social dynamics of scientific activity and how agreements about objectivity are or could be achieved.

Longino's ideas were presented in the context of the natural sciences. The second position, which is compatible with Longino's, comes from the social sciences (Williams 2000, 2005). Williams has addressed the issue of the possibility of objectivity in sociology, and has claimed that if we are to have a science of the social world, we must have some way of determining what are true accounts of the social world. While accepting that objectivity based on value freedom is untenable, because value freedom itself is impossible, he has argued that 'a version of objectivity that begins from values and is therefore situated within particular social contexts is possible' (Williams 2005: 99). He has defined objectivity as *'the purposeful search for truth about the properties of objects'* (2005: 110).

Williams has contended that objectivity, like truth, is a social value, and that, as a consequence, it will be regarded differently in different contexts. It is social to the extent that it is supported by some community that is the arbiter of its achievement. Objectivity in science is different from objectivity in other fields, such as the law.

The desire for true accounts of the social world has to be tempered by the recognition that there is no ultimate way of evaluating the truthfulness of explanations. Another solution is to sidestep the problem of finding impartial criteria and focus on the usefulness of explanations – a pragmatic approach. If theories do what we need them to do, such as help us to solve some problems, maybe that is all we need to be concerned about. Of course, we could go further and argue that if a theory works, it must be true.

What use should social researchers make of the way in which research participants conceptualize and understand their world?

This question poses a further dilemma, by bringing us back to two issues discussed in chapter 1. The first concerns the fundamentally different ways in which knowledge is produced: that is, by a researcher working 'top down' or 'bottom up'. The second concerns the two different postures that a researcher can adopt toward the people they research: that is, as an 'outside expert' or an 'inside learner'. The dilemma concerns how much credence should be given to what people can tell you about their social world as against the so-called expert knowledge that an experienced social scientist can bring to any research problem. The way in which we deal with this issue will depend largely on how we responded to the previous question about whether there is one social reality or many.

If we adopt the view that there is only one social reality, and that it exists independently of what social actors think about it, then the answer to this question is that, as we are the experts, social scientific theories will provide a more reliable basis for answering our RQs than social participants' perceptions and understandings. If, however, we are inclined to the multiple social reality view, and we accept the epistemology of *constructionism*, we will want to give a great deal of credence to the knowledge that social participants have of their world. How else can we find out about the socially constructed world they inhabit? While we may differ in terms of how much credence we give to what they tell us, one way or the other we will want to listen to their accounts. Just how we do this will be a matter of choosing between what we consider to be the most appropriate method or methods.

What should the relationship be between everyday, lay language and social scientific, technical language?

The final dilemma to be considered here derives from a combination of most of the other epistemological dilemmas. This choice is about whether the social scientific concepts to be used in a research project should come from existing research and/or theory, or whether they should be derived from the everyday language of those being researched. Should social scientific language be imposed on everyday life, or should it be derived from everyday, lay language? Should the starting point for answering RQs be with existing social scientific knowledge or with everyday knowledge?

In those RPs that adopt a 'top down' approach to research, the language that the participants use to deal with that part of the social world in which the social researcher is interested, and their ideas about what is going on, are considered to be, at best, unreliable, and, at worst, irrelevant. RPs that adopt a 'bottom up' approach argue that all accounts of social life must either be expressed in the language of the participants, or at least be based on the way in which they conceptualize and understand their reality. Of all the questions being examined here, this is probably the most central one, as well as being the most controversial. Bhaskar (1979: 198) has identified it as the central methodological question in the social sciences.

We will come back to these dilemmas in chapter 6, albeit in a different guise, and after exploring the RPs in some detail.

The Postmodern Turn

The postmodern turn, or *postmodernism*, refers to a group of perspectives on social theory and research that challenge the way in which the social sciences were traditionally understood about fifty years ago. A somewhat parallel process has been occurring in the arts, architecture and literature.

As *postmodernism* means many things to many people, it is difficult to define concisely. The easiest way to think about *postmodernism* is to contrast it with modernism. Potter has characterized the differences, in the context of the social sciences, in terms of caricatures of the differences between two friends.

> The modernist is well meaning and hard working, but she has not got much of a sense of humour: she is constantly struggling to get to the best understanding of what is going on in any situation. She knows what she is like: confident, honest and forthright. The postmodernist talks more about work than actually doing it; she is witty and ironic – you never know whether she is making fun of you or sending herself up. You would be hard put to say whether she has a particular personality or not; she is many things at once, and none of them seems more true than any other. (Potter 1996: 88)

What follows spells out the significance of these differences.

Types and origins of *postmodernism*

The concept of *postmodernism* has been used to refer to three different types of development. The first describes changes in art and architecture involving a rejection of the idea of representation in the former and the adoption of local and mixed styles in the latter. The second describes changes in contemporary society to post-industrial and post-capitalist forms, or to cultural changes within capitalism generally associated with consumerism, popular culture, mass media and economic globalization. The third refers to developments in French and Anglo-Saxon philosophy and social theory that have come to have a significant impact on social research. It is the third development that concerns us here.

The ideas that have emerged in postmodern philosophy are a reaction against the views of science and knowledge that emanated from Europe during the fifteenth, sixteenth and seventeenth centuries and reached their culmination in the eighteenth century in what is known as the 'Age of Enlightenment'. The central idea of modernity was a belief in rationality and progress, a radical break with history and tradition that was intended to liberate human beings from irrationality, ignorance and superstition. This rationality is most clearly evident in the precision and certainty of science in its attempt to understand, control and manipulate nature.

A new epoch?

Most writers locate the advent of postmodern society after the Second World War in advanced capitalist societies (Dickens and Fontana 1994: 3). Whether *postmodernism* constitutes a new epoch (postmodernity), or whether it is just 'modernism coming to terms with its limitations' (Sayer 2000: 30), is a much debated issue (B. Smart 1996). Certainly, *postmodernism* can be viewed as the emergence of a period of reflection on the assumptions, claims and practices established in modernity.

Developments in modernist society and philosophy have laid the foundation for the more radical ideas of *postmodernism*. To begin with, the past century has seen a growing diversity in the world, resulting from the effects of colonialism, population growth, major wars, global capitalism and migration. The mixing and blending of cultures within nation-states, as well as the changing social structures of inequality and power, have led to unprecedented diversity.

At the same time, a plurality of competing theoretical perspectives has emerged within the social sciences, each claiming to provide superior understanding. On its own, this development has the potential to challenge the idea of universal truth. However, the growing fragmentation of societies and the perspectivization of social scientific knowledge have been accompanied by challenges to the dominant (inductive) logic of *empiricism* as a way to develop scientific knowledge. As we have seen, some philosophers began to argue that all scientific knowledge is tentative and open to revision, thus undermining one of the central tenets of science, the claim to certain knowledge. In addition, ideas about the socially constructed nature of reality had begun to emerge some time before ideas of *postmodernism* were articulated.

Whether or not we prefer to view *postmodernism* as constituting a new epoch or as a refining process within modernism, it is tempting to see it as completely rejecting all that modernism stood for and as undermining its very foundations. 'Where modernism purports to base itself on generalised, indubitable truths about the way things really are, *postmodernism* abandons the entire epistemological basis for any such claims to truth. Instead of espousing clarity, certitude, wholeness and continuity, *postmodernism* commits itself to ambiguity, relativity, fragmentation, particularity and discontinuity' (Crotty 1998: 185). *Postmodernism* has also challenged the idea of human progress through universal reason.

Characteristics

In spite of the variety of concepts that have been used to identify *postmodernism*, and the variety of views that have been presented on the relationship of the modern to the postmodern, it is possible to identify a number of themes that represent breaks with modern ideas (Best and Kellner 1997: 255–8; Alvesson and Sköldberg 2000; Alvesson 2002, 2004). However, this is not to suggest that *postmodernism* is a unified set of ideas; rather, that within this diversity there are some dominant ideas.

1 *The rejection of grand narratives.* Grand or meta-narratives refer to major philosophical systems, or grand, overarching social theories, which claim to describe and explain total societies or even world systems. Examples of these include Marxism, systems theories and liberal economic theories (Lyotard 1984). *Postmodernism* denies that such theories provide universal explanations, and accords them no privileged status; they are regarded as stories, grand tales about social life, told from the point of view and interests of the story-teller, and are designed to maintain established power bases. Further, postmodern theorists, such as Baudrillard, Lyotard and Foucault, contend that with the end of the modern era, modern social theory is now obsolete.

Postmodernists advocate non-totalizing theorizing of societies and cultures, preferring instead mini-narratives, 'which provide explanations for small-scale situations located within particular contexts where no pretensions of abstract theory, universality or generalisability are involved' (Grbich 2004: 26). Emphasis is placed on 'difference, plurality, fragmentation, and complexity' (Best and Kellner 1997: 255–6). Lyotard's (1984) view on this can be summarized as follows.

> Different groups (institutions, disciplines, communities) tell different stories about what they know and what they do. Their knowledge does not take the form of a logically structured and complete whole, but rather takes the form of narratives that are instrumental in allowing them to achieve their goals and to make sense of what they are doing. Since these narratives are all local, they cannot be linked together to form a grand narrative which unifies all knowledge. The postmodern condition is characterised by the coexistence of a multiplicity of heterogeneous discourses – a state of affairs assessed differently by different parties. (Cillers 1998: 114)

2 *Rejection of absolute truths.* Because *postmodernism* regards social realities as multiple social constructions, subject to re-formation and reconstruction, notions of objective reality and absolute truths are rejected. Truth and reality are embedded in the meanings that are intersubjectively negotiated between social actors from their shared, subjective life experiences. Knowledge itself is regarded as a social construction that is negotiated through dialogue. The result is that there can be many truths. Neither everyday nor scientific truths can be regarded as absolute, because they are based on local, negotiated knowledge. '[A]bsolute knowledge becomes unattainable, and all knowledge becomes relative and subject to negotiation' (Grbich 2004: 25).

3 *Critique of representation.* One of the dominant characteristics of *postmodernism* is a rejection of the idea that language mirrors or maps reality. In *empiricism*, language was used to describe facts about the world that emerged from disciplined observation. However, *postmodernism* not only claims that there are no such things as facts, but also examines the discourses used to support such an idea and the simple relationships that are claimed between words and objects.

Postmodernists are concerned with how images of reality are produced, particularly in written and electronic forms. Rather than being concerned with what these images are meant to represent, they focus on understanding the images themselves.

In *postmodernism*, representation is more rhetorical than reportorial. Researchers do not describe reality or report their findings; they engage in persuasive arguments about the meaning of texts. Language is no longer a mirror of reality or a means of conveying meaning; it is accepted as context-dependent, metaphorical and as constituting reality. The result is that the boundaries between fact and fiction become blurred, the distinction between reality and illusion has disappeared (Hollinger 1994: 128).

4 *Centrality of discourse.* Postmodern theorizing involves close-up interpretive analysis of social texts, written or visual accounts of both social participants and researchers. Texts become synonymous with empirical data, but data that have no relationship with a reality beyond the text (Antonio and Kellner 1994: 129). 'Postmodernists, defining everything as a text, seek to "locate" meaning rather than to "discover" it' (Rosenau 1992: 8). *Postmodernism* shifts the agenda from a concern with using empirical evidence in the development and testing of explanations to a conversation about texts by scholars or rhetors whose concern is to guide and convince themselves and each other (Brown 1994: 231).

5 *Fragmented identities.* The humanist idea of the individual as unique – with intentions, motives and meanings, and possessing a dynamic, integrated consciousness – is regarded as a Western ethnocentricity. The person is now seen as a collection of separate identities, rather than as an individual. These identities may form and re-form, may change and disappear, in unpredictable ways. This is the death of the individual, autonomous, meaning-giving subject (Alvesson 2004: 844).

6 *Adoption of cultural relativism.* Relativism is a reaction against objectivism. The latter asserts that there is 'some permanent, ahistorical matrix or framework

to which we can ultimately appeal in determining the nature of rationality, knowledge, truth, reality, goodness, or rightness' (Bernstein 1983: 8). Instead, there is an acceptance of the inescapable role of rhetoric in claims to truth and objective foundations of knowledge.

Objective criteria that are presented as a basis for distinguishing truth from falsity are seen to be nothing more than forms of persuasion that are designed to show that what is claimed is true. Concerns with 'validity' and 'reliability' give way to a concern with variations in social constructions that change over time and differ across contexts. All social constructions are considered to be valid, and none is privileged over any other.

Postmodernists endorse all forms of relativism. Relativism denies the right of members of one culture to make judgements about the values or practices of another culture, on the grounds that there is no culturally neutral position from which any human being can make objective judgements about anything, let alone about another culture. In so far as judgements of this kind are made, they must be seen to be based, at best, on broader human values and, at worst, on specific cultural values, not on some ultimate criteria.

Postmodernism and social enquiry

Postmodernism does not lead to a specific research programme, and lacks its own social scientific research area. Many postmodernists are not interested in advancing knowledge or in producing anything of general theoretical value (Alvesson and Sköldberg 2000: 175–6). Instead of seeing social research as dealing with a single theoretical frame of reference and searching for logical results and unified interpretations, postmodern research problematizes the authority of the researcher and the research itself, and strives for fragmented knowledge and multiple interpretations.

Some writers, such as Rorty (1989), see *postmodernism* as having a parasitic bias, because it condemns everything and proposes nothing. However, other writers have argued that its influence has been in two different directions, described by Rosenau (1992) as being either sceptical or affirmative, and by Best and Kellner (1997) as extreme or moderate.

> The sceptical version promotes a 'negative' agenda, based on the idea of the impossibility of establishing any truth. Representation becomes a matter of imposing arbitrary meaning on something. Research becomes a matter of deconstruction . . . This approach strongly discourages empirical work, at least as conventionally and positively understood.
>
> Affirmative postmodernism also questions the idea of truth and validity but has a more positive view of social research. . . . This version is not antithetical to empirical work and empirical claims, but issues around description, interpretation, and researcher authority become problematic. (Alvesson 2004: 845)

In spite of it lacking its own research agenda, *postmodernism* has had a profound influence on social enquiry. In terms of research practice, the view that data

collection produces descriptions and understanding of social and cultural phenomena is replaced by a focus on the social constructions of both research participants and the researcher. The focus is on discourses that occur in small-scale local
settings, discourses that create and maintain multiple realities and identities, and
that are open to multiple interpretations.

> Interviews can, for example, be seen not as simple reports of reality or sites for the
> expression of the meanings and experiences of the interviewees but as local settings in
> which dominant discourses constitute subjects and their responses. Ethnographies are
> less viewed as the authoritative reports of other cultures based on carefully carried out
> fieldwork and more as fictional texts in which the authorship and the constructions
> of those being studied matter as much or more than the phenomena 'out there' claimed
> to be studied. Rather than capturing meanings, finding patterns, and arriving at firm
> conclusions, postmodernistically inspired social research shows the indecisiveness of
> meaning, gives space for multiple voices, and opens up for alternative readings.
> (Alvesson 2004: 845)

While accepting the complexity of the social world and the situated and per-
spectival character of knowledge, some features of *postmodernism* have been
rejected by critical or *neo-realists* (Sayer 2000) and many feminists (e.g. Farganis
1994; Ramazanoğlu and Holland 2002).

> Feminists need not reject postmodern thought, or ignore criticisms of modern notions
> of methodology. But taking up the productive freedoms that postmodernism offers
> does not escape epistemology or dispense with the problems of what connections are
> made or refused between knowledge and power, or between ideas, experiences and
> reality. Feminist and postmodern thinkers continue to have different concerns.
> (Ramazanoğlu and Holland 2002: 103)

Sayer (2000: 30), in particular, has argued that, in spite of all the issues raised by
postmodernism, by adopting an affirmative orientation, it is still possible to
develop reliable knowledge.

The strong anti-science thread that runs through the work of postmodernists
has forced social researchers to examine closely their approaches to social enquiry.
There are three possible ways of responding. First, to give up all hope of being able
to provide any kind of systematic understanding of social life and, maybe, turn to
writing novels instead; this is the *defeatist* stance. Second, to accept the claims of
postmodernism and be content with the kind of products that it allows; this is the
converted stance. Or, third, to take on board those ontological and epistemological criticisms of modernist science that cannot be avoided, such as the claims for
context-specific, multiple and socially constructed realities, and the need to recognize both the tentative nature of knowledge, with its time and space limitations,
and the researcher's role in knowledge production. It is then necessary to be
content with much more limited aspirations in terms of research outcomes and
knowledge production; this is the *reformist* stance.

Other alternatives have emerged more recently coming out of the research
paradigms of Social Realism (or at least the version that has adopted the *depth*

realist ontology and the epistemology of *neo-realism*) and *complexity theory* (see chapter 5 and Postscript). While it is accepted that explanations need to be more complex, and knowledge is more tentative than that claimed by earlier traditions of science, the relativist view of knowledge advocated by *postmodernism* is not accepted.

The position I take in this book is that social science *is* possible, that a number of methods or logics of enquiry (RSs) need to be used, including those used in the natural sciences (but with some modifications), and that the social sciences also have a special logic that is not relevant to the natural sciences. The issues raised by negativists can be dealt with in this special logic. I believe that as social researchers need all four RSs in their armoury, it is necessary to reconstruct their classical formulations, particularly the Inductive and Deductive RSs, to make them viable for use in answering RQs. While being sympathetic to many aspects of *postmodernism*, I believe that it is possible and necessary to undertake viable social enquiry, with all its limitations, thus enabling social researchers to provide useful knowledge of social life. As we shall see in the Postscript, writers who advocate the use of *complexity theory* argue for the need to reject the idea of universal knowledge and restrict our ambitions to tentative and local but, nevertheless, useful knowledge. Whether this allows us to reject the ideas that make up *postmodernism* in their entirety is a matter of dispute.

In chapter 3, the four RSs are reviewed, the limitations of the Inductive and Deductive RSs exposed, and modifications made to overcome these. Ten RPs are outlined and discussed in chapters 4 and 5. In the final chapter, the RPs are reviewed and compared in terms of their ontological and epistemological assumptions, and inter-paradigm critiques discussed. The chapter ends with a review of some major dilemmas that have been signalled in this chapter.

Chapter Summary

- A major controversy, which has divided social scientists for more than a century, has centred on two related questions. Are social sciences possible? Can the social sciences use the same methods and procedures that have been so successful in the natural sciences?
- Four main attitudes to answering these questions have emerged, represented by *naturalism, negativism, historicism* and *postmodernism*.
- *Naturalism* claims that all sciences should use the same method, or logic of enquiry, regardless of the nature of their subject matters.
- *Negativism* claims that the methods of the natural sciences cannot be used in the social sciences.
- *Historicism* claims that only some methods of the natural sciences can be used: that is, those relevant to making predictions of future events on the basis of past trends.
- This view of prediction has been attacked as being non-scientific and more like prophecy.
- It is commonly assumed that there is only one scientific method, in which sci-

entists make careful observations and conduct experiments that lead to new discoveries.
- This view of the scientific method has been challenged as being both logically unsatisfactory and as not reflecting good scientific practice.
- Three main methods have emerged in the literature as being or having been used in the natural sciences, based on the logics of induction, deduction and retroduction.
- In making choices about how to answer research questions, researchers have to face a number of dilemmas.
- Ontological dilemmas are concerned with two main questions:

  - Is there only one social reality in any situation?
  - Where, within this reality or these realities, do we look for answers to 'why' research questions?

- There is more than one way of dealing with these dilemmas, but it is not possible to establish which one is correct.
- Epistemological dilemmas are expressed in a further set of questions that a researcher must answer:

  - Is it possible to be objective in social enquiry?
  - Is it possible to determine whether explanations are true or false?
  - Is it possible to observe directly a social reality that is assumed to exist independently of the social participants?
  - What use should social researchers make of the ways in which research participants conceptualize and understand their world?
  - What should be the relationship between everyday, lay language and social scientific, technical language?

- Again, there are no correct answers, only alternatives.
- *Postmodernism* has emerged since the Second World War in the context of growing diversity in the world resulting from the effects of colonialism, population growth, major wars, global capitalism and migration, with the resultant mixing and blending of cultures within nation-states, as well as the changing social structures of inequality and power.
- The concept of *postmodernism* refers to three different types of development:

  - changes in art and architecture;
  - changes in contemporary society associated with consumerism, popular culture, mass media and economic globalization; and
  - developments in French and Anglo-Saxon philosophy and social theory.

- *Postmodernism* has been described as involving a complete rejection of, or as a reflection on, the assumptions, claims and practices established in modernity.
- The central idea of modernity was a belief in rationality and progress that was intended to liberate human beings from ignorance and superstition and,

through the precision and certainty of science, to lead to the understanding,
control and manipulation of nature for the benefit of all.
- However, the growing fragmentation of societies and the perspectivization of
  social scientific knowledge have been accompanied by challenges to *empiricism*
  as a basis for advancing knowledge.
- Claims to certain knowledge have been undermined, involving the rejection of

  - the grand narratives of major philosophical systems and overarching social
    theories, in favour of mini-narratives that have none of the universalizing and
    generalizing pretensions of abstract theory;
  - objective reality and absolute truth, in favour of socially constructed, multi-
    ple realities and local, negotiated knowledge;
  - the representation view of language contained in *empiricism*, in favour of lan-
    guage constituting reality;
  - the idea of empirical evidence, in favour of texts that are treated as data with
    no reality beyond the text;
  - the integrated view of human beings, in favour of the idea of fragmented
    identities; and
  - objectivism, in favour of relativism.

- Postmodern research problematizes the authority of the researcher and, instead,
  strives for fragmented knowledge and multiple interpretations.
- The postmodern turn leaves researchers with three choices:

  - the *defeatist* stance, in which all hope of being able to provide a systematic
    understanding of social life is abandoned;
  - the *converted* stance, in which the claims of *postmodernism* are accepted and
    the researcher is content with the kinds of products it allows; and
  - the *reformist* stance, in which some aspects of *postmodernism* are accepted,
    such as the existence of context-specific, multiple socially constructed reali-
    ties, the tentative nature of knowledge, and the researcher's role in knowl-
    edge production, with resulting limited aspirations in terms of research
    outcomes and knowledge production.

- The *reformist* stance is adopted in this book, particularly to deal with deficiencies in the four research strategies.

Further Reading

Alvesson, M. 2002. *Postmodernism and Social Research*.
——2004. 'Postmodernism'.
Bauman, Z. 1990. 'Philosophical affinities of postmodern sociology'.
Best, S. and D. Kellner. 1997. *The Postmodern Turn*.
Crotty, M. 1998. *The Foundations of Social Research*.
Dickens, D. R. and A. Fontana (eds). 1994. *Postmodernism and Social Inquiry*.
Grbich, C. 2004. *New Approaches in Social Research*.

Hollinger, R. 1994. *Postmodernism and the Social Sciences.*
Popper, K. 1961. *The Poverty of Historicism.*
Rosenau, P. M. 1992. *Post-modernism and the Social Sciences.*
Seidman, S. (ed.). 1994. *The Postmodern Turn.*
Trigg, R. 1985. *Understanding Social Science.*
Williams, M. 2000. *Science and Social Science.*
——and T. May. 1996. *Introduction to the Philosophy of Social Research.*

3

Advancing Knowledge Using Four Research Strategies

Introduction

In order to generate new knowledge about social phenomena, researchers need to adopt a logic of enquiry, a research strategy (RS), to answer research questions. We shall examine three of the major natural science RSs: the Inductive, Deductive and Retroductive. There are, or have been, advocates for the use of each of these three natural science RSs in the social sciences. However, in addition to them, there is a fourth one that is appropriate only in the social sciences, the Abductive RS.

The literature abounds with debates about the relative merits of using each of these four RSs in the social sciences. The arguments are based on logical, theoretical and ideological grounds. The outcome is that all RSs have had weaknesses exposed, although what is regarded as a weakness depends very much on which RS the particular critic prefers. The debates are complex and sometimes inconclusive.

This book adopts a pragmatic approach to these debates. Each RS is outlined in the form in which it has been presented by its initiators and followers. Then, in response to its strengths and weaknesses, modifications are proposed to make them available to practising social researchers. This means being less dogmatic than the original advocates about what they can do.

The four RSs solve puzzles in very different ways. They differ in their

- ontological assumptions;
- starting points;
- steps or logic;
- use of concepts and theory;
- styles of explanation or understanding; and
- the status of their products.

They constitute four different ways of generating new social scientific knowledge by addressing the problem of where to begin and how to proceed. As we saw in chapter 1, one involves collecting data and generalizing from them; another starts by finding a suitable theory that will provide some hypotheses to test; a third searches for underlying causal mechanisms; and the fourth begins by trying to discover social actors' meanings and interpretations, and uses these to generate social scientific descriptions and understanding.

The principles behind two of the RSs, the Inductive and the Deductive, are more widely known than those of the Retroductive and Abductive RSs. The application of inductive and deductive reasoning to research is now well established in the social science literature on research methods, particularly with regard to theory building (see, e.g., Babbie 1992; de Vaus 1995, 2001; Neuman 2000; Wallace 1971, 1983).

It is important to note that the RSs described here owe more to philosophers and social scientists who are concerned about logics of knowledge generation than they do to the practices of social researchers. They represent idealized ways of knowledge production rather than summaries of how social researchers do their research. They are arguments for, rather than examples of, how research should be done. This creates problems for finding empirical illustrations, with the result that the examples used tend to be reconstructions of what some social researchers seem to have done, rather than how they set out with a particular logic in mind. They are reconstructed logics rather than logics in use (Kaplan 1964).

Styles of Reasoning

The Inductive and Deductive RSs are based on two contrasting styles of reasoning, both of which are linear in nature; that is, they move logically from one idea to another. However, alleged deficiencies in the Inductive and Deductive RSs have led to the development, perhaps reclaiming, of two other alternative forms of reasoning: retroduction and abduction. The latter are based on cyclic or spiral processes, rather than linear logic.

The styles of reasoning used in the Inductive and Deductive RSs are, not surprisingly, induction and deduction. Both styles consist of two main kinds of statements: *singular statements*, which refer to a particular event or state of affairs at a particular time and place; and *general statements*, which refer to all events of a particular kind at all places and times. Here is an example of a singular statement that might result from undertaking an investigation into a specific problem in a particular context.

This long-term unemployed factory worker from Erehwon has lost his self-respect.

The general form of this statement is:

Long-term unemployed people lose their self-respect.

An *inductive argument* begins with a number of singular statements and concludes with a general or universal statement. The premises of the argument are statements about specific instances of some event or state of affairs, and the conclusion is a generalization drawn from these premises. The premises might consist of statements about many unemployed factory workers who have lost their self-respect. If all these statements were consistent, and no instances were observed of unemployed workers who have not lost their self-respect to some degree, then it might be concluded that long-term unemployed people lose their self-respect. This general statement makes no restrictions about the type of former employment, where people live, or how long they have been unemployed. However, if some of the singular statements about unemployed people did not refer to loss of self-respect, the argument might conclude with another form of general statement.

Long-term unemployed people are at risk of losing their self-respect.

This statement is general but not universal, because it leaves open the possibility that some long-term unemployed people, under certain conditions, may not lose their self-respect. In either case, in an inductive argument, the conclusion makes claims that exceed what is contained in the premisses; it promises to extend knowledge by going beyond observed instances of some phenomenon.

A deductive argument is the reverse of this. The argument moves from premisses, at least one of which is a general or universal statement, to a conclusion that is a singular statement. The conclusion contains less than the premisses. Using the same example, the deductive form of argument might set out to explain why a particular individual, or category of individuals, suffers from loss of self-respect. Put simply, the argument might read as follows:

1 Long-term unemployed people lose their self-respect.
2 Mary Smith has been unemployed for two years.
3 Therefore, Mary Smith suffers from loss of self-respect.

The premisses (statements 1 and 2) include a general statement and a singular statement, and the conclusion (statement 3) is a singular statement. Nothing has been added to the premisses to get to the conclusion; the truth of the premisses guarantees the truth of the conclusion.

In addition to induction and deduction, Aristotle added a third, *reduction*. Writing mainly in the second half of the nineteenth century and the early part of the twentieth century, Peirce (1934) translated this third form of reasoning as 'abduction' or 'retroduction', and sometimes as 'hypothesis'. Peirce's view of retroductive/abductive reasoning involves 'making an hypothesis' that appears to explain what has been observed; it involves observing some phenomenon and then claiming what it was that gave rise to it.

Peirce argued that all enquiry begins with the observation of some surprising phenomenon. This is followed by a search for a point of view that will resolve the puzzle. Science, according to Peirce, is much more a struggle for intelligibility than it is a matter of strictly following logical procedures. He expressed the form of inference in retroduction as follows:

> The surprising fact, C, is observed;
>> But if A were true, C would be a matter of course,
>> Hence, there is reason to suspect that A is true. (Peirce 1934: 117)

He regarded the process of retroduction as akin to finding the right key for the lock, although the key may never have been observed before.

Peirce regarded Kepler's discovery that the planets move in elliptical orbits around the sun as being the greatest piece of retroductive reasoning ever performed. Kepler did not merely describe or generalize from what had been observed. Through a long process of investigation and the most careful and judicious reflection, he was able to modify his theory until it was in a form that fitted the observations. This was not a random process of casting around for ideas; it was methodical and thoughtful. Retroduction, therefore, is no easy task, which, while involving a process of reasoning, does not lead to certainty; it culminates in finding *a* solution to a research problem.

The use of retroductive reasoning in the Retroductive RS draws heavily on Peirce's ideas. However, as Peirce saw retroductive and abductive reasoning as being equivalent, we will need to search elsewhere for a basis for the Abductive RS. However, what we will end up with draws some inspiration from his ideas.

The Inductive Research Strategy

The Inductive RS represents a very seductive view of science. It corresponds to a popular conception of the activities of scientists: namely, making careful observations,[1] conducting experiments, rigorously analysing the data obtained, and hence producing new discoveries or new theories. Personal opinions are excluded from this process, in order to arrive at what is believed to be true knowledge.

The earliest form of induction used to develop knowledge about the world has been attributed to Aristotle and his disciples. Known as 'enumerative induction', it is referred to here as *naïve induction*. Knowledge is produced about a restricted class of things or events from a limited number of observations. However, a more challenging use of induction is to produce general conclusions about open or unrestricted classes of things and events (Quinton 1980).

This view of science is sometimes referred to as *empiricism*, because of the stress on observation as the foundation of scientific knowledge, in preference to relying on Greek philosophy and the Bible. According to this view, if you want to understand nature, then you must consult nature, and not the writings of Aristotle or religious texts. Science was seen to be built on facts gained by observation, not on some preconceived notions about how the world works.

The Inductive RS has been described by Harré (1972: 42) as consisting of three principles:

- *Accumulation*: knowledge grows by the addition of further well-attested facts such that each new fact does not require any alteration to the previous ones.
- *Induction*: from true statements describing observations and the results of experiments, true generalizations can be inferred.

- *Instance confirmation*: the level of our belief in the truth of a generalization is proportional to the number of instances that have been observed.

This RS has also been characterized as consisting of four main stages (Hempel 1966: 11):

1 All facts are observed and recorded without selection or guesses as to their relative importance.
2 These facts are analysed, compared and classified, without using hypotheses.
3 From this analysis, generalizations are inductively drawn as to the relations between them.
4 These generalizations are subjected to further testing.

Medawar (1969a: 40) expressed the Inductive RS this way.

Let us first assemble the data; let us by observation and by making experiments compile the true record of the state of Nature, taking care that our vision is not corrupted by preconceived ideas; then inductive reasoning can go to work and reveal laws and principles and necessary connections.

Apart from the necessary observational equipment and skills, and the ability to set aside preconceptions, all that the researcher needs to be able to do is to think logically. The generalizations will follow from the data. If these generalizations are challenged, the defence of the inductive scientist will be that they are based on the facts, and only objective and logical procedures have been used.

The Inductive RS embodies the *shallow realist* ontology, which assumes that there is a reality 'out there' with regularities that can be described and explained. It adopts the epistemological principle of *empiricism*, that the task of observing this reality is essentially unproblematic as long as the researcher adopts objective procedures. It claims that reality impinges directly on the senses; that what we 'see' is what exists. As shall be seen, the other RSs have different ontological and epistemological assumptions.

The Inductive RS had its origins in the work of Francis Bacon (1889) and John Stuart Mill (1947). Bacon, the first major philosopher of science of the modern period, set out in his *Novum Organum* an elaborate account of the method of induction[2] that is still regarded by many as *the* scientific method.[3] Rather than simply accumulating knowledge by generalizing from observations, Bacon argued that it is necessary to focus on negative instances. His became an *eliminative* method of induction. By stressing negative instances, rather than just positive ones, Bacon argued that this method had a better chance of producing true theories than was possible by other forms of induction. He claimed that it controls the tendency to jump to conclusions from a few cases; it forces the researcher to examine a wide range of different cases; and it involves a search for possible causes, one of which he believed is associated with every natural phenomenon we can observe.

Bacon's view of science was dominant for more than two centuries. In elaborating these ideas, Mill (1947) believed that the purpose of science was to discover causes and hence produce general laws. He set out a number of methods, or Canons of Induction, the most important of which are the method of agreement and the method of difference. In the method of agreement, two instances of a phenomenon need to be different in all but one characteristic, while in the method of difference, two situations are required to be similar in all characteristics but one, the phenomenon being present with this characteristic. In both cases, the different characteristic can be considered as either the cause or the effect of the phenomenon.

Social science advocate

An early advocate of the use of the Inductive RS in sociology was Emile Durkheim (1858–1917). He was not the first sociologist to argue for a science of society, having continued a tradition already established by Comte in France and Spencer in England. However, he largely rejected their ideas on what a science of society should look like and, in the process, determined the dominant style of empirical research in the developing discipline.

Durkheim differed from these earlier social theorists in that he focused his attention on very limited problems, rather than searching for grand theories of society. His approach is set out in *The Rules of Sociological Method* (Durkheim 1964) and is illustrated in his research on suicide (Durkheim 1970). He moved away from the modes of explanation of social life that were dominant in his day, based on the analysis and combination of ideas, to a process of observing, describing and comparing things. He wanted social scientists to base their explanations on empirical evidence, rather than on philosophical or metaphysical theories. More particularly, he wished to avoid forms of explanation in which an argument is supported by examples, even if based on observation, in favour of one in which generalizations (or theories) are produced *from* observations. In short, he argued for the use of the logic of induction.

Durkheim insisted that explanations of social phenomena must be in terms of independently existing forces that act on individuals from without, and that these forces, while lacking the more tangible form of forces that act in nature, nevertheless have the same objective, thing-like quality. If nothing else, their presence can be established by the effects that they produce, somewhat analogous to gravity.

According to Durkheim (1964), as social phenomena have an independent existence, they can and should be treated as if they are things, and observed in a manner similar to natural phenomena. However, he believed that there is a danger that the observer may allow common-sense ideas or preconceptions to distort the process of observation. Hence, he argued that if these preconceptions are set aside, and the phenomenon under investigation is defined in advance, it will be possible to recognize the relevant facts that must be accumulated in order to arrive at a scientific explanation. The aim is to produce objective data and thus true generalizations about an independent reality.[4] For an empirical example, see box 3.1.

Box 3.1 Empirical example: occupational prestige

I have chosen not to use Durkheim's study of suicide as an example of the Inductive RS, as a reconstruction of his work will serve as an example of the Deductive RS. Instead, we turn to the extensive work that has been conducted around the world, since the Second World War, on social differentiation and inequality. The heyday of this research was from the 1950s to the early 1980s, when positivism and empiricism ruled, particularly in American sociology.

This phenomenon is variously referred to by labels such as 'social class',[a] 'social status' or 'socio-economic status', and it has been measured in various ways. While the concepts and categories are not consistent, researchers in this field generally assumed the existence of some kind of social hierarchy associated with occupation and, sometimes, also with income and education. This structure of occupations is seen to have an independent existence, and is occupied by people whose position is partly determined by their educational qualifications and who are then in a position to earn different levels of income.

Researchers developed various methods for measuring this social reality. Samples of people were usually asked how they view the social standing, or prestige, of occupations, and then their responses were consolidated into a hierarchy of occupational scores. Various ranking and rating methods have been used to achieve this. The landmark study was conducted by the National Opinion Research Centre (NORC) in the USA in 1947 (see Duncan 1961; Lasswell 1965). Numerous similar studies were conducted in different parts of the world about this time and in the following decades (see, e.g., in the UK, Hall and Jones 1950; Moser and Hall 1954; Goldthorpe and Hope 1974; Stewart, Prandy and Blackburn 1980; in the USA, Hodge, Siegel and Rossi 1966; Blau and Duncan 1967; in Canada, Blishen 1967; Pineo and Porter 1967; and in Australia, Broom, Jones and Zubrzski 1968; Congalton 1969; Daniel 1983). Alternatively, the educational qualifications and incomes of incumbents of occupations have been used to establish occupational scores or categories. This occupational hierarchy is viewed either as a continuum of scores, or is divided into a set of 'social class' categories. A common practice, particularly in national censuses, is to establish social classes by categorizing occupations in terms of their relative skill levels and/or their authority, responsibility and control in the processes of production.

Once these scales or sets of categories have been established, individuals can be located in the class or status structure. A further method has been used to assign individuals directly to a class category, either by asking them to nominate the social class in which they consider themselves to be, or by providing a set of class categories and asking them to identify the one they consider applies to them. The assumption here is that people are aware of a class structure, and they know where they are located. Regardless of the fact that different ontological assumptions are used in this method – social classes rather than an occupational hierarchy – the two are frequently used interchangeably, and have been regarded as measuring the same thing.

A major conclusion that has been drawn from studies of occupational status/prestige is that, in spite of the different ways in which it has been measured, there is a consensus of views amongst people about both the existence of such a hierarchy and the positions of occupations in it (see, e.g., Hodge, Siegel and Rossi 1966). Furthermore, on the basis of twenty-eight national studies of occupational prestige, conducted between 1947 and 1963, Hodge, Treiman and Rossi concluded that all societies have social structural features in common: 'occupations stand roughly in the same order of popular evaluation across a wide variety of nations of varying levels of industrialization and varying cultural backgrounds' (1966: 310; see also Treiman 1977). Very strong associations between national measures of occupational prestige have been regarded as establishing the validity of each scale (see, e.g., Jones and Jones 1972). Some writers have gone so far as to claim that occupational prestige is sociology's 'great empirical invariant' (Marsh 1971; Featherman, Jones and Hauser 1975).

In spite of the variety of ways in which structures of inequality have been studied, this field of research bears all the hallmarks of the use of inductive logic in association with a *shallow realist* ontology and the epistemology of *empiricism*. While these structures cannot be observed directly, and while a variety of measures have been used to 'reveal' them, researchers have been confident that they constitute a universal feature of all societies.

There are many problems with this tradition of research, some of which are associated with the deficiencies of inductive logic itself (see the next section).[b]

[a] In this context, 'social class' is used as a generic concept for social hierarchies, and should not be confused with Marxian notions of 'class'.

[b] Some years ago, I became embroiled in a heated debate about these ontological and epistemological assumptions with some Australian exponents of this tradition (see Blaikie 1977, 1978, 1981).

Problems

In spite of convincing critiques dating back to the 1930s, the use of induction persisted as a major RS in some scientific and philosophical circles until the 1960s. However, in its classical form, it is now rejected by most natural and social scientists, and is regarded by philosophers of science as flawed.

Justifying the principle

The first difficulty is how to justify the principle of induction. Can inductive inferences be logically justified? Some earlier philosophers argued that as the principle of induction is widely accepted in both science and everyday life, its truth is based on experience. Popper responded by arguing that to claim that the principle of induction is a universal statement derived from experience is to use the principle in order to justify it; this involves an infinite regress (1959: 29). It therefore follows that there is no purely logical or mechanical induction process for establishing the validity of universal statements from a set of singular statements (Hempel 1966: 15).

Making claims beyond the evidence

The first deficiency alone is enough to demolish the claims of the Inductive RS. However, there are a number of other important criticisms that need to be examined. In an inductive argument, if the premises are true, it does not follow that the conclusion will also be true. It may be the case that all observed cases of long-term unemployment exhibit loss of self-respect, but a further observation may reveal a case that is different. Hence, on the basis of the original observations, the conclusion that long-term unemployed people lose their self-respect cannot be regarded as true.

The response of an inductivist might be that while we cannot be 100 per cent sure of the conclusion to an inductive argument, it might be regarded as true at some level of probability. The greater the number of observations, and the greater the variety of conditions under which the observations are made, the greater the probability that the conclusion will be true. However, a major difficulty with this modification is that it is not possible to establish just how probable a conclusion might be. Until all possible observations are made (and that can never happen), it is not possible to be certain about the proportion of observation statements that are not consistent with the universal statement.

How many observations?

Another problem concerns the number of observations that need to be made before a generalization is possible. To be sure of the truth of an inductively derived generalization, it would be necessary to observe all instances of a phenomenon, in the present, past and future. Clearly, this is not possible; but even if the period of observation is restricted to a current time period, there is still the problem of when to stop observing.

An inductivist might argue that it is simply necessary to make all 'relevant' observations. But relevant to what? All research is directed towards answering questions or solving some problem. If the research question was, 'What factors lead to loss of self-respect?', long-term unemployment is only one possible area on which to focus attention; other factors may be more relevant. But how do we know where to look for them, and why do we think that unemployment might be relevant? Whether we are aware of it or not, we make choices in what we observe.

Description not explanation

The Inductive RS implies that all that is required in research is numerous observations of the phenomenon under investigation. If we study enough cases of loss of self-respect, we will discover those factors with which it is associated, and hence be able to provide an explanation for it: e.g. that it is a consequence of long-term unemployment. However, at best, what this RS produces are descriptions of patterns of association. But no matter how confident we are about an association, we cannot conclude that loss of self-respect is a *consequence* of long-term unemployment. It could be that loss of self-respect was produced by something else, and that this led to unsatisfactory performance at work, which then led to unemployment.

Therefore, an explanation for loss of self-respect requires more than a description of it. Even a well-established association still requires an explanation. It is necessary to go beyond the reporting of events in order to explain them. The critical question is where to look for the explanation. The Inductive RS provides no answer. In fact, it deliberately prohibits the researcher from even pursuing any hunches. 'The facts must speak for themselves.'

Relying on Bacon's and Mill's methods is no real help, as both require the scientist to have some ideas about possible causes of the phenomenon in order to know to which 'circumstance' to pay attention. As Harré (1972) has suggested, if we wish to explain why plants grow more vigorously in warm weather than in cold, the choice between heat and light as possible causes could not be made using Mill's methods. It would be possible to set up a controlled experiment to test the independent effects of heat and light, and we might come to the conclusion that light seems to be the predominant cause, but that some heat is also necessary. However, would this process lead us to photosynthesis as the mechanism of growth? Mill's methods may be useful guides for the preliminary stages of an investigation, but, according to Harré, they are inadequate as a method for discovering or testing theories.

Observation involves interpretation

This leads us to another more serious objection to the Inductive RS, which has to do with the activity of observing. The inductivist operates with two important assumptions about observation: that all science starts with observation, and that observation provides a secure basis from which knowledge can be derived (Chalmers 1982: 22). However, Popper has argued that all observation involves interpretation. In fact, 'in the social sciences it is even more obvious than in the natural sciences that we cannot see and observe our objects before we have thought about them. For most of the objects of the social sciences, if not all of them, are abstract objects; they are *theoretical* constructions' (Popper 1961: 135). For example, 'self-respect' is a theoretical idea that could not have been induced mechanically from observing unemployed people. We have to know what we want to observe before we can see it. We will keep bumping into this problem in the following chapters.

Summary

Two of the early critics of the Inductive RS, Popper and Hempel, summarized their views as follows.

> I do not believe that we ever make inductive generalizations in the sense that we start with observations and try to derive our theories from them. I believe that the prejudice that we proceed in this way is a kind of optical illusion, and that at no stage of scientific development do we begin without something in the nature of a theory, such as a hypothesis, or a prejudice, or a problem – often a technological one – which in some way *guides* our observations, and helps us to select from the innumerable objects of observation those which may be of interest. (Popper 1961: 134)

There are, then, no generally applicable 'rules of induction', by which hypotheses or theories can be mechanically derived or inferred from empirical data. The transition from data to theory requires creative imagination. Scientific hypotheses and theories are not *derived* from observed facts, but *invented* in order to account for them. They constitute guesses at the connections that might obtain between the phenomena under study, at uniformities and patterns that might underlie their occurrence . . . [T]he ways in which fruitful scientific guesses are arrived at are very different from any process of systematic inference. (Hempel 1966: 15)

The application of the Inductive RS has been illustrated in a somewhat exaggerated form in the context of medical practice by the eminent biologist and Nobel Laureate, Peter Medawar.

A patient comes to his physician feeling wretched, and the physician sets out to discover what is wrong. In the inductive view the physician empties his mind of all prejudices and preconceptions and *observes* his patient intently. He records the patient's colour, measures his pulse rate, tests his reflexes and inspects his tongue (an organ that seldom stands up to public scrutiny). He then proceeds to other, more sophisticated actions: the patient's urine will be tested; blood counts and blood cultures will be made; biopsies of liver and marrow are sent to the pathology department; tubing is inserted into all apertures and electrodes applied to all exposed surfaces. The factual evidence thus assembled can now be classified and 'processed' according to the canons of induction. A diagnosis (e.g. 'It was something he ate') will thereupon be arrived at by reasoning which, being logical, could in principle be entrusted to a computer, and the diagnosis will be the right one unless the raw factual information was either erroneous or incomplete. (Medawar 1969a: 42–3)

If researchers are influenced by their past experiences, knowledge and expectations, and they must work from within some language, and all observations entail theoretical assumptions, how is objectivity possible? Different researchers, from different cultural backgrounds and biographical trajectories, working with different theoretical assumptions, will, at best, have different views of reality. If objectivity is not possible, then the discovery of truth is also impossible.

Revision

It is on the claim that it can produce universal generalizations and true explanations that the Inductive RS founders. For the reasons just discussed, such claims are untenable. Why, then, persist in using this RS?

Social researchers need descriptions of social phenomena in order to answer 'what' RQs. It is possible to produce elementary descriptions that refer to single individuals or events. However, researchers need more general descriptions to answer their questions. To answer the RQ, 'What kinds of people are unemployed?', data are needed on a range of unemployed people. A description to answer this RQ requires the use of inductive logic. We take the descriptions of all the unemployed people in our study, and we produce a general description of their characteristics. For example, our sample of unemployed people may have a low level of education and limited job skills, and lack a sense of their own worth (self-respect). Whatever description is produced to answer the RQ requires a choice to be made from amongst an endless array of possible characteristics.

How do we know what characteristics to look for? We cannot decide this just from collecting data, because we have to make decisions about what data to collect. The result is that we have infringed most of the principles of inductive logic. We have decided in advance what to look for – although we may stumble across some other characteristics in the course of our research – and we have limited our data collection to a specific location, however narrow or extensive. The answer to our 'what' question will have been influenced by our background knowledge, from both theory and previous research, and will be limited in time and space. What we are not claiming is that we have produced an explanation for unemployment. All that we have been able to do is produce the best description we can of unemployed people within the confines of our research project and the state of knowledge at the time.

In addition to the use of one or more individual characteristics, descriptions can also be made of the patterns of association between these characteristics. For example, we could establish the relationships between level of self-respect and age and gender. Such patterns are just more elaborate descriptions, and would answer a RQ such as, 'What socio-demographic characteristics are associated with loss of self-respect?' However, to make the pursuit of this question worthwhile, we would first need to establish that the people in our sample differ in their levels of self-respect.

The use of inductive logic in this way requires the adoption of different onto-logical and epistemological assumptions than were used in the classical version. Table 3.1 sets out the aims, assumptions and logic of a revised Inductive RS as well as the other three.

The aim of the revised Inductive RS is to establish limited generalizations about the distribution of, and patterns of association amongst, observed or measured characteristics of some social phenomenon. Typical characteristics in research populations and samples are either demographic (e.g. gender, age, education, religion) or are based on theoretical concepts (e.g. social class, religiosity, attitudes of various kinds). When an outside/expert researcher stance is adopted towards the researched, the social world can be observed or measured only through the use of such researcher-defined concepts.

Whereas a *shallow realist* ontology was adopted in the classical version of the Inductive RS, this is no longer tenable. Also, a *conceptual realist* ontology has little relevance to empirical social research. Hence, the ontological assumptions used in this revision of the Inductive RS will be one of the other realist versions, *cautious*, *depth* or *subtle*. If descriptive associations are to be explained by the Deductive or Retroductive RS, the ontologies are likely to be *cautious realist* or *depth realist*, respectively. If the data used are qualitative, as in ethnography, a *subtle realist* ontology could be adopted.

As the epistemology of *empiricism* is no longer tenable, another needs to be adopted. If the Inductive RS is used on its own, the epistemology of *convention-alism* would be appropriate. However, if the RS is used in combination with either

Table 3.1 Revised research strategies

	Inductive	Deductive	Retroductive	Abductive
Aim:	To establish descriptions of characteristics and patterns	To test theories, to eliminate false ones and corroborate the survivor	To discover underlying mechanisms to explain observed regularities	To describe and understand social life in terms of social actors' motives and understanding
Ontology:	Cautious, depth or subtle realist	Cautious or subtle realist	Depth or subtle realist	Idealist or subtle realist
Epistemology:	Conventionalism	Conventionalism Falsificationism	Modified neo-realism	Constructionism
Start:	Collect data on characteristics and/or patterns	Identify a regularity to be explained	Document and model a regularity	Discover everyday lay concepts, meanings and motives
	Produce descriptions	Construct a theory and deduce hypotheses	Describe the context and possible mechanisms	Produce a technical account from lay accounts
Finish:	Relate these to the research questions	Test the hypotheses by matching them with data	Establish which mechanism(s) provide(s) the best explanation in that context	Develop a theory and elaborate it iteratively

the Deductive or Retroductive RS, their revised epistemologies could be adopted instead.

The descriptions produced by the revised Inductive RS, whether they be univariate or bivariate descriptions,[5] are limited in time and space. While they are commonly quantitative, they are not restricted to data of this type. However, the selection of characteristics to be studied, and their definition and measurement, are all conducted from the researcher's point of view. See box 3.2.

Box 3.2 Application of the revised Inductive Research Strategy

To illustrate the use of the revised version of the Inductive RS, let us return to the research topic on long-term unemployment that was introduced in chapter 1. Two 'what' questions and one 'why' question were posed.

1 What kinds of people experience long-term unemployment?
2 What is it like to be unemployed for an extended period?
3 Why are these people unemployed?

The revised Inductive RS is a very suitable choice to answer RQ 1. The answer will be in the form of a description of the characteristics of these people. However, the researcher needs some guidance in the choice of characteristics to be included. Previous research in the area will be useful, as may an exploratory study with a small sample from the population under consideration. While experienced researchers will have a storehouse of ideas to draw on, their knowledge and past experiences, as well as their preferred RP(s), will both facilitate and limit their choice. There is no alternative to this.

If the choice of methods is quantitative, then measures of each characteristic will need to be devised.[a] Some obvious examples are age, gender, level and type of education, marital/family situation, area of residence, employment experience and duration of unemployment. There have to be good reasons for selecting characteristics. Also, to be meaningful, distributions on most of these characteristics would need to be compared with those of the population within which the study is conducted. What we are looking for is what makes these people different.

A description can also include an analysis of patterns in the relationships between some of these characteristics. For example, younger unemployed people may be different from older people, particularly in education, marital/family situation and employment experience. The establishment of such patterns will prompt further 'why' questions. This is not to suggest that we should engage in what some have called 'mindless empiricism', just measuring variables and correlating them. What these patterns will provide is more detailed descriptions and, hence, fuller answers to 'what' questions. Of course, it is possible to answer RQ 1 using qualitative methods. Even here, but perhaps to a lesser extent, the researcher will have to have some idea of what to look for.

RQ 2 could require a major study on its own. If quantitative methods are used, the researcher will need a great deal of guidance as to what to observe and what questions to ask members of the population, or a sample of them. Qualitative methods lend themselves to answering this RQ, possibly by means of in-depth interviews. Whatever methods are used, the outcome will be a detailed description arrived at by the use of inductive logic, by drawing together data from many people into general statements. Many statistical procedures, such as measures of central tendency and dispersion, and measures of association, imply inductive logic.

Inductive logic is not particularly useful for answering 'why' questions. Established patterns between characteristics, or very detailed qualitative descriptions, *can* point in the direction of possible answers. However, different RSs are required to answer RQ 3.

[a] I refer to characteristics rather than variables throughout the discussion of this illustration. Variables come into being only when measures for these characteristics have been devised. The illustration will stop short of this stage in research and, as well, will leave open the possibility of qualitative descriptions that do not use variables.

The Deductive Research Strategy

The Deductive RS was proposed as an alternative to the Inductive RS. The contrast between the two RSs is illustrated in Medawar's example of how a second type of clinician might go about the task of arriving at a diagnosis.

The second clinician always observes his patient with a purpose, with an idea in mind. From the moment the patient enters he sets himself questions, prompted by foreknowledge or by sensory cues; and these questions direct his thought, guiding him towards new observations which will tell him whether the provisional views he is constantly forming are acceptable or unsound. Is he ill at all? Was it indeed something he ate? An upper respiratory virus is going around: perhaps this is relevant to the case? Has he at last done his liver an irreparable disservice? Here there is a rapid reciprocation between an imaginative and a critical process, between imaginative conjecture and critical evaluation. As it proceeds, a hypothesis will take shape which affords a reasonable basis for treatment or for further examination, though the clinician will not often take it to be conclusive. (Medawar 1969a: 44)

Naïve and sophisticated falsification

Support for the logic of deduction can be traced back to antiquity. More than 2,000 years ago Euclid developed a system of geometry in which a large number of propositions (theorems) are demonstrated, or proved, if they can be deduced from a few assumptions (axioms or postulates). Euclidian geometry was later followed by Aristotelian logic – simple syllogisms used as a basis for developing knowledge by logical argument. So powerful were these axiomatic and syllogistic systems that they led to the view that scientific theories should also be constructed in this deductive form.

The Deductive RS is sometimes referred to as the *hypothetico-deductive* method, or the method of conjecture and refutation. It is based on the *cautious realist* ontology and the epistemology of *falsificationism*. Karl Popper is its pioneer and most outspoken advocate.

Whereas the classical inductivists looked for evidence to confirm their general-izations, sometimes referred to as *justificationism*, deductivists try to falsify their hypotheses. The use of the Deductive RS begins with a question or a problem that needs to be understood or explained. Instead of starting with observations, the first stage is to produce a possible answer to the question; to look for an explana-tion for the problem in existing theory, or to invent a new theory.

Braithwaite saw the Deductive RS as one in which the natural scientist has great freedom to propose a theory, but has to hand over to Nature the task of deciding whether any of the conclusions drawn from it are false (1953: 368). The 'aim is not to save the lives of untenable systems, but, on the contrary, to select the one which is by comparison the fittest, by exposing them all to the fiercest struggle for survival' (Popper 1959: 42).

Popper's version of the RS (1959: 32–3) can be summarized as follows.

1 Begin by putting forward a tentative idea, a conjecture, a hypothesis or a set of hypotheses that form a theory.
2 With the help, perhaps, of other previously accepted hypotheses, or by specify-ing conditions under which the hypotheses are expected to hold, deduce a con-clusion, or a number of conclusions.
3 Examine the conclusions and the logic of the argument that produced them. Compare this argument with existing theories to see if it constitutes an advance in our understanding. If you are satisfied with this examination,
4 Test the conclusion by gathering appropriate data; make the necessary observ-ations or conduct the necessary experiments.
5 If the test fails, i.e. if the data are not consistent with the conclusion, the 'theory' must be false. The original conjecture does not match up with reality and must therefore be rejected.
6 If, however, the conclusion passes the test, i.e. the data are consistent with it, the 'theory' is temporarily supported; it is *corroborated*, not proven to be true.

Popper also set out a number of requirements for this strategy. First, for any theory to be regarded as scientific, it must be possible, at least in principle, to falsify it – to use evidence to challenge it. A theory that is not capable of being tested cannot be called scientific (Popper 1959: 40, 48). A good theory is falsifi-able, because it makes definite claims about the world. This requirement is known as the 'demarcation criterion' because it separates scientific theories from other forms of explanation. Second, tests should be as demanding as possible, for a theory that can survive such a test must be more acceptable than one that has been subjected to weaker tests (Popper 1961: 134). Also, the more precisely a theory is stated, the more falsifiable it becomes, and the more falsifiable it is, the better (Chalmers 1982: 42). For an empirical example, see box 3.3.

Box 3.3 Empirical example: Durkheim's theory of egoistic suicide

Durkheim (1858–1917), as we have seen, was a staunch advocate of the Inductive RS. He chose to study suicide to demonstrate the superiority of inductive sociological explanations (Durkheim 1970). However, when his research is examined closely, it appears that the underlying logic of his explanations is deductive. This deductive reconstruction of his egoistic theory of suicide follows his procedures closely. However, it is important to note that this reconstruction is not designed to deal with problems his critics have raised (see, e.g., Douglas 1967; Atkinson 1978), although it does reduce the impact of some of them.

Durkheim set out with a definition of suicide as 'all cases of death resulting directly or indirectly from a positive or negative act of the victim himself [*sic*], which he knows will produce this result' (1970: 44). He believed that such a definition would give him comparable data.[a] He then presented some data to support his argument that suicide has social causes. First, he compared absolute figures, from 1841 to 1872, for France, England, Denmark and states that are now part of Germany: Prussia, Saxony and Bavaria. He found the rates were fairly constant over this period, with both marked and stable differences between countries. He also noted some rises and falls across all countries, which he attributed to European-wide events, and country fluctuations, which he attributed to internal events. Durkheim claimed that these 'facts' were evidence for social causes.

He then proceeded to eliminate some non-social causes, such as mental illness, age, race, ethnicity and heredity, as well as possible physical causes, such as latitude, seasonal changes, time of day and month of the year. He also explored the possibility that suicide may be imitative behaviour. The outcome of these investigations was that while variations were present, Durkheim believed that these factors could not account for the differences in suicide rates that he had established.

One other difference in suicide rates became his focus of attention: namely, that Protestant countries had higher suicide rates than Catholic countries, and that countries of mixed religious faith had moderate rates. 'If one casts a glance at the map of European suicide, it is at once clear that in purely Catholic countries like Spain, Portugal, Italy, suicide is very little developed, while it is at its maximum in Protestant countries, in Prussia, Saxony, Denmark' (Durkheim 1970: 152). He also established that within the states of Germany, suicide rates are in direct proportion to the number of Protestants and in inverse proportion to the number of Catholics. The non-social and physical factors just reviewed were not able to help him explain these differences.

To tackle this problem, Durkheim divided suicide into three types: egoistic, altruistic and anomic. Egoistic suicide occurs when a person experiences a weakening in commitments to group goals and norms, and has to depend on his or her own resources. Altruistic suicide is the reverse, and occurs when a person is deeply committed to group goals and norms, even when suicide is a duty (e.g. Japanese samurai and kamikaze bomber pilots, and, in traditional India, widows at their husband's funeral). Anomic suicide occurs when periods of crisis or rapid social change undermine group norms; a person becomes unsure about how to behave. 'Egoistic suicide results from man's [*sic*] no longer finding a basis for existence in life; altruistic suicide, because this basis for existence appears to man situated beyond life itself. The third sort of suicide . . . results from man's activity's lacking regulation and his consequent sufferings' (Durkheim 1970: 258). Note that the descriptions of these types of suicide are as much theories as they are definitions. It is at this point that Durkheim began to stray from his professed use of the Inductive Research Strategy; he brought theoretical ideas to the data.

Durkheim used the idea of egoistic suicide to explain the religious differences in suicide rates. He argued that Catholicism is a unified religion in which religious activities are constant and regular, thus creating solidarity and a sense of belonging. Protestantism, he argued, encourages people to think for themselves rather than subscribe to doctrine without question. This 'spirit of free enquiry' encourages controversy and schisms. 'So if Protestantism concedes a greater freedom to individual thought than Catholicism, it is because it has fewer common beliefs and practices. . . . [T]he superiority of Protestantism with respect to suicide results from its being a less strongly integrated church than the Catholic church' (Durkheim 1970: 159).

Durkheim's ideas about egoistic suicide have been formulated into five propositions, using three main concepts: 'suicide rate' (the number of suicides per thousand of a population); 'individualism' (the tendency for people to think for themselves and act independently, rather than conform to the beliefs and norms of some group);[b] and 'Protestantism' (a collection of Christian groups formed as a result of the Reformation in Europe).

1 In any social grouping, the suicide rate varies directly with the degree of individualism (egoism).
2 The degree of individualism varies directly with the incidence of Protestantism.
3 Therefore, the suicide rate varies with the incidence of Protestantism.
4 The incidence of Protestantism in Spain is low.
5 Therefore, the suicide rate in Spain is low. (Homans 1964: 951)[c]

The theory contains two universal propositions (1 and 2) that state the form of the relationships between pairs of concepts. The meaning of each proposition could be elaborated, and reasons given for its inclusion. The third proposition follows logically from the first two and links suicide rate with 'Protestantism', a less abstract concept than 'individualism'. On its own, each proposition explains nothing, but all three propositions together constitute an explanation for differences in suicide rates. The addition of proposition 4, a descriptive statement, allows for a prediction (proposition 5) that can be tested (assuming that relative suicide rates can be satisfactorily established). Similarly, predictions could be made about other countries (e.g. Republic of Ireland) to provide further tests of the theory. Alternatively, if proposition 5 needs to be explained, then the preceding propositions provide the explanation.

In this particular theory it would be possible to test propositions 1–3 directly by gathering data on these pairs of concepts in various populations. All that is required is a description of the form and strength of association between the two concepts, or variables based on them. Hence, according to Popper, when theories are structured in this deductive way, the differences between explanation, prediction and testing are just a matter of emphasis.

Durkheim's research went through a number of stages that are characteristic of the Deductive RS. He established a regularity that cried out for an explanation: the relationship between suicide rates and religion. He examined a number of existing theories and found that they were of no help. So he invented a theory which made sense of the regularity. While he did not express this theory as a deductive argument, it lends itself to this. The theory of egoistic suicide can be tested by comparing other religious groups or societies, and can be reformulated to compare other types of social groups. In effect, this is what Durkheim did when he found that suicide rates vary according to marital status; the lowest rate is for people married with children, followed by married people without children, widowed, divorced and unmarried. This suggests that lack of integration into both domestic and religious groups can have the same consequences.

[a] Unfortunately, as critics have pointed out, his data depended on the definitions of those who were responsible for categorizing the causes of death, and not necessarily in terms of the 'victim's' motives, which Durkheim's definition required. This has undermined the comparability of suicide rates across groups and societies, thus weakening Durkheim's arguments.

[b] An alternative concept, 'social integration', refers to the acceptance and practice of a group's beliefs and norms by its members. Durkheim argued that free enquiry in a religious group can lead to schisms, while strict adherence to beliefs and practices that some groups require, can socially integrate the members.

[c] Another reconstruction of Durkheim's theory, using different concepts, can be found in Merton 1957: 97.

This view of the process of advancing knowledge is rather paradoxical. Why do we not try to find support for a fledgling theory, rather than try to destroy it? Popper argued that

if we are uncritical we shall always find what we want: we shall look for, and find, confirmations, and we shall look away from, and not see, whatever might be dangerous to our pet theories. In this way it is only too easy to obtain what appears to be overwhelming evidence in favour of a theory which, if approached critically, would have been refuted. (Popper 1961: 134)

While Popper's view of science began to gain acceptance in the 1960s, there were features of it with which some commentators were dissatisfied. In his early work, he regarded a single refutation as being sufficient for the demise of a theory. However, he later allowed for theories to be modified, as long as further testing was done.

Popper's view of the logic of science has come to be known as *naïve falsificationism*. Lakatos (1970) set out to improve on Popper's method by developing what he called *sophisticated falsificationism*. He moved the emphasis away from establishing the level of falsifiability of a single theory to a comparison of the degree of falsifiability of competing theories.

Problems

As with the Inductive RS, the Deductive RS has been subjected to a variety of criticisms.

Cannot escape induction

It has been argued that deduction involves the use of induction. In spite of his strong support for the logic of deduction, Hempel has claimed that in the case where a theory has not been falsified, its acceptance relies on data that lend 'inductive support' (1966: 18).

More recently, O'Hear (1989) has discussed Popper's claim that the best theory at any time is the one that has survived the severest tests. He has suggested that it is difficult to talk of severe tests without using some notion of inductive reasoning. The degree of corroboration of a theory is always based on its past performance, and the judgement of the severity of a test is based on past evidence. But how is it possible to move from past experience to the calculation of present or future probability? 'The crucial point is that it is only against a background of expectations built up from past experience that we can speak of some outcomes being improbable, and hence of severe tests in the Popperian sense. Without some sort of inductive argument, all tests are liable to look equally severe' (O'Hear 1989: 40). Knowledge concerning the past success of a theory to pass tests is not an adequate basis for future actions based on the theory, except on the basis of inductive assumptions. Therefore, according to O'Hear, the Popperian method of falsification does not provide a basis for believing in theories that have survived severe tests.

Source of propositions in a theory

An important issue for the practising researcher is where to find the propositions that make up a deductive theory. Popper had no interest in this question. He distinguished between what he called the *logic of knowledge* – the method by which theories are justified – and the *psychology of knowledge* – the process by which a new idea is conceived.

LIVERPOOL
JOHN MOORES UNIVERSITY

I.M. MARSH LRC
Tel: 0151 231 5216

The initial stage, the act of conceiving or inventing a theory, seems to me neither to call for logical analysis nor to be susceptible to it. The question of how it happens that a new idea occurs to a man [*sic*] – whether it is a musical theme, a dramatic conflict, or a scientific theory – may be of great interest to empirical psychology; but it is irrelevant to the logical analysis of scientific knowledge . . . [T]here is no such thing as a logical method of having new ideas, or a logical reconstruction of this process. (Popper 1959: 31–2)

According to Popper, every discovery contains an 'irrational element' or a 'creative intuition'. For him, the issue of how theories are tested is the only scientifically relevant one. Similar arguments have been presented by Reichenbach (1948: 382) and Braithwaite (1953: 20–1). Unfortunately, this is not particularly helpful to the practising researcher. Are the propositions derived by imaginative conjecture, as Popper maintained, or by some form of inductive reasoning, which Popper wished to avoid (Hesse 1974: 2)?

Like Medawar (1969a) before her, Hesse was critical of this aspect of the Deductive RS and stressed the role of creative imagination, as well as logic, in the process of scientific discovery.

I have maintained that scientific theories are not constructed solely out of sense-data or out of operational definitions, but are 'hypothetico-deductive' in form; that is, they consist of hypotheses which may not in themselves have any reference to immediate observations, but from which deductions can be drawn which correspond to the results of experiments when suitably translated into experimental language. The main point that emerges from such a description of theories is that there can be no set of rules given for the procedure of scientific discovery – a hypothesis is not produced by a deductive machine by feeding experimental observations into it: it is a product of creative imagination, of a mind which absorbs the experimental data until it sees them fall into a pattern, giving the scientific theorist the sense that he [*sic*] is penetrating beneath the flux of phenomena to the real structure of nature. (Hesse 1953: 198)

Stated like this, the process of scientific discovery may seem to be relatively straightforward. However, as we shall see later in the chapter, seeing data 'fall into a pattern' is a complex and difficult process.

Limitations of data

Another area of criticism of the Deductive RS concerns the problem of using data to test a theory. From a practical point of view, the process of testing a theory is dependent not only on making accurate observations, but also on the stage of development of both the theories behind the observations and the measuring instruments that are used. Popper recognized this problem, but gave it only limited attention; he was unable to provide a satisfactory solution. 'In point of fact, no conclusive disproof of a theory can ever be produced; for it is always possible to say that the experimental results are not reliable or that the discrepancies that are asserted to exist between the experimental results and the theory are only apparent and that they will disappear with the advance of our understanding' (Popper 1959: 50).

Medawar and Chalmers have echoed the same concern, but they saw it as being serious. 'We could be mistaken in thinking that our observations falsified a hypothesis: the observations may themselves have been faulty, or may have been made against a background of misconceptions; or our experiments may have been ill-designed' (Medawar 1969a: 53–4). 'Conclusive falsifications are ruled out by the lack of a perfectly secure observation base on which they depend' (Chalmers 1982: 63–4).

Theory dependence of observations

An area of criticism, touched on briefly in chapter 2, derives from the problem of the theory dependence of observation; it is the problem of the relationship between theories and 'reality'. One of the central features of the Inductive RS is the distinction made between observation languages and theoretical languages, between statements about uncontaminated, objective data and theories derived by induction. Deductivists argue that, at least to some degree, all statements must be in a theoretical language, because of the theory dependence of observations. Therefore, if there is no such observation language, and all observations are interpretations, there is no way of comparing theoretical statements with 'reality'; they can only be compared with observations produced by theory-impregnated concepts and measurements. Hence, there is no way of knowing whether theoretical statements match 'reality', because reality cannot be observed directly.

In order to avoid this circularity problem, Pawson (1989) has adopted a *transformation model of measurement* based on the notion of information transfer. He provided an example of how the heat produced by an internal combustion engine might be measured. 'The basic strategy in the measurement of a physical property is to harness an output of energy from a physical system, transforming that output into some kind of "signal" and transmitting that information to some kind of recording device' (Pawson 1989: 110). The consequence of viewing measurement this way is that, rather than the theory that is being tested providing guidance for observations, a whole family of theories is called upon to produce data. '[C]ircularity is avoided since theories or expectations which lead us to inquire about the measured are not the theories and principles used in the measurement' (1989: 115).

Role of scientific communities

Another category of criticism has to do with the intellectual and social contexts within which science is practised. The history of science provides many examples of theories for which there was disconfirming evidence but that were nevertheless not rejected. A classic example is the theory of planetary motion developed by Copernicus in the sixteenth century as an alternative to that developed by the early Greek astronomers. More recent examples are Newton's gravitational theory, Bohr's theory of the atom, and the kinetic theory of gases (Chalmers 1982). Why did this happen? Answers to this question are concerned with the role of scientific communities (see chapter 6).

Recognition of the role of scientific communities is also related to the issue of the source of hypotheses. These ideas can be drawn from what P. S. Cohen (1968) has called 'meta-theories', Inkeles (1964) has called 'models', Willer (1967) has called 'general models', Cuff et al. (1998) and others have called 'perspectives', and Kuhn (1970a) has called 'paradigms'. Although there are differences in the meaning of these various concepts, they all recognize that social theorists and researchers operate in the context of abstract ontological and epistemological assumptions. These ideas are frequently taken for granted; they may not be formulated explicitly; they are not subjected to critical scrutiny or testing; and they may be modified, but cannot be refuted. They provide the backdrop to research; they make 'observation' and 'understanding' of the social world possible; and they set limits to what is 'seen' and 'known'. If intuition or creativity is at work, it occurs within the possibilities and limits of a body of ideas held by the community within which a researcher works.

Kuhn (1970a), Polanyi (1958), Lakatos (1970), Hesse (1974), Laudan (1977) and Feyerabend (1978) have helped to discard the limited views of science proposed by both the Inductive and Deductive RSs. 'These investigations have taught us how vital and central the role of theory is for any scientific discipline. And they have also shown that even the . . . concept of scientific theory as consisting of hypothetical-deductive systems is far too narrow and misleading to account for the varied functions of theory in science' (Bernstein 1976: 105).

Too much logic

The concern to find a strictly logical strategy for science has been attacked by Feyerabend (1978), who claimed that adherence to rational procedures inhibits scientific progress. He turned this criticism into a proposal for scientific anarchism.

> The idea of a method that contains firm, unchanging, and absolutely binding principles for conducting the business of science meets considerable difficulty when confronted with the results of historical research. We find then, that there is not a single rule, however plausible, and however firmly grounded in epistemology, that is not violated at some time or other. It becomes evident that such violations are not accidental events, they are not the results of insufficient knowledge or of inattention which might have been avoided. On the contrary, we see that they are necessary for progress . . . There is only *one* principle that can be defended under *all* circumstances and in all stages of human development. It is the principle: *anything goes*. (Feyerabend 1978: 23, 28)

This principle seems to have received an enthusiastic reception, particularly among social science students who find the intricacies of philosophical debate difficult and tedious, and the prescription of research procedures inhibiting. However, it can become an excuse for sloppy research.

Revision

Social researchers have to be able to answer 'why' RQs, to be able to explain patterns which they or others have observed. Using an existing theory, or inventing a new theory, is one way of achieving this.

The aim of the revised Deductive RS is to find an explanation for a pattern of association between two concepts (e.g. between long-term unemployment and loss of self-respect) by proposing a theory, the relevance of which can be tested. The pattern itself can be established by the use of the revised Inductive RS, although descriptions produced by the use of the Abductive RS can also provide the starting point (see table 3.1).

Once this has happened, the first stage is to borrow or construct a theory to explain the pattern of association. This theory needs to be expressed in the form of a deductive argument, the conclusion of which is the association to be explained (e.g. 'Long-term unemployment is associated with loss of self-respect'). The second stage is to collect data on the explanatory concepts in the argument. The third stage is to test the propositions in the argument: that is, the patterns of association between these concepts and those to be explained (see the reconstruction of Durkheim's theory of egoistic suicide, box 3.3), by comparing the patterns and strengths of association in the data with the form of the propositions in the argument. As conclusive refutations of a theory are not possible, a judgement has then to be made as to the extent to which the theoretical argument answers the 'why' RQ.

When the data are quantitative, some version of the *cautious realist* ontology could be used with this revised Deductive RS. However, the *subtle realist* ontology may be more appropriate when qualitative data are used.

While the status of explanations produced by the classical Deductive RS was always regarded as being tentative and, therefore, subject to modification or replacement, nevertheless, the aim was to find the 'true' explanation. As Popper admitted, there is no way of knowing when this has been achieved. As long as the researcher is willing to assume that an external reality exists, this position could still be adopted. However, the revised version of the Deductive RS needs to be less ambitious and more pragmatic. Rather than searching for *the* truth, any deductive explanation would be regarded as one amongst other possible explanations. If it meets the research objectives in a particular context, satisfies the stakeholders, and produces useful outcomes, it can be accepted until something better comes along. Hence, the epistemology of *falsificationism* could be modified to make it consistent with a *conventionalism* view of truth, a position which Popper appears to have adopted in his earlier work (see Kuhn 1970b, 1970c). See box 3.4.

Combining the Inductive and Deductive Strategies

The relationship between the logics of induction and deduction has been debated for about 150 years. For example, in 1874 Jevons (1958) suggested that all inductive reasoning is the inverse application of deductive reasoning, and Whewell (1847) argued that induction and deduction go upstairs and downstairs on the same staircase. Is it possible to combine these two RSs and thereby capitalize on their strengths and minimize their weaknesses?

Wallace (1971) has proposed such a scheme and, in the process, has endeavoured to overcome the deficiencies of both *naïve induction* and *naïve falsification*.

Box 3.4 Application of the revised Deductive Research Strategy

Returning to the research topic of long-term unemployment, the first thing to recognize is that the Deductive RS is not capable of providing answers to 'what' RQs. As its forte is answering 'why' questions, the focus of attention needs to be RQ 3.

3 Why are these people unemployed?

The key concept here is 'these people', i.e. people with the characteristics that were discovered in the answer to the first RQ. In particular, the Deductive RS can provide explanations for patterns or relationships between characteristics.

Let us assume that one of the patterns revealed by the use of the Inductive RS in answering RQ 1 indicated that the level of unemployment was higher amongst younger and older people and lower amongst middle-aged people. We want to know why this is so. The following RQ is a specific version of RQ 3.

3a Why are younger and older people over-represented amongst the unemployed and middle-aged people under-represented?

The Deductive RS requires us to find or develop a theory that would answer this question. Such a theory could include ideas about extent of employment experience and duration and type of education. Propositions in the theory could suggest that young people have a higher rate of unemployment because they lack the work experience that employers are looking for, particularly in a tight job market, and that older people lack the kind of education that would enable them to change occupations if the field in which they had worked for most of their lives was eliminated, say, by the application of new technology. Young people could be seen to be doubly at risk if their education is limited and, perhaps, is also non-vocational. These ideas, put together in the form of a deductive argument, would provide a theory that could be tested. You might like to try constructing a suitable theory.

In Wallace's scheme (see fig. 3.1),[6] two sets of overlapping processes are involved: theorizing and doing research; and induction and deduction. These processes are related in a series of cyclical stages that, for example, could occur in the following order: start with observation, then move to empirical generalization, to theory, to hypotheses, to tests, and then to further observations. Wallace was at pains to point out that this reconstruction of the scientific process is not intended to imply inflexibility. For example, the process of moving from one stage to another may involve a series of preliminary trials, including mental experiments, pre-tests and pilot studies; that is, feedback loops may be built in. It is also possible to begin the process at any stage in the cycle. However, he discussed the process beginning with observations.

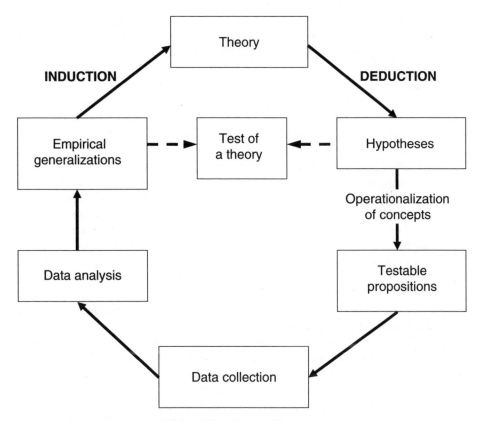

Source: Adapted from Wallace 1971, 1983; de Vaus 1995.

Figure 3.1 The cycle of theory construction and testing

Wallace is not a naïve inductivist as far as observation is concerned. He argued that while observations are almost the prime arbiters of the scientific process, 'the primacy of observations in science should not be taken to mean that observations are "immediately given" or wholly detached in their origins from empirical generalizations, theories, and hypotheses to which they then give rise' (Wallace 1971: 33). Thus, observations provide information for, as well as being the output of, the scientific process. In social research, data gathered from samples of some population can, by means of techniques of statistical inference, produce statistical (i.e. empirical) generalizations. Following Merton (1957), he regarded these empirical generalizations as nothing more than summaries of observed uniformities, not the universal laws as claimed by the naïve inductivists. This is the position taken here in the revision to the Inductive RS. For Wallace, this process is the *inductive research stage* of the cycle in which concepts are measured and statistical associations established. In the reconstruction of Durkheim's theory of suicide (box 3.3), this would be between 'religious affiliation' and 'suicide rate'.

The next stage in the process is to construct theories from empirical generalizations by forming concepts and developing and arranging propositions – the *inductive theorizing stage*. According to Wallace, these processes involve making the terms in the empirical generalizations and their relationships more abstract. A creative jump has to be made to identify 'degree of individualism' as a theoretical concept related to the descriptive variable 'religious affiliation'. Thus, the most abstract proposition in the theory, that 'the suicide rate varies directly with the degree of individualism', is arrived at, and it can now be arranged with propositions of similar abstractness to form a theory. Unfortunately, Wallace appears to have underestimated the complexity of this process, which can hardly be called inductive. We return to this issue later in the chapter.

Assuming for the moment that it is possible to construct a theory from empirical generalizations, in *deductive theorizing*, the first step in the next stage, the theory is examined for internal consistency and compared with other theories to see whether it is superior in terms of having greater breadth of scope, a higher level of abstraction, and whether it is more parsimonious. It is then possible to deduce hypotheses or predictions from the theory in the manner already discussed.

The *deductive research stage* requires the translation of the concepts in the hypotheses into measurement procedures involving instruments, scales and sampling techniques.[7] It is then possible to test the theory by making new observations. The latter can be compared with the predictions, and a decision made as to whether the theory has been corroborated or confirmed, whether it has been refuted, or whether it can be modified for further testing. By measuring the theoretical concepts in various ways and in different contexts, several tests of an initially corroborated theory are possible. Results that do not fully corroborate a theory may provide a stimulus for the modification of the theory or the development of a new theory. Merton has described this as the 'serendipity' component of research, 'the fairly common experience of observing an *unanticipated, anomalous and strategic* datum which becomes the occasion for developing a new theory or for extending a different theory' (1957: 104).

As Wallace's use of the Inductive and Deductive RSs differs from their original formulations, and as his views are consistent with the revisions made to these two RSs here, his scheme can easily be adopted. However, it is important to recognize that this scheme makes no provision for the socially constructed character of social reality. Any attempt to graft on to this scheme an input from social actors' constructions could lead only to ontological and epistemological confusion.

More recently, Rubinstein et al. (1984) have argued that science is a process that progressively explores the world by means of a systematic alternation between induction and deduction, an iterative process for refining and testing ideas. However, this process offers no assistance in the difficult activity of finding ideas that make sense of collected data. We have to turn to the Retroductive and Abductive RSs for help with this.

The Retroductive Research Strategy

Recognition of deficiencies in the Inductive and Deductive RSs has led to the development, or perhaps reclaiming, of two alternative RSs, the Retroductive and the Abductive. They are based on cyclic or spiral processes, rather than linear logic. Retroduction is advocated for use in both the natural and the social sciences.

The Retroductive RS has been discussed by philosophers for many years, and, it is claimed, has been used since the beginning of science. However, its incorporation into an articulated philosophy of science is a recent development. The central problem for the Retroductive RS is how to arrive at the structures and mechanisms that are postulated to explain observed regularities. Is there an appropriate mode of reasoning that will assist the researcher to find these ideas? Is there a *logic of discovery*?

This issue has been a matter of some dispute. A number of sympathetic writers have suggested that, if there is a logic of discovery, it involves creative imagination (Hempel 1966), intuition (Medawar 1969b), guesswork (Feynman 1967), or the free creation of our minds (Popper 1972). Both the Retroductive and Abductive RSs require the use of a logic of discovery.

The Retroductive RS adopts a *depth realist* ontology – with its three domains of reality, the empirical, the actual and the real – and uses the epistemology of *neo-realism*, or a combination of *neo-realism* and *constructionism*.

Structures and mechanisms

Following Bhaskar's suggestion (1979: 15), the logic of retroduction refers to the process of building hypothetical models of structures and mechanisms that are assumed to produce empirical phenomena. This requires a disciplined scientific imagination.

The Retroductive RS can be summarized as follows:

1 In order to explain observable phenomena, and the regularities that obtain between them, scientists must attempt to discover appropriate structures and mechanisms.
2 Since these structures and mechanisms will typically be unavailable to observation, we first construct a model of them.
3 The model is such that, were it to represent correctly these structures and mechanisms, the phenomena would then be causally explained.
4 We then proceed to test the model as a hypothetical description of actually existing entities and their relations. To do so, we work out further consequences of the model (i.e. additional to the phenomena we are trying to explain), that can be stated in a manner open to empirical testing.
5 If these tests are successful, this gives good reason to believe in the existence of these structures and mechanisms.
6 It may be possible to obtain more direct confirmation of these existential claims, by the development and use of suitable instruments.
7 The whole process of model building is then repeated, in order to explain the structures and mechanisms already discovered (Harré 1961; Keat and Urry 1975: 35).

For Bhaskar, science conceived in this way is analogous to peeling the layers off the proverbial onion. As one set of structures and mechanisms is postulated, tested and 'revealed', others at a 'lower' level go through the same process.

Distinctions between the domains of the *actual* and the *real* therefore keep changing as the strata of reality are unfolded. Hence, reality has *ontological depth* (Bhaskar 1979: 15).

The idea of the Retroductive RS was developed initially by Harré (1961, 1970, 1972), and later by Bhaskar (1978), to show how explanation does or should occur in the natural sciences. Later they applied retroductive logic to the social sciences. Harré (1970) has devoted considerable attention to the use of models in the natural sciences, and has adapted their use to the social sciences (Harré and Secord 1972; Harré 1974, 1976, 1977). Space does not allow a rehearsal of the use of models in the natural sciences here,[8] but some attention needs to be given to their use in the social sciences.

The use of models in the social sciences

One common view of the concept 'model' in the social sciences is that it is a formalized theory, i.e. an integrated set of propositions that state relationships between various concepts and that has been successfully subjected to empirical testing. This is sometimes referred to as a *theoretical* model. When the propositions are translated into particular symbolic terms, it is referred to as a *mathematical* model. Alternatively, the concept 'theory' is sometimes regarded as being synonymous with a particular perspective or paradigm – e.g. conflict theory or consensus theory – leading to expressions such as 'theoretical perspective' or 'general model'. Such perspectives might be more usefully regarded as 'meta-theories', or, as they are in this book, Research Paradigms. They contain the principles and assumptions upon which the propositions of a theory are based.

What Harré (1972, 1976) had in mind for theories and models in both the natural and the social sciences was different from these uses. Theories provide answers to the question, 'Why is it that the patterns of phenomena are the way they are?' The theory supplies an account of the constitution and behaviour of those things which, in their interactions with each other, produce the manifested pattern. Models, on the other hand, are pictures or images that are intended to represent an explanatory mechanism (Harré has called them *icons*). They indicate what a mechanism might look like, and thus help researchers in the search for them.

These iconic models can come from many sources. Harré used the example of the relationships between stage actors, social role-players and the patterned behaviour of people. The behaviour of people can be seen to be like social role-players (hence the use of the concept 'social actors'), and these role-players are, at least in some respects, like stage actors. The stage provides the source for the iconic model, which, in turn, provides a hypothetical mechanism for the explanation of patterned behaviour (Harré 1979).

Harré (1976) used models in what he has called the *ethogenic* point of view, an approach which draws on many aspects of *constructionism*. Human beings are regarded not as passive responders to the contingencies of their social world, but as agents who use theories about people and their situations, and a related social technology.

A person's social capacities are viewed as being related to the cognitive equipment she or he possesses. As this cognitive equipment is not readily available for inspection by the social actor, by other social actors or by social scientists, it is necessary to construct models of the way a person thinks. According to Harré, social actors do this in their interaction with each other, and social scientists need to do it in order to explain patterns in social life. Social actors construct models of people who they know well and with whom they interact on a regular basis, as well as of people who are more remote. Like Schütz before him and Giddens after him, Harré considered social scientific methods of understanding as being of the same form as these everyday methods (1976: 25).

Ethogenists see the social world primarily in social episodes of encounters between individuals. Social episodes range from formal social acts that can be identified as rituals, to informal interactions that lack any explicit rules, the ceremonial nature of which actors may not be aware. People bring their cognitive resources to these micro-social situations, which are constrained by rules and social sanctions. In order to grasp these episodes, it is necessary to construct an abstract description, an image of them (what Harré called *homeomorphs*). Then explanatory models of the largely unknown natures of people, their cognitive resources, or psychological 'mechanisms' (called *paramorphs*), need to be constructed. And, finally, the macro-structures of the social world need to be identified.

Harré regarded the images people have of the social order, such as 'the class structure', as nothing more than models that are part of the cognitive resources used in the management of social interaction (1976: 37). These images of society are models in a double sense: they are models for a reality that has to be constructed for people to inhabit; and they are modelled *on* some real or imagined view of the world. These models of the social order may be realistic, in that they relate to real differences in the world, such as people being viewed as either male or female, or they may be fictitious, in that they picture the social world as a structure which is 'brought to the world' rather than being 'derived from it'.

An important difference between the natural and the social sciences with regard to model building is that the natural scientist creates models of an existing world, whereas social actors create the world based on some model.

> In an analysis of the theories about people and their social actions that we deploy in the management of ourselves and our interaction with others, images of society have the place that metaphysical visions of the world have in natural science. The image of society gives us our ideas of what roles there can be, and then we discover empirically if they are filled, how and by whom – the only difference from natural science being the crucial fact that we can and do construct worlds to fulfil images. (Harré 1976: 36)

These constructions of the social world need to be used as elements in explanations.

Some models need to go beyond what participants can report about a social episode, and involve elements and structures of which they are unaware and, perhaps, could never become aware. However, according to Harré, their authenticity can be checked by endeavouring to replicate the social processes based on the assumptions contained in the model. If this is successful, the model can be assumed to be analogous to those cognitive structures that produced the patterns of behaviour. He considered that the best check on the model would be to locate the physiological mechanisms that produced the social behaviour, although he recognized that this is impossible at present and will be unlikely for some time to come.

Harré's use of models implies a *subtle realist* ontology and an epistemology of *neo-realism*. However, retroductive logic is also used with a *depth realist* ontology. In the latter case, models need to be constructed of hidden social structures and processes.

To a large extent, models will be regarded as being plausible if they conform to the scientific worldview dominant at the time in a particular discipline or scientific community. Models that lie outside the ontological assumptions of the worldview will have great difficulty in being accepted; the discipline or sub-discipline worldview – research paradigm – determines what will be considered as real. For an empirical example, see box 3.5.

Box 3.5 Empirical example: applying realist logic

It is not difficult to find empirical examples of the use of retroductive logic in the natural sciences, although the scientists concerned would probably not have recognized their use of it. A frequently quoted example is the case of the discovery of viruses. Certain diseases could not be explained by the presence of bacterial agents. Viruses were postulated to explain their occurrence, and, in time, their existence and mode of operation were demonstrated. The same process led to the 'discovery' of the structure of the atom. Initially, atoms were hypothetical entities; it was only after some time that they were actually observed. Similarly, the genetic explanation for inherited characteristics started out as such an idea but took hundreds of years to establish. An example from linguistics can be found in Chomsky's notion of 'deep structure', which he used to explain linguistic competence (Taylor 1982: 163). In all these cases, because the causal structures and/or mechanisms had never been observed, it was necessary first to imagine what they might be like, and then to formulate these ideas into some image or model.

These examples have all been reconstructed from a retroductive point of view and, conversely, have no doubt contributed to the way in which the ideal type Retroductive RS was constructed. This ideal type does not seem to relate as well to the social sciences, and this may account for the fact that little if any social research seems to have used this logic explicitly. There is a coterie of social scientists, particularly in the UK, who advocate the *depth realist* ontology, but do not seem to use the epistemology of *neo-realism*. Instead, known structures and mechanisms tend to be postulated, and their relevance established.

A seminal attempt to conduct social research with a *depth realist* ontology can be found in Pawson's work (1989, 2000; Pawson and Tilley 1997) using the 'logic of realist explanation'. For him, realist explanations of observed regularities 'involve uncovering certain of the "causal powers" of individuals and institutions', of showing how structure and agency combine to produce such regularities. 'Realists thus think of the underlying engine of social reality in terms of people's reasoning as well as the resources available to them' (Pawson 2000: 294, 295). His position is summarized in the following quotation.

> *Explanations focus on interesting, puzzling, socially significant outcome patterns (O). Explanation takes the form of positing some underlying mechanism (M) that generates the outcome, which will consist of propositions about how structural resources and agent's reasoning have constituted the regularity. The workings of such mechanisms are always contingent and conditional, and hypotheses will also be constructed in respect of which local, institutional and historical contexts (C) are conducive to the action of the mechanism.* (Pawson 2000: 298)

The basic elements of this logic of explanation are represented in the figure (adapted from Pawson 2000: 298 and Pawson and Tilley 1997: 72).

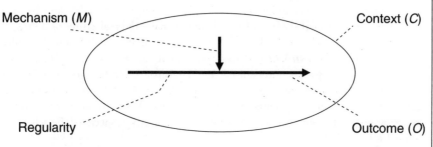

The task of the researcher is to postulate both the underlying mechanism that gives rise to empirical outcomes and the balance of contextual conditions that enable, modify or nullify the action of mechanisms (Pawson 2000: 297).[a] Pawson applied his realist logic of explanation to two classic studies: Marshall, Newby, Rose and Vogler's *Social Class in Modern Britain* (1988) and Rossi, Berk and Lenihan's *Money, Work and Crime* (1980) (Pawson 2000: 300–20).

As an elaborator of Merton's (1957) 'middle range theory', Pawson has given a realist gloss to Durkheim's work on suicide. In terms of anomic suicide, he has argued that the explanation for different suicide rates is to be found in individual actions and social constraints. '[W]hilst the decision to commit suicide is a matter of the individual's desperation, misery, isolation and so on, such dispositions are socially structured and thus will vary with the social cohesion and support that different communities are able to bring to marginalized members. Generalizing, we can say that researchers should search for social mechanisms in choices people make and the capacities they derive from group membership' (2000: 295). Hence, according to Pawson, anomie is not simply correlated with suicide; it is the mechanism that produces the different rates across different communities.

What appears to be missing in this version of the RS is an emphasis on the creative process needed to invent new explanatory structures and mechanisms. Perhaps at this stage in the development of the social sciences it is necessary to exhaust the explanatory capacity of known types of structures and mechanisms before launching too far into the difficult territory of discovering new ones. Possible mechanisms can be gleaned from existing theories.

An exception is Taylor's (1982) attempt to develop an alternative to Durkheim's theory of suicide. While acknowledging the importance of Durkheim's work, he adopted a *depth realist* ontology and used what he called theoretical reflection and abstraction, i.e. retroductive logic, to identify explanatory mechanisms. He argued that as most suicides are risk-taking behaviour, there is no clear distinction between genuine suicide acts and those that are not intended to succeed. Unlike Durkheim, he paid attention to social actors' meanings, and attempted to show how a variety of specific suicidal performances are produced by one of four interrelated states of meaning. None of this was derived from observation or experience.

---

[a] Hedström has presented a somewhat similar model in which a combination of beliefs, desires and opportunities is used to explain action. Beliefs and desires are mental states with motivational force, and opportunities make the realization of desires possible or not possible (2005: 38–42). Archer has taken these models further by addressing the question of how *structures* (Pawson's 'context' and Hedström's 'circumstances') influence *agency* (Pawson's 'mechanisms' and Hedström's combination of 'beliefs' and 'desires'). She has argued that social agents deliberate reflexively on the social circumstances, the constraints and enablements, which they confront by means of an 'internal conversation', a dialogue between objective and subjective aspects of the self (Archer 2003: 130).

Revision

The empirical illustration in box 3.5 indicates the modifications that have been made to the ideal-typical view of the Retroductive RS by a major practitioner. The aim still remains the discovery of underlying mechanisms that, in particular contexts, explain observed regularities. The first stage is to provide an adequate description of the regularity to be explained. As with the Deductive RS, this stage requires the use of either the revised Inductive RS or the Abductive RS. What follows after this is likely to include an examination of the characteristics of the context under investigation and an examination of possible contending mechanisms. The relevance of these mechanisms would need to be investigated, and the features of the context, in terms of the ways in which it facilitates or inhibits the operation of the mechanism(s), would need to be established (see table 3.1). See box 3.6.

The Abductive Research Strategy

Abductive logic was originally proposed as a method for generating hypotheses in the natural sciences, but is now advocated as the appropriate method of theory

Box 3.6 Application of the revised Retroductive Research Strategy

The Retroductive RS can also be used to answer RQ 3a on why there is a curvilinear association between age and level of unemployment. We have two alternatives: the *structuralist* or the *constructionist* versions. As we shall see, the *constructionist* version has much in common with the Abductive RS, the differences being mainly in their epistemologies. The *idealist* ontology of the Abductive RS lacks a belief in the existence of an independent, external social reality, whereas the *subtle realist* ontology of the *constructionist* version still entertains this belief, and the *depth realist* ontology of the *structuralist* version has an unwavering commitment to it. The *structuralist* version seeks an explanation in terms of underlying social structures, and the constructionist version pays attention to cognitive mechanisms.

A *structuralist* answer to RQ 3a could focus on social locations that limit access to education in terms of proximity to good-quality educational institutions, and structures of inequality, which mean that some people lack the economic resources to take advantage of available facilities, particularly good-quality ones that charge high fees. The national and international labour markets are other possible areas for investigation. The important point is that the researcher has to construct models or images of these structures, and then has to set about establishing their relative presence or absence in the lives of these people.

A *constructionist* answer could focus on restricted constructions of the educational and occupational worlds that lead to limited educational and occupational aspirations; low self-respect as a result of a history of past, poor educational performance; and the internalization of subcultural lifestyle rules and expectations that influence individual choices. These types of cognitive resources would place severe restrictions on a person's decision-making and problem-solving skills. Again, establishing the presence of these hypothesized aspects of an individual's cognitive resources would constitute an answer to the question.

While these two versions of the Retroductive RS look in different places for their answers, they are not mutually exclusive. In Pawson's logic of explanation, mechanisms and structures (context) are seen to be operating together; mechanisms (people's reasonings) are enabled or inhibited by the context (structural resources). Different age cohorts have lived in different contexts; their biographies have intersected with history at different points. Opportunities and limitations are different in different contexts, in different periods of a societal and world history. This can explain the curvilinear association between age and level of unemployment.

construction in interpretive social science. This RS involves constructing theories that are derived from social actors' language, meanings and accounts in the context of everyday activities. Such research begins by describing these activities and meanings, and then derives from them categories and concepts that can form the basis of an understanding or an explanation of the problem at hand. It is based on an *idealist* ontology and the epistemology of *constructionism*.

The Abductive RS incorporates what the Inductive and Deductive RSs ignore – the meanings and interpretations, the motives and intentions, that people use in their everyday lives, and which direct their behaviour – and elevates them to the central place in social theory and research. As a consequence, the social world *is* the world perceived and experienced by its members, from the 'inside'. The social scientist's task is to discover and describe this 'insider' view, not to impose an 'outsider' view on it. Therefore, the aim is to discover why people do what they do by uncovering the largely tacit, mutual knowledge, the symbolic meanings, intentions and rules, which provide the orientations for their actions. Mutual knowledge is background knowledge that is largely unarticulated but which is constantly used and modified by social actors as they interact with each other.

The Abductive RS has many layers to it. The basic access to any social world is the accounts that people can give of their own actions and the actions of others. These accounts contain the concepts that participants use to structure their world and the 'theories' they use to account for what goes on. However, much of the activity of social life is routine, and is conducted in a taken-for-granted, unreflective manner. It is when enquiries are made about their behaviour by others (such as social scientists), or when social life is disrupted, and/or ceases to be predictable, that social actors are forced to search for or construct meanings and interpretations. Therefore, the social scientist may have to resort to procedures that encourage this reflection in order to discover the meanings and theories.

For some social scientists, reporting social actors' accounts is all that is possible and necessary in order to understand social life. Others are prepared to turn these accounts into social scientific descriptions of the way of life of a particular social group (community or society), but would insist on keeping these descriptions tied closely to the language used by social actors. However, once these descriptions are produced, it is possible to understand them in terms of some existing social theory or perspective. Still others will want to generate abstract descriptions, or even theories, from the descriptions produced from social actors' accounts.

These layers can be summarized as follows:

Everyday concepts and meanings
provide the basis for
social action/interaction
about which
social actors can give accounts
from which
social scientific description can be made
from which
social theories can be generated
or which can be understood in terms of existing
social theories or perspectives

According to Bhaskar (1979, 1986), the relationship between everyday or lay concepts and meanings and social scientific or technical concepts and theories is the central question of method in the social sciences. However, it remains a largely neglected area of concern among social theorists and social researchers. *It is to the process of moving from lay descriptions of social life, to technical descriptions of that social life, that the notion of abduction is applied.*

Advocates

While not labelled as the Abductive RS, a number of writers have advocated the use of social actors' concepts, meanings and theories as the basis for generating new social scientific knowledge. The following review of such writers is selective; it includes only those who are concerned with achieving understanding, even explanation, and excludes those concerned primarily with description (e.g. ethnomethodologists). The review begins with Weber's use of ideal types as a means of developing explanations. Schütz took this idea further and, together with Winch, provided the foundation for the Abductive RS. A review of their work is followed by that of a US contributor (Douglas) and two British ones (Rex and Giddens). Finally, a rather different use of abductive logic is discussed – the Grounded Theory of Glaser and Strauss (1968).

Weber's ideal types

Weber wanted sociology to be a generalizing science in which abstract concepts are used to represent actual historical events and concrete courses of action. For him, sociology is concerned with generalizations and causal explanations of historically and culturally important phenomena, and with the analysis of individual actions, structures and processes possessing cultural significance.

He dealt with the relationship between such abstract concepts of meaningful action and concrete historical meaningful action by means of ideal types. They are abstractions, constructed by the social scientist to approximate an actual state of affairs, and they must, according to Weber (1964: 110), be adequate on the level of meaning. This notion of adequacy was central to his concern with both generating explanations and ensuring that these explanations are related to the actual meaning that actors use. The action under consideration must constitute a regular pattern, but, no matter how regular (statistically probable) it is, it is not explained without providing the meanings that are typically associated with such action. Further, the meanings contained in ideal types must fit with *normal* expectations about the motives people acting in that particular situation would have. However, the question of whose view of normal is critical here.

Weber recognized that the process of constructing ideal types of subjective meaning associated with particular action entails some practical difficulties for the social scientist, mainly because people are not always aware of the meanings they are using. He argued that it is up to the social scientist to construct a hypothetical ideal type of meaning that might account for the action under consideration, and then proceed to test this hypothesis. This latter process could be seen as using either deductive or retroductive logic. Weber's strategy for developing ideal types is able to circumvent a direct exploration of the actual meanings used by social actors. However, it must be acknowledged that in his own historical work he had little option but to proceed in this way.

Schütz's first-order and second-order constructs

Schütz, like Weber, was concerned with the problem of how to generate social scientific concepts and theories of subjective meaning structures. He accepted Weber's view that this can be achieved by the use of ideal types, but he adopted a different conception of their nature and origin. Whereas Weber was prepared to allow the sociologist to attribute typical meaning to an ideal type, Schütz insisted that social scientists' types (second-order constructs) must be derived from everyday typifications (first-order constructs) that constitute social actors' social reality.

> The thought objects constructed by the social scientist, in order to grasp this social reality, have to be founded upon the thought objects constructed by the common-sense thinking of men [*sic*], living their daily life within their social world. Thus, the constructs of the social sciences are, so to speak, constructs of the second degree, that is, constructs of the constructs made by the actors on the social scene, whose behaviour the social scientist has to observe and to explain. (Schütz 1963a: 242)

The critical difference between first-order and second-order constructs is that they are devised with different purposes in mind and within different contexts. The first-order constructs used by social actors take a particular stock of everyday knowledge for granted, and are designed to deal with a social problem – to make social interaction possible and understandable to the participants. Second-order constructs are designed to deal with a social scientific problem – to describe and explain social phenomena – and have to relate to a sometimes taken-for-granted social scientific stock of knowledge (Schütz 1963b: 337–9).

The move from first-order to second-order constructs requires the social scientist to select from the activities and meanings of everyday life those considered to be relevant to the purpose at hand and to construct models of the social world – typical social actors with typical motives and typical courses of action in typical situations.

Schütz claimed that all scientific knowledge of the social world is indirect. The social sciences cannot understand people as living individuals, each with a unique consciousness. Rather, people can only be understood as personal ideal types existing in an impersonal and anonymous time, which no one has actually experienced or can experience.

According to Schütz, ideal types are constructed by the social scientist on the assumption that social action is rational: that if a person were to perform the typified action with full knowledge of all the elements that the social scientist has included as being relevant, and only those elements, then using the most appropriate means available she or he would achieve the goals as defined by the ideal type (Schütz 1963b: 334). Thus, ideal types are models of rational (means–end) action and, as such, can be compared with actual social action as a way of developing understanding. In addition, elements of a model can be varied in order to produce several models, the outcomes of which can be compared.

Like Weber, Schütz wished to develop explanations from ideal types, and he regarded them as theoretical systems embodying testable hypotheses (Schütz 1963a: 246).

The ultimate constraint on a researcher in constructing ideal types is contained in Schütz's *postulate of adequacy*. He argued that the concepts of social science have to remain consistent with common sense, with first-order concepts. In short, if social actors cannot identify with types that have been constructed to represent their actions or situations, then the researcher has either got it wrong or has strayed too far from the concepts of everyday life.

Winch's lay language and technical language

Whereas Weber and Schütz were concerned with meanings and motives, Winch (1958) argued that social behaviour is to be understood as rule-following behaviour, and not as causally regular behaviour; rules provide the reasons and the motives, the meaning for behaviour. Like Schütz, Winch was concerned with the relationship between the language of the social actors and the language used by investigators. He recognized that the only language available in the natural sciences is that of the investigator. However, in the social sciences, two languages are available: the social scientists' and the participants'. Research needs to be done from the context of the investigation, not from the context of the investigator; or, if you like, it has to start from social realities, not sociological realities.

Winch was also concerned with the problem of understanding other forms of life, particularly those with a very different language and culture from that of the investigator. He was concerned that distortion not occur in attempts to understand, interpret and explain alien societies (Bernstein 1983: 28). It is the problem of 'how to make intelligible in our terms institutions belonging to a primitive [*sic*] culture, whose standards of rationality and intelligibility are apparently quite at odds with our own' (Winch 1964: 315).

Winch took the position 'that the concepts used by primitive peoples can only be interpreted in the context of the way of life of those peoples' (1964: 315). He objected to the ethnocentric attitude in which the rationality of alien cultures is judged in terms of criteria of rationality used in the culture of the investigator.

For Winch, the relationship between lay language and technical language involves building the latter on the former; but he was not dogmatic about restricting technical concepts to those derived from lay concepts. He considered that while the social scientist may find it necessary to draw on technical concepts in a discipline, such concepts will, nevertheless, imply an understanding of social actors' concepts. He used the example of the concept of 'liquidity preference' in economics, a concept that is not generally used by people in business to conduct their everyday activities but which is used by economists to explain certain kinds of business behaviour.

Douglas's theoretic stance

Douglas's existential sociology relies heavily on the ideas of Schütz and of Garfinkel's ethnomethodology, but went beyond both of them. The critical questions for

Douglas were what stance to adopt towards everyday life and what methods of analysis to use.

A major feature of Douglas's position is that everyday life must be studied on its own terms, and *'make use only of methods of observation and analysis that retain the integrity of the phenomena.* This means most simply that the phenomena to be studied must be the phenomena as experienced in everyday life, not phenomena created by (or strained through) experimental situations' (Douglas 1971: 16). However, he argued that in addition to systematically studying the common-sense meanings and actions of everyday life on their own terms, the social scientist 'must then seek an ever more general, trans-situational (objective) understanding of everyday life' (1971: p. x). He objected to naturalistic sociologies that restrict themselves to descriptions of everyday actions and meanings on the assumption that this can be done in some pure form, uncontaminated by a researcher's preconceptions – that is, by using naïve induction.

In taking this position, Douglas recognized that the problem of objectivity had to be addressed. If presuppositions do enter into the research process, and the empiricist strategies for establishing objectivity cannot be accepted, some other solution must be found. In brief, his solution was to define objective knowledge as useful knowledge, and useful knowledge as shareable knowledge. The share-ability of knowledge is achieved

> by progressively freeing the knowledge of concrete phenomena from the situation in which they are known . . . Moreover, this freeing is done not by making the knowledge objectlike or thinglike but by so examining the situation in which we do the knowing that we are able to (partially) specify the ways in which another observer would go about constructing the same kind of situation. (Douglas 1971: 28)

He was interested not in establishing fundamental truths about everyday life, but in seeking partial (objective) truths that will be replaced as 'deeper' analyses of everyday life are undertaken. Douglas's position turns out to have a close affinity with the British tradition represented by Winch, Rex and Giddens.

Rex's neo-Weberianism

Like Schütz before him, Rex (1971, 1974) used Weber as the major foundation for his approach to sociology. He wished to develop Weber's position, while at the same time avoiding the extremes of the Inductive and Deductive RSs – which neglect social actors' meanings – and what he called empirical phenomenology – which is concerned with them exclusively. Rex drew on Schütz and Garfinkel, and he was sympathetic with Habermas's Critical Theory (see chapter 5).

Rex also addressed the question of the relationship between social actors' constructs and sociologists' theories. For him, the language and meanings used by social actors in everyday life are the 'first and most elementary givens' for the sociologist; it is necessary to 'learn the language' before establishing ideal types. The question then becomes in what ways, and to what extent, are these ideal types different from the concepts and meanings used by the social actors.

While recognizing that actors' theories have some role in the process of formulating ideal types, he acknowledged that the former are distinct from the latter.

> For, whereas the actor's use of meanings is open-ended, situation-bound, and often inconsistent, the sociologist who uses these meanings in order to provide definitions and rules of transformation in his [sic] ideal typical theory when he uses it for explanatory purposes can, if he wishes, always subject the interpretations and meanings which he takes over from the actor to some kind of test, and he is likely to do so when he finds himself in dispute with his fellow sociologists. He may then argue with them about the internal consistency of the concepts being used and about whether or not the descriptions of the social and cultural world used by the actor are justifiable or not. It should be noted here that, although the ethnomethodologists and other phenomenologically-oriented sociologists believe that the 'integrity of the phenomenon' should be preserved and that meddling with or seeking to alter 'members' theories' is undesirable, they do none the less probe the members' meanings which they encounter. (Rex 1974: 47)

Hence, Rex did not believe that actors' meanings and accounts should be accepted uncritically. Like Marx, he acknowledged that people may suffer from 'false consciousness', that they may have an inadequate understanding of the broader social context and their place within it. He argued that there has to be a role for social scientists to offer different accounts of social actors' activities. However, this creates a problem for social scientists in being able to demonstrate that their accounts have a greater claim to acceptance. In the end, Rex proposed that 'sociology can give a different and competing account of the meaning of action, not that it can give a true and objective account. Nonetheless, this does not mean that the sociologist's account is yet another account, no better than that of any ideologist or of the actor himself [sic]' (1974: 48).

Rex did not provide any details of how ideal types are to be derived from everyday language except to say that a process of abstraction is involved. He was nevertheless adamant that social theories are founded on everyday meanings. But he was not averse to the sociologist both criticizing and generalizing from actors' accounts, and he wished, ultimately, to build sociological concepts and theories that include reference to 'real' social structures, or at least those that sociologists regard as real and of which social actors may be unaware. In this regard, he distanced himself from both Schütz and Douglas and from other phenomenologists and ethnomethodologists.

Giddens's immersion in a form of life

Drawing mainly on Schütz, Giddens has made the most significant contemporary contribution to the establishment of the Abductive RS. He argued that the mutual knowledge that social actors use to negotiate their encounters with others, and to make sense of social activity, is the fundamental subject matter of social science. The social scientist cannot begin to describe any social activity without knowing what social actors know, either what they can report or what they tacitly assume, while engaging in social activity.

The processes involved in producing social scientific descriptions of this mutual knowledge are complex and diverse. According to Giddens, it depends on 'the hermeneutic task of penetrating the frames of meaning' used by social actors, and requires the social scientist to immerse herself or himself in the way of life of a group. This is particularly necessary when the culture of a group is very different from that of the researcher, as has traditionally been the case for anthropologists, but also for social scientists who conduct research within their own society. As developed societies are made up of many subcultures based, for example, on social class, ethnicity, age, gender and region, social researchers cannot assume that their mutual knowledge is necessarily similar to that of other subcultures in their society. Giddens argued that while it is not necessary or usually possible for social researchers to become full members of such groups or communities, it is necessary that they learn enough about these ways of life to be able to participate in them at least to some degree.

The techniques available to a researcher to learn a way of life are the same as those available to any person who wishes to become a member of a group or community. Understanding the meaning of what other people say and do is a skilled accomplishment of competent social actors, not the preserve of the professional social investigator (Giddens 1976b: 322). These techniques involve observing and listening; asking questions about what is appropriate or inappropriate behaviour, and why it is appropriate or inappropriate; and reflexively monitoring trial-and-error behaviour.

Social scientists must draw on the same 'mutual knowledge' that social actors use to make sense of their activity. Without immersion, there is no adequate understanding of what lies behind and structures overt behaviour. Social research has to deal with a social world that is already constituted as meaningful by its participants. In order to grasp this world, it is necessary to get to know what social actors already know, and need to know, in order to go about their daily activities.

Early in his work, Giddens consolidated his views into a set of 'rules of sociological method' (1976a: 160–2). Like Rex, he was concerned that basing social theory on everyday language could lead to a 'paralysis of the critical will'.

> It is right to claim that the condition of generating valid descriptions of a form of life entails being able in principle to participate in it (without necessarily having done so in practice). . . . In this sense, hermeneutic tasks are integral to the social sciences. But it does not follow from such a conclusion that the beliefs and practices involved in forms of life cannot be subjected to critical assessment – including within this the critique of ideology. We must distinguish between *respect for the authenticity of belief . . .* and the *critical evaluation of the justification of belief . . .* [W]e must differentiate what I call 'mutual knowledge' from what might simply be called 'common sense' . . . [M]utual knowledge is not corrigible to the sociological observer . . . Common sense is corrigible in the light of claimed findings of social and natural science . . . [W]e should not therefore succumb passively to a paralysis of the critical will. . . . [T]he critical evaluation of beliefs and practices is an inescapable feature of the discourse of the social sciences. (Giddens 1979: 251–3)

In short, mutual knowledge must be taken seriously if social activity is to be understood from the point of view of the participants; it is not open to correction by the social scientist. However, everyday explanations embodied in common sense can be corrected in terms of the findings of the natural and social sciences. For an empirical example that is consistent with the views of Schütz and Giddens, see box 3.7.

Box 3.7 Empirical example: limitations of ageing

This study was concerned with factors that influence the kind and quality of care that old people receive as they experience the limitations of ageing (Stacy 1977, 1983; Blaikie and Stacy 1984). It was conducted in two stages. The first stage focused on seven two-generation families that saw themselves as having to make decisions about a member of the older generation. In-depth interviews with individual family members, participant observation at family gatherings, and informal visits were conducted over a twelve-month period. More time was spent with the member of the older generation than with other family members. The first-order concepts that emerged – for example, 'independence', 'sickness' and 'responsibility' – were found to be used in relation to decision-making. A range of meanings of these concepts was found both within and between families. Attention was also paid to the type of relationships that the older member had with the rest of their family. After several months, the families were written up as descriptive case studies, and the sociological literature consulted for ideas that might bring some order to the diversity of ways in which individuals viewed their situations and the ways in which they related to each other. In short, the researcher was searching for suitable second-order concepts by conducting a dialogue between the first-order concepts and sociological concepts that were considered to be useful.

In the course of this dialogue, it became evident that differences between families centred on two processes: giving and receiving, and decision-making. To understand the first, the second-order concepts of 'obligations', 'reciprocity' and 'rights' proved to be useful. Decision-making processes occurred when an actual or potential change in the older person's situation was recognized, and someone felt that a decision needed to be made. Differences were noted in how change was perceived (as temporary or permanent), who took the initiative in identifying the need for a decision to be made and how others responded to this, who made the decision, and whether the decision-maker took others into account. It was found that the various meanings given to the three first-order concepts could be accommodated within these two processes.

Two typologies emerged: one concerned with *family relationships*, the other with the older person's *worldview*. Three types of *family relationships* were identified: 'independent', 'dependent' and 'reciprocal'. In the 'independent' type, the older person maintains their independence in decision-making, while also expecting their family members to facilitate their decisions without interference. In the 'dependent' type, the older member expects their family to identify problems and make decisions about them, which they accept. In 'reciprocal' families, alternatives are discussed and, if necessary, compromises reached.

The old people were found to have three types of *worldviews*: 'progressing through', 'present living' and 'accumulated experience'. In the 'progressing through' type, the past, present and future are seen to be predestined. Maintenance of values, rather than the pursuit of goals, and attachment to physical surroundings are important. Relationships with people and events occur within this environment on the older person's terms. The world of the 'present living' type of old person is centred on people with whom they happen to be associated at any time. They adapt to their physical environment and conform to the expectations of others. The past and the future have little significance, and such persons derive meaning and gratification from social attachments in the present. The world of 'accumulated experience' type includes both people and physical surroundings. These people pursue goals and believe they have influenced past events in their lives and can influence their future. Meaning is derived from social interaction and achieving goals.

The two typologies were found to be related: 'independent' with 'progressing through'; 'dependent' with 'present living'; and 'reciprocal' with 'accumulated experience'.

Typologies were constructed by engaging in a number of dialogues: between the researcher and the social actors; by the researcher relating first-order concepts to ideas gleaned from the literature; by the researcher relating the emerging types back to the accumulated information in field notes, memos, etc.; and between the researcher and one or more 'empathetic' outsiders, such as a supervisor or colleague. The aim of this iterative and very demanding process was to produce a clustering amongst observed personal and/or social activities and characteristics, without, initially, having any idea of what the finished product will look like. The process was one of observation and active participation, accumulating information, reflecting on this, and testing ideas.

The development of these particular types involved examining the ways in which the older people and their families differ with respect to how their views and actions relate to the first-order concepts and the emerging second-order concepts. It involved searching for explanations of observed behaviour, and testing the emerging ideas by making predictions about aspects of family relationships and the ways in which older people might respond to the kinds of caring offered them. Once developed, the types were described in a language to which family members could relate and were presented to them informally. This process confirmed that they found the types relevant to their situation both acceptable and meaningful. It was possible to locate all older people and their families.

The second stage of the research involved trying out these typologies with a larger group (219 case studies of older people), and with a different purpose in mind: i.e. to understand how interaction with members of health and welfare agencies influences the kind and quality of care that older people receive. Keeping the previous typologies in the background, a much wider range of first-order concepts emerged this time, requiring a more extensive range of ideas from the literature. The outcome was four types of older people – the 'controlling', 'striving', 'responding' and 'negotiating' types – each described in terms of major identifying characteristics, types of social relationships, conceptions of time and space, purpose in life, sources of rewards, views of possible alternatives and futures, and responses to the limitations of ageing.[a] Only thirteen of the cases could not readily be located in one of the types: one moved between types at different times; three showed so few characteristics that locating them was not possible; seven had mixed characteristics; and in only two cases did the types seem to be inappropriate.

A second typology was developed from a sample of health and welfare professionals in community organizations, by focusing on their orientations to the older people with whom they worked. Two types emerged by using the same processes: the 'looking after' and the 'enabling' types. Very briefly, the 'looking after' type of professional believes that older people have the right to good physical care; they know what is best for older people, and expect them to accept and be grateful for the help offered. The 'enabling' professional believes that older people have the right to receive help that enables them to look after themselves; they help older people to be independent, to be active and to take responsibility within the programmes offered.

When the two typologies developed in the second stage are related, it is possible to predict the likely outcome when carers of either type work with older people of different types.

[a] Unfortunately, space does not permit a full description of the types here (see Stacy 1983: 164–70).

Glaser and Strauss's Grounded Theory

Finally, it is appropriate to review Grounded Theory as an example of a logic of discovery. However, it differs from the other uses of abductive logic just reviewed, in that it is grounded not on lay language and understandings, but only on data conceived very broadly.

Grounded Theory originated in the United States when empiricist methods were in the ascendancy and interpretive research was largely descriptive. Its founders, Glaser and Strauss, argued that sociological research methods in the 1960s were primarily concerned with improving the accuracy of measurement and with the rigorous testing of theory, to the neglect of the prior step of discovering what concepts and hypotheses might be appropriate for the area under investigation. For them, the generation and testing of theories are of equal importance, and the two activities are intimately related (1968: 2).

Their solution was to generate theory from data by a process they described as 'inductive'. This, they argued, can produce a theory that will fit and work; that is, its concepts and categories will be appropriate, it will be meaningfully relevant, and it will be able to both explain and predict the phenomena under investigation. Theory generation is seen to be intimately involved in the process of research, rather than something that precedes it. 'Generating a theory from data means that most hypotheses and concepts not only come from the data, but are systematically worked out in relation to the data during the course of the research' (Glaser and Strauss 1968: 6). This means that theoretical ideas that come from other sources – such as existing theories or one's own or others' insights – are not simply tested during the course of the research, as is the case with the Deductive RS, but have to be worked out in relation to the data in a much less formal trial-and-error process. Theory generation is, therefore, an evolving process.

In Grounded Theory, comparative analysis is used to generate two types of theory: substantive and formal. Substantive theory is generated in specific contexts, and is related to a specific social process, such as dying (Glaser and Strauss 1965). Formal theory, on the other hand, is generated at a higher level of generality, and involves concepts that can be applied to a number of substantive areas, such as power and social mobility (Glaser and Strauss 1968: 32).

The process of theory generation is one of trial and error, in which tentative hypotheses are entertained and informally tested in the context of continuing data gathering.

> Whether the sociologist, as he [*sic*] jointly collects and analyzes qualitative data, starts out in a confused state of noting almost everything he sees because it all seems significant, or whether he starts out with a more defined purpose, his work quickly leads to the generation of hypotheses. When he begins to hypothesize with the explicit purpose of generating theory, the researcher is no longer a passive receiver of impressions but is drawn naturally into actively generating and verifying his hypotheses through comparison of groups. Characteristically, in this kind of joint data collection and analysis, multiple hypotheses are pursued simultaneously. Some are pursued over long periods of time because their generation and verification are linked with developing events. Meanwhile, new hypotheses are continually sought. (Glaser and Strauss 1968: 39)

The emphasis is on a process of observation and reflection, and on continuing comparative analysis. As this proceeds, the emerging hypotheses may be integrated with other hypotheses into a formal theory.

While Grounded Theory construction requires an integrated process of data collection, coding and analysis, Glaser and Strauss suggested that these aspects of research activity need to be separated into alternating stages. In the early stages, more time will be spent on collection than on coding and analysis, but, as the research proceeds, the balance changes; towards the end, analysis predominates, with only brief periods of collection to pick up loose ends. Analysis requires periods of detachment and reflection, especially in the early stages. Later, as categories become clearer, some analysis may occur simultaneously with data collection. They argued that Grounded Theories are not easily refuted, because they are intimately linked to data, but they are likely to be modified and reformulated as the research process continues. The publication of a report on the research is only a pause in the never-ending process of theory generation.

Grounded Theory is the most explicit exposition of a practical method that comes close to what is designated here as the Abductive RS. However, its concepts are not explicitly derived from lay language; they are labels that the researcher constructs for categories that are used to organize the data. It is essentially a method of qualitative data gathering and analysis, albeit one that departs radically from the linear logic and procedures characteristic of the Inductive and Deductive RSs.[9]

Revision

The various social scientists who have contributed to the Abductive RS have also presented a variety of views. While all but Glaser and Strauss agreed that social scientific description and understanding need to use social actors' concepts and meanings as their foundation, they disagreed about what happens from then on. The following summary draws together the dominant themes into a point of view rather than a revision of any writer's work.

This RS differs from the other three in many ways, and in its ontological and epistemological assumptions in particular; it is traditionally based on an *idealist* ontology and the epistemology of *constructionism*. However, there is no reason why the *subtle realist* ontology could not be adopted as an alternative to a pure *idealist* position.

The first stage of any version of the Abductive RS is to discover how social actors view and understand that part of their world of interest to the researcher. To begin with, the researcher needs to discover both the everyday concepts that social actors use to typify features of their world and the meanings they give to them. It may also be necessary to discern the social actors' motives and their ways of interpreting and understanding their own actions, others' actions and social situations (see table 3.1).

For some researchers, this is all that is necessary. The task is to report these concepts, meanings, motives and interpretations in language that stays as close as possible to that of the social actors. If research stops at this point, abductive logic has not really come into play. Those researchers who wish to go further have a choice between one or two more stages. The first of these, and the second stage in the sequence, is for the researcher to abstract or generate second-order concepts from these first-order lay concepts. The language that the researcher uses to describe and understand the actors' social world needs both to be derived from lay language and to stay as close as possible to it. Abductive logic requires a hermeneutic dialogue to occur between first-order, lay concepts and meanings and second-order, technical concepts and interpretations.

While this technical language removes the researcher somewhat from the social actors' world, it is necessary to constrain the process of generating second-order concepts in order to maintain a close connection with it. Social actors need to be able to recognize themselves and others in the second-order accounts. There are a number of reasons for this: first, the researcher needs to know whether the social actors' world has been adequately grasped; and second, that the second-order account has not been overly 'contaminated' by the researcher's constructions. The second-order account needs to have 'integrity' (see Douglas 1971: 16), and social actors can provide the best check, a process described by ethnomethodologists as 'member checking'. In some circumstances, a reverse 'translation' of second-order concepts may be required to make this possible.

At the third stage, the understanding obtained in the second stage can be taken in at least two directions. One is the refinement and further elaboration of this understanding by the continuing use of the RS, perhaps with other social actors in the same context, or by moving into similar or comparative social contexts. The other possibility is to take the understanding obtained in the second stage and translate it into a form that can be used in another RS. For example, it would be possible to move to the constructionist version of the Retroductive RS and search for explanatory mechanisms of which social actors are unaware. This would involve supplementing understanding derived from their point of view with an explanatory account from the researcher's point of view. Taken together, they could provide a researcher with richer answers to RQs, using complementary ontological assumptions.

Another way to extend this process is to use the second-stage understanding as a basis for a theory that could be tested using the Deductive RS. As this may require a shift in both ontological and epistemological assumptions, the resulting explanation will be of a different kind to the understanding produced by the use of the Abductive RS alone. Nevertheless, if a researcher can cope with making this change in assumptions, a broader understanding of the social phenomenon may be possible. Whether this is necessary will depend on the way in which the RQs have been formulated. See box 3.8 for the final application of the revised Research Strategies to the proposed study on long-term unemployment.

Box 3.8 Application of the revised Abductive Research Strategy

The Abductive RS can provide answers to all three of the RQs in our study of long-term unemployment.

1 What kinds of people experience long-term unemployment?
2 What is it like to be unemployed for an extended period?
3 Why are these people unemployed?

Research on a population or sample of unemployed people, using qualitative methods such as some form of participant observation and/or in-depth interviewing, would allow a researcher to create typologies of the characteristics of unemployed people, their experiences of being unemployed, and their accounts of why they think they are unemployed.

To answer RQ 1, a researcher would need to explore a range of characteristics. However, the selection of characteristics would need to be determined, at least initially, by what people reveal about themselves, rather than a researcher setting out with what she or he thinks is important. Once a researcher is satisfied with the description of the characteristics, the next stage would be to try and establish whether they cluster together. For example, three types of long-term unemployment may emerge from the data: young people with minimum education, little or no vocational training, and little or no work experience; older, unskilled people with limited education, whose type of work has been taken over by machines and computers; people of all ages, and various skill levels, who have been made redundant because the business in which they have been employed has relocated to a low-wage country. The first could be labelled the 'Struggling' type, the second the 'Superseded' type, and the third the 'Sacrificed' type.

Let us assume that these three types cover almost all the people included in the study. In combination, they might lead to the same curvilinear association between age and unemployment that was found using the Inductive RS (see RQ 3a). However, in this case, the association would be expressed discursively rather than statistically. The detailed descriptions of each type are likely to suggest that different explanations are needed for each type of unemployment. They might also hint at a possible explanation for this association.

While the data used to construct these types will have come from the accounts of themselves and their situation provided by the people studied, the degree of abstraction required to move from their everyday language to the researcher's descriptions of the types will be limited. However, this issue becomes more critical in answering RQs 2 and 3.

An answer to RQ 2 would come from detailed individual accounts of unemployment experiences. These would be reviewed to look for commonalities. Again, the researcher would try to establish whether, within the range of experiences, subgroups of individuals shared similar experiences. As these experiences will be expressed in a variety of ways, the researcher will have to abstract typical experiences from the social actors' accounts.

RQ 3 requires an initial exploration of everyday explanations for unemployment, using the same data collection methods as above. Again, it should be possible to establish a typology of everyday explanations from amongst the range of accounts. The researcher could then use this typology to construct another level of explanation, into which some existing theoretical ideas, or some new ones, are imported. At this point, the researcher has moved further away from everyday accounts, to include reference to structures and processes of which social actors may be unaware, and such a theory could be tested using either the Deductive or Retroductive RS.

It is important to note that answering these three research questions would not require three separate studies. An ongoing dialogue with these unemployed people, perhaps through a series of interviews, would allow the RQs to be addressed in sequence. However, as this type of interviewing is very flexible, it is possible that some people may talk about why they think they are unemployed in the first interview. Others, who have not raised the matter, may need to be prompted to talk about it in later interviews.

The essential characteristic of this process is the interplay between the ways in which social actors view and understand their world and social scientists' attempt to make sense of the diversity of views and accounts. This usually requires a process of immersion in the social world being investigated, then withdrawal from it for reflection and analysis, followed by further stages of immersion and withdrawal. A series of in-depth interviews, and/or periods of participant observation, is a useful way of doing this.

Schütz (1963a) and Giddens (1976a) have provided the principles behind the Abductive RS (see chapters 4 and 5). However, a detailed outline of how ideal types are generated from everyday accounts is not yet readily accessible. It resides in conference papers (Blaikie and Stacy 1982, 1984) and in a collection of post-graduate theses (see, e.g., Stacy 1983; Drysdale 1985, 1996; Balnaves 1990; Priest 1997, 2000; Ong 2005).[10] Other examples of how these RSs are used can be found in Blaikie 2000.[11]

Combining the Retroductive and Abductive Strategies

As we shall see in chapter 5, aspects of the Abductive RS have been incorporated into a number of contemporary RPs. Some form of abduction provides the starting point for Critical Theory, Social Realism and Structuration Theory, and is the dominant strategy in Feminism. All these RPs accept that it is essential to have a description of the social world on its own terms, at least as the basis for other RSs.

Habermas recognized the relevance of both Retroductive and Abductive RSs for an emancipatory social science, and Fay incorporated the Abductive RS into his version of Critical Theory. However, it is in the work of Harré that the logics of abduction and retroduction are combined. Harré and Secord have argued that lay explanations of behaviour provide the best model for psychological theory (1972: 29).

> At the heart of the explanation of social behaviour is the identification of the meanings that underlie it. Part of the approach to discovering them involves the obtaining of *accounts* – the actor's own statements about why he [*sic*] performed the acts in question, what social meanings he gave to the actions of himself and others. These must be collected and analysed, often leading to the discovery of the rules that underlie the behaviour . . . An important tool in obtaining these meanings is ordinary language which is well adapted for explaining a pattern of social interaction in terms of reasons and rules. (Harré and Secord 1972: 9–10)

In contrast to the dominant schools of psychology, which have used the Inductive and Deductive RSs, ethogeny (so-called by Harré) insists that it is necessary to respect 'the intellectual capacities of ordinary human beings as managers and interpreters of the social world. Everyone is, in a certain sense, a fairly competent social scientist, *and we must not treat his (or her) theory about the social world and his place in it with contempt*' (Harré 1974: 244). However, while social actors' accounts are the starting point, and are taken seriously, they are not accepted uncritically (Harré and Secord 1972: 101).

Therefore, one version of the Retroductive RS incorporates aspects of both a *depth realist* and an *idealist* ontology and combines the epistemologies of *neo-realism* and *constructionism*. As we shall see, other RPs also allow for the use of the Abductive RS, at least in the preliminary stages of research, and then proceed to use another RS in later stages.

Chapter Summary

- The research strategies are based on four different styles of reasoning; the Inductive and Deductive strategies are based on linear reasoning, while the Retroductive and Abductive strategies are based on cyclic or spiral processes.
- Inductive and deductive forms of reasoning are generally well known, and are frequently presented as being the only two available.
- An inductive argument begins with a number of singular or particular statements (premises) and concludes with a general or universal statement; the conclusion makes claims that exceed what is contained in the premises.
- A deductive argument moves from premises, at least one of which is a general or universal statement, to a conclusion that is a singular statement; the conclusion contains less than the premises.
- The Inductive and Deductive research strategies have dominated philosophical views on the processes whereby theories are generated in both the natural and the social sciences.
- The Inductive research strategy represents a popular view of *the* scientific method, which can be traced back to the establishment of the natural sciences, and it was vigorously advocated as being appropriate for the social sciences as their foundations were being laid.
- The Inductive research strategy embodies the *shallow realist* ontology that assumes that there is a reality 'out there' with regularities that can be described and explained, and it adopts the epistemological principle of *empiricism* that the task of observing this reality is essentially unproblematic as long as the researcher adopts objective procedures.
- The logic behind the Inductive research strategy has been described as

  - assembling data, without making any judgements about their relative importance, by making 'objective' observations and conducting experiments;
  - using inductive reasoning to arrive at generalizations about patterns in the data;
  - subjecting these patterns to further testing in order to establish scientific laws of nature or social life.

- In time, the Inductive research strategy came under attack, particularly because of its naïve view of the role of observation and the unsatisfactory nature of inductive logic on which it was based.
- The Deductive research strategy was intended to overcome the deficiencies of the Inductive strategy.
- Its advocates claimed that it solved the problems of the truth status of scientific theories and provided a criterion for demarcating science from non-science.
- The logic behind the Deductive research strategy is to

  - put forward a hypothesis or set of hypotheses that form a theory;
  - deduce one or more conclusions, perhaps with the aid of previously accepted hypotheses;

- critically examine the logic of the argument in the theory, and determine whether the conclusion constitutes an advance in knowledge;
- test the conclusion by gathering appropriate data;
- if the data are not consistent with the conclusion, the theory must be judged to be false;
- however, if the data are consistent with the theory, it is temporarily supported; it is *corroborated* but not proven.

- In this research strategy, scientific research was seen to be about refuting false conjectures rather than inductively confirming derived generalizations; falsification rather than verification became the catch cry.
- Various attempts have been made to refine and elaborate the Deductive research strategy and in some cases to transform it.
- One suggestion was to replace naïve falsification with sophisticated falsification; the testing of isolated hypotheses was replaced with the notion of theories as structured wholes, as networks or paradigms.
- In addition, the worldviews of scientific communities were elevated to the status of mutually exclusive and incommensurate ontological and epistemological arbiters.
- This shift in approach involved some fundamental changes:

  - In the Inductive research strategy, it is claimed that the truth of theories can be established conclusively.
  - In the Deductive research strategy, it is claimed that while the pursuit of truth is the goal of science, all scientific theories are tentative.
  - This has led to the conventionalist position that all scientific theories are regarded as the relativistic products of scientific communities.

- While retroductive and abductive forms of reasoning are not well known, they may nevertheless be used implicitly by many researchers.
- Retroductive reasoning differs fundamentally from inductive and deductive logic in that it is used to discover the premises of an argument from its conclusions.
- It involves working back from observations to an explanation; once the explanatory idea has emerged, it will be overwhelming and irresistible.
- As abductive and retroductive reasoning were seen by Peirce as being equivalent, inspiration for the use of the abductive form in the Abductive research strategy has to be found elsewhere.
- As an alternative to Induction and Deduction, the strategy of Retroduction has been advocated as an appropriate strategy for the social sciences.
- This research strategy is used to generate hypothetical models of structures and mechanisms which may not have been observed previously, but which are assumed to produce observed phenomena.
- By the use of disciplined scientific imagination, a plausible model of what is producing an observed regularity is invented; it involves working back from observations to an explanation.
- The reality of the hypothesized structures and mechanisms is initially assumed, but has to be empirically demonstrated.

- Once this has been achieved, and their status is transformed from the 'real' to the 'actual', they become the phenomena to be explained.
- This idealized view of the Retroductive research strategy has been modified by some social scientists.
- Abduction, a strategy that is implicit in a number of research paradigms, has been advocated as either the only suitable one for the social sciences, or as an essential adjunct to other research strategies.
- Abduction characterizes those research paradigms concerned with deriving expert accounts of social life from the everyday accounts that social actors can provide.
- In view of the fact that much social life is routine and habitual, and takes place in an unreflective, taken-for-granted manner, the accounts of social actors do not usually reveal the largely tacit meanings that underpin their interactions.
- It is therefore necessary for the social scientist to piece together the fragments of meanings that can be gleaned from these accounts; this is a hermeneutic process of trying to grasp the unknown whole from the known parts (see chapters 4 and 5).
- While the versions of the Abductive research strategy discussed here have many features in common, they also differ in important respects:

  - on the issue of retaining the integrity of the phenomenon;
  - on the extent to which it is appropriate to generalize from and thus decontextualize lay accounts;
  - on the extent to which explanation is the aim; and
  - on whether it is appropriate to correct or interpret lay accounts in the light of sociological theory.

- Much still remains to be done to develop appropriate techniques for generating second-order concepts from first-order concepts, for moving from lay language to technical language.

Further Reading

Bhaskar, R. 1979. *The Possibility of Naturalism.*
Blaikie, N. 2000. *Designing Social Research*, ch. 4.
Chalmers, A. F. 1982. *What is this Thing Called Science?*
Durkheim, E. 1964. *The Rules of Sociological Method.*
——1970. *Suicide.*
Giddens, A. 1976a. *New Rules of Sociological Method.*
——1984. *The Constitution of Society.*
Harré, R. 1974. 'Blueprint for a new science'.
——1977. 'The ethogenic approach: theory and practice'.
——and P. F. Secord. 1972. *The Explanation of Social Behaviour.*
Hempel, C. E. 1966. *Philosophy of Natural Science.*
Medawar, P. B. 1969a. *Induction and Intuition in Scientific Thought.*
——1969b. *The Art of the Soluble.*

O'Hear, A. 1989. *An Introduction to the Philosophy of Science.*
Outhwaite, W. 1975. *Understanding Social Life.*
——1983. 'Towards a realist perspective'.
Pawson, R. 2000. 'Middle-range realism'.
Popper, K. R. 1959. *The Logic of Scientific Discovery.*
——1961. *The Poverty of Historicism.*
Riggs, P. L. 1992. *Whys and Ways of Science.*
Schütz, A. 1963a. 'Concept and theory formation in the social sciences'.
——1963b. 'Common-sense and scientific interpretation of human action'.
Winch, P. 1958. *The Idea of Social Science and its Relation to Philosophy.*

4

Classical Research Paradigms

Introduction

Social researchers approach research problems from different theoretical and methodological perspectives by using what are referred to here as Research Paradigms (RPs). Overarching or underpinning the choice of research problem, the formulation of Research Questions and the selection of one or more Research Strategies, is a RP. Embodied in each RP is a particular combination of ontological and epistemological assumptions, and these have a bearing on the kind of research outcomes achieved.

Ten RPs are reviewed and discussed in this and the next chapter. The first four, identified here as 'classical', represent the earliest attempts at either applying the methods of the natural sciences to the social sciences, or rejecting such an application.[1] Most of the contributors were writing during the nineteenth century and the early part of the twentieth century, although many of the ideas pre-date this period. The classical RPs are Positivism, Critical Rationalism, Classical Hermeneutics and Interpretivism.

Each RP provides its own particular answer to the question, 'Can the methods of the natural sciences be applied to the social sciences?' Positivism's answer is a straightforward 'Yes'; it advocates that all sciences, whether natural or social, should use the epistemology of *empiricism*. The second answer, given by Critical Rationalism, is 'Yes and No'; it argues for the use of the same methods, or logics for advancing knowledge, but rejects the view of science associated with Positivism in favour of a different one. The third answer, from Classical Hermeneutics, is a definite 'No'; it claims that the aim of explanation in the natural sciences is not relevant to the social sciences. It is concerned with interpretation, particularly the interpretation of texts. The fourth answer of Interpretivism is also 'No'; it rejects the methods of the natural sciences as appropriate for the social sciences, arguing that, because of the qualitative differences in their subject matters, a different approach is required.

Positivism

In its various forms, Positivism has presented the classical view of science. In the nineteenth century, Positivism was not merely a philosophy of science; it expressed a more general worldview that lauded the achievements of science. As it relates to the social sciences, Positivism is based on the thesis of *naturalism*. The concept of 'positivism' was invented by Comte in 1970; he was one of the founding fathers of sociology, but he did not formulate the doctrine.[2]

Characteristics

Numerous attempts have been made to identify the central tenets of Positivism (see, e.g., Abbagano 1967; von Wright 1971; Kolakowski 1972; Giedymin 1975; Hacking 1983; Stockman 1983). The following rules are generally accepted as representing its characteristics.

Phenomenalism. This rule asserts the uniqueness of experience as the only reliable basis for scientific knowledge. What is to count as knowledge must be based on what an observer can perceive by his or her senses. This perception must be 'pure experience' with an empty consciousness. Hence, it is a passive model of knowledge. 'An episode of scientific discovery begins with the plain and unembroidered evidence of the senses – with innocent, unprejudiced observation' (Medawar 1969b: 147).

Nominalism. The rule of nominalism asserts that abstract concepts used in scientific explanations must also be derived from experience; metaphysical notions for which observation is not possible have no legitimate existence except as names or words. For example, the concept of 'God' cannot be regarded as scientific, as it is not possible to observe God, and statements such as 'God exists' or 'God does not exist' are meaningless, because no observational evidence can have any bearing on them. A development of this rule is the belief that language used to describe observations must be uncontaminated by any theoretical notions, and that statements in this language can be readily established as true or false by reference to 'reality'. It is a theoretically neutral observation language in which the descriptive terms correspond to real objects. Hence, terms that do not belong to this privileged language, that is, theoretical terms that refer to what is unobservable, must either be able to be translated into observables, or they are regarded as being meaningless.

Atomism. The objects of experience, of observation, are regarded as discrete and independent events that constitute the ultimate, fundamental elements of the world. In so far as these isolatable impressions are formed into generalizations, they do not refer to abstract objects in the world, only to regularities among such events (Harré 1970).

General laws. Scientific theories are regarded as a set of highly general, law-like statements, and establishing such general laws is the aim of science. These scientific laws summarize observations by specifying simple relations or constant conjunctions between phenomena. Explanations are achieved by subsuming individual cases under appropriate laws. These laws are general in scope, in that they cover a broad range of observations, and they are universal in form, in that they apply, without exception, across time and space.

Value judgements and normative statements. This rule requires a separation of 'facts' and 'values', and denies to values the status of knowledge. Giddens has expressed this rule as 'the idea that judgments of value have no empirical content of a sort which renders them accessible to any tests of their "validity" in the light of experience' (1974: 3).

Verification. This rule is concerned with the way in which the truth or falsity of any scientific statement can be settled. Scientific laws are verified with reference to an observable state of affairs. Initial generalizations derived from observations are further confirmed by the accumulation of evidence. The greater the weight of confirming evidence, the greater their claim to be true statements about the world.

Causation. A central tenet of Positivism is that there is no causation in nature, only regularities or constant conjunctions between events, such that events of one kind are always followed by events of another kind. For example, if sufficient heat is applied to a suitable container of water, it can be observed that it will change from a liquid to a gas. For pure water, at normal air pressure (at sea level), this change can be observed to occur at a constant temperature. In Positivism, the only concern is to determine this temperature and, if it *is* constant, a constant conjunction, between the event of applying heat and the event of the change of status of water, can be asserted as being true. Causal language, such as, 'heating water causes it to change from a liquid to a gas', is unnecessary; all that we need to know is that one event follows the other. Therefore, to explain an observed event requires only that it be located within a wider-ranging regularity. How do we know why water changes its state? Because this happens after heat is applied. Similarly, all we need to know to be able to predict what will happen when heat is applied to water is the constant conjunction, 'water changes from liquid to gas after it is heated'.

Varieties

According to Halfpenny (1982), it is possible to identify twelve varieties of Positivism. Outhwaite (1987) has suggested that these can be reduced to three. The first variety was formulated by Comte as an alternative to theological and metaphysical ways of understanding the world. In this view, all scientific knowledge is based on laws derived from observation, and all sciences are unified in a hierarchy of related levels, building on mathematics at the lowest level, followed by astronomy, physics, chemistry, biology and, finally, sociology. However, Comte believed in the existence of a social reality independent of the realities of the sciences at lower levels in the hierarchy, a reality that is governed by laws that cannot be reduced to the laws of the other sciences; in other words, he rejected reductionism.

LIVERPOOL JOHN MOORES UNIVERSITY
LEARNING & INFORMATION SERVICES

The second variety, known as logical positivism, was founded in Vienna in the 1920s. The catch cry of these philosophers was that any concept or proposition that does not correspond to some state of affairs, that is, that cannot be verified by experience, is regarded as meaningless (the 'phenomenalism' rule). At the same time, it was argued that the concepts and propositions of the higher-level sciences *can* be reduced to those of the lower ones; that is, the propositions of the social sciences can ultimately be analysed down to those of physics. This is reductionism.

The third variety of Positivism, which was derived from the second, and is sometimes referred to as the 'standard view' in the philosophy of science, dominated the English-speaking world after the Second World War. Its fundamental tenet is that all sciences, including the social sciences, are concerned with developing explanations in the form of universal laws or generalizations. Any phenomenon can be explained by demonstrating that it is a specific case of some such law (the 'general law' rule).

The various brands of Positivism, while differing in some details, have a particular view of the methods of the natural sciences. Other responses to the question of whether the methods of the natural sciences can be used in the social sciences have not accepted this view. It is therefore useful to distinguish between *naturalism*, as a positive response to the question, and the specific features that have come to be identified with Positivism as a philosophy of science, thus making it possible to adopt a naturalism based on a non-positivist view of science (Keat and Urry 1975: 2).

Positivism in the social sciences

It was through the work of Comte (1970) and Durkheim (1964) that Positivism was introduced into sociology. Durkheim's views on this were discussed in chapter 3. Forms of Positivism have dominated sociology, particularly in the decades immediately following the Second World War, and continue to do so today in disciplines such as psychology and economics. During the past twenty-five years, Positivism has been the subject of much criticism within sociology (see, e.g., Giddens 1974; Fay 1975; Keat and Urry 1975, 1982; Adorno et al. 1976; Benton 1977; Hindess 1977; Halfpenny 1982; Bryant 1985).

Summary

Positivism regards reality as consisting of discrete events that can be observed by the human senses. The only knowledge of this reality that is acceptable is that which is derived from experience, the recording of the 'unembroidered evidence of the senses'. The language used to describe this knowledge consists of concepts that correspond to real objects, and the truth of statements in this language can be determined by observations that are uncontaminated by any theoretical notions.

It is assumed that there is order in this reality that can be summarized in terms of the constant conjunctions between observed events or objects. These regularities, which are considered to apply across time and space, constitute general laws, but not causes; explanations are achieved by demonstrating that any regularity is a specific case of some more general law. Positivism, but particularly the version known as logical positivism, rejects all theoretical or metaphysical notions that are not derived from experience. In the same way, value judgements are excluded from scientific knowledge, as their validity cannot be tested by experience. It is argued that anything that cannot be verified by experience is meaningless.

Critical Rationalism

Critical Rationalism adopts the position that the natural and the social sciences differ in their content, but not in the logic behind their methods. It incorporates the *cautious realist* ontology and the epistemology of *falsificationism*. As it rejects Positivism's epistemology of *empiricism*, it is sometimes referred to as post-positivism (Guba 1990b; Lincoln and Guba 2000). The idea behind Critical Rationalism is a logic of explanation based on a critical method of trial and error, in which theories are tested against 'reality'. This approach, commonly known as the 'method of hypothesis', the hypothetico-deductive method or the method of falsificationism, provides the foundation for the Deductive RS (see chapter 3).

Early foundations

The early foundations of this RP were laid by the English mathematician and theologian, William Whewell (1794–1866), in his monumental work, *The Philosophy of the Inductive Sciences* (1847). Whereas Bacon's view of science had been based on what he believed it *should* be, Whewell examined how scientists actually carry out their activities. It has been argued that 'Whewell's exposition of the classical hypothetico-deductive theory of science is probably the most masterful one written before the philosophy of science became a full-bodied discipline in the twentieth century' (Butts 1973: 57).

Whewell was a contemporary of John Stuart Mill, and debated the nature of induction with him. He was critical of Mill's view that scientific knowledge consists of forming generalizations from a number of particular observations, and he challenged the view that observations can be made without preconceptions. He rejected the idea that generalizing from observations is the universally appropriate scientific method, and argued that hypotheses must be invented at an early stage in scientific research, in order to account for what is observed. For him, observations do not make much sense until they have been organized by some 'conception', a *colligation* or organizing idea, supplied by the researcher. These fundamental ideas cannot be deduced from observations; they cannot be seen in the facts, because 'all facts involve ideas unconsciously'. Facts are bound together by a new thought, by 'an act of the mind'. In other words, hypotheses must be applied to bring some order to data.

These conceptions involve the use of new concepts or statements that have not been applied to these 'facts' previously. In the case of Kepler, it was *elliptical orbit*, and for Newton it was *gravitate*. However, Whewell was not able to offer rules for producing these 'conceptions'; nor did he believe that the process could be taught. Rather, it requires 'inventive talent'; it is a matter of guessing several conceptions, and then selecting the right one. He shifted the source of explanations from observations to constructions in the mind of the scientist.

> To hit upon the right conception is a difficult step; and when this step is once made, the facts assume a different aspect from what they had before: that done, they are seen in a new point of view; and the catching this point of view is a special mental operation, requiring special endowments and habits of thought. Before this, the facts are seen as detached, separate, lawless; afterwards, they are seen as connected, simple, regular; as parts of one general fact, and thereby possessing innumerable new relations before unseen. (Whewell, quoted in Brody and Capaldi 1968: 137)

Not all such conceptions produce good theories. However, Whewell thought that it was impossible to doubt the truth of a hypothesis if it fits the facts well. In spite of this kind of self-validation, he was prepared to put hypotheses to the test by making predictions and appropriate observations. It is in this latter view of science that Whewell anticipated Popper's approach.[3] Popper was not particularly interested in the notion of hypotheses as organizing ideas; this, as we have seen, is more relevant to the logic of retroduction. Rather, he was concerned with the view of science in which hypotheses, or conjectures, were produced as tentative answers to a research problem, and were then tested.

Popper's version

Karl Popper, the founding father of Critical Rationalism, first published his ideas in German in 1934, translated into English in 1959 as *The Logic of Scientific Discovery*, and then in later works (Popper 1961, 1972, 1976, 1979). While not a member of the Vienna Circle (the group of scientists, philosophers and mathematicians who founded logical positivism in the 1920s), Popper had a close intellectual contact with it. He shared with this tradition the view that scientific knowledge, imperfect though it may be, is the most certain and reliable knowledge available to human beings. However, he was critical of Positivism, particularly logical positivism, and was at pains to distance himself from it. He rejected the idea that observations are the foundation of scientific theories, and he recognized the important historical role played by metaphysical ideas in the formation of scientific theories.

According to Popper, to imagine that we can start with pure observation, as the Positivists have claimed, without anything in the nature of a theory, is absurd. He argued that observations are always selective, and that they occur within a frame of reference, or a 'horizon of expectations'. Rather than wait for regularities to impose themselves on us from our observations, we must actively impose regularities upon the world. We must jump to conclusions, although these may be discarded later if observations show that they are wrong. It is a process of trial and error, of conjecture and refutation (Popper 1972). Hence, Popper concluded that it is up to the scientist to invent regularities in the form of theories; but these theories must then be tested by making appropriate observations; the attitude must be critical, rather than dogmatic. The theories produced by this process are passed on, not as dogmas, but with the injunction that they be further improved.

This critical attitude makes use of both verbal argument and observation.

> [T]he role of logical argument, of deductive logical reasoning, remains all-important for the critical approach; not because it allows us to prove our theories, or to infer them from observation statements, but because only by pure deductive reasoning is it possible for us to discover what our theories imply, and thus to criticize them effectively. Criticism . . . is an attempt to find the weak spots in a theory, and these, as a rule, can be found only in the more remote logical consequences which can be derived from it. It is here that purely logical reasoning plays an important part in science. (Popper 1972: 51)

The question of whether theories or observations come first was not a problem for Popper. It is observations that produce the problem that needs to be explained. 'But these observations, in their turn, presupposed the adoption of a frame of reference: a frame of expectations: a frame of theories' (Popper 1972: 47).

Critical Rationalism, as expounded by Popper, is a search for truths about the world. However, he argued that we can never hope to establish whether theories are in fact true; all we can do is to eliminate those that are false. Science aims to get as near the truth as possible by a process of rational criticism and the testing of theories against descriptions of observed states of affairs. These theories are either rejected or provisionally accepted, and are then subjected to further tests. We never know when we have produced a true theory; all we have are those theories that have, for the present, survived this critical testing process.

In addressing the methods of the social sciences in one of his later publications, Popper summarized what he called his main thesis (1976: 89–90).

1 The method of the social sciences, like that of the natural sciences, consists in trying out tentative solutions to certain problems: the problems from which our investigations start, and those that turn up during our investigation. Solutions are proposed and criticized.
2 If the attempted solution is open to pertinent criticism, then we attempt to refute it; for all criticism consists of attempts at refutation.
3 If an attempted solution is refuted through our criticism, we make another attempt.
4 If it withstands criticism, we accept it temporarily; and we accept it, above all, as worthy of being further discussed and criticized.
5 Thus the method of science is one of tentative attempts to solve our problems, by conjectures that are controlled by severe criticism. It is a consciously critical development of the method of 'trial and error'.
6 The so-called objectivity of science lies in the objectivity of the critical method. This means, above all, that no theory is beyond attack by criticism.

Demarcating science from pseudo-science

For reasons similar to those that motivated the logical positivists to want to demarcate science from metaphysics, one of Popper's major concerns was to develop a secure criterion for demarcating science from pseudo-science. He argued that science is distinct from other forms of knowledge by the fact that its theories are capable of being exposed to rigorous empirical testing and, therefore, to the possibility of being falsified. Marx's theory of history (*historicism*) and Freud's psychoanalysis were regarded by him as non-scientific theories. Psychoanalysis can explain everything an individual can do or experience, while in the case of Marx's theory, it may be less a matter of whether the theory can be falsified than of it having been falsified and still being retained. The adherents of the theory may reject what might be regarded as falsifying evidence by constantly modifying the theory. 'Once your eyes were thus opened you saw confirming instances everywhere; the world was full of verifications of the theory' (Popper 1972: 35). Because all observations can be explained or excused by such theories, no observation can challenge them. Therefore, according to Popper, as the theories cannot be falsified, they do not have scientific status. He did not intend to show that nonscience was meaningless; rather, that if metaphysical notions were included in theories, the testing process would soon establish whether they had any scientific status.

Summary

Critical Rationalism has attacked Positivism and advocated a very different view of the methods of the natural sciences. It rejects sensory experience as a secure foundation for scientific theories, thus making 'pure' observation impossible. It therefore regards all such theories as being tentative rather than absolutely true. Observations are always made within a frame of reference, with certain expectations in mind. Hence, it is argued, generalizing from a limited set of 'impure' observations is not a satisfactory basis for developing scientific theories.

Critical Rationalism makes no distinction between observational and theoretical statements; all observations are theory-dependent and occur within a 'horizon of expectations'. Observation is used in the service of deductive reasoning, and theories are invented to account for observations, not derived from them.

Observations may furnish evidence of regularities that need to be explained, but the process of explanation must begin with a tentative theory, an idea that could account for what has been observed. Such a conjecture must then be subjected to critical examination and rigorous testing against 'reality'. Rather than scientists waiting for nature to reveal its regularities, they must impose regularities (deductive theories) on the world and, by a process of trial and error, using observations, try to reject false theories. Observations need to be made to collect data relevant to the theory. If these data are not consistent with the theory, the theory must be rejected, or at least modified and retested. As Popper has argued, *'there is no more rational procedure than the method of trial and error – of conjecture and refutation: of boldly proposing theories; of trying our best to show that these are* erroneous; and of accepting them tentatively if our critical efforts are unsuccessful' (Popper 1972: 51).

Classical Hermeneutics

Of all the RPs to be considered in this chapter, Classical Hermeneutics is the most diverse and complex, and the least well understood by social scientists. 'Hermeneutic' literally means making the obscure plain, but is generally translated as 'to interpret'.[4] For the most part, hermeneutics has been concerned with the interpretation of texts. However, the relevance of hermeneutics to contemporary social science lies in the possibility of regarding as texts the records made of social life, and in the application of these approaches to their interpretation.

Origins

Hermeneutics emerged in the seventeenth century in Germany, and referred initially to the principles of biblical interpretation developed by Protestant scholars to provide clergy with manuals for scriptural exegesis. However, textual exegesis, and theories of interpretation in religious, literary and legal fields, date back to antiquity. In time, the English usage of the word came to refer to non-biblical interpretation, particularly to texts that are obscure or symbolic, in order to get at hidden meaning. The advent of *rationalism* in the eighteenth century led to the Bible being interpreted to make it relevant to 'enlightened rational' people. Its mythical elements were purged, and, by natural reason, great moral truths were extracted from the historical context in which they were hidden (an activity known as *philological hermeneutics*). Hence, the aim of early hermeneutics was to understand texts written in radically different times and situations.

Schleiermacher's *hermeneutic circle*

The next stage, developed by Schleiermacher (1768–1834), provided the foundation for modern hermeneutics. Because he saw hermeneutics as a science for understanding any utterance in language, he moved from a concern with the analysis of texts from the past to the problem of how a member of one culture or historical period grasps the experiences of a member of another culture or period. It became the study of understanding itself, of the conditions of dialogue between historical periods (known as *general hermeneutics*).

For Schleiermacher, understanding has two dimensions: *grammatical* interpretation, which corresponds to the linguistic aspect of understanding and which sets the boundaries within which thought operates, and *psychological* interpretation, which attempts to reconstruct the creative act that produced the text or social activity. Psychological interpretation involves trying to place oneself within the mind of the author or social actor in order to know what was known by this person as she or he wrote the text or prepared for and engaged in some social act.

It is the art of re-experiencing the mental processes of the author of a text or the speech of a social actor. This is the reverse of the process that produced the text or conversation, as it starts with the finished expression or activity and goes back to the mental activity of its production. This involves a laborious process of endeavouring to construct the life context in which the activity has taken place and in which it makes sense. The process is known as the *hermeneutic circle*, of endeavouring to grasp the unknown whole in order to understand the known parts.

> We understand the meaning of an individual word by seeing it in reference to the whole of the sentence; and reciprocally, the sentence's meaning as a whole is dependent on the meaning of individual words. By extension, an individual concept derives its meaning from a context or horizon within which it stands; yet the horizon is made up of the very elements to which it gives meaning. By dialectical interaction between the whole and the part, each gives the other meaning; understanding is circular. (Palmer 1969: 87)

Since communication is a dialogical relationship, the *hermeneutic circle* assumes a community of meaning shared by the speaker (or author) and the hearer (or reader). However, evidence of these shared meanings consists of largely incomprehensible fragments of elements in the 'conversation'. The task is to piece these together to reconstruct the shared meanings.

The grammatical approach to interpretation uses a comparative method, and proceeds from the general to the particular. The psychological approach is intuitive, and uses both the comparative method and the 'divinatory' method. In the latter, the interpreter attempts to transform himself or herself into the author, to grasp the mental processes involved. Although these two approaches have equal status, Schleiermacher argued that they cannot be practised at the same time: in considering the common language, the writer is forgotten; in understanding the author, the language is forgotten. Ultimately, the aim in understanding the author or social actor from the psychological point of view is to gain access to what is meant in the text or in the social activity.

This process of interpretation is considerably more laborious and difficult for the interpreter than is the activity of understanding in which participants in a 'conversation' need to engage. Much of this latter understanding is taken for granted, and is drawn on without reflection. However, as Schleiermacher has argued, the interpreter, as an outsider, is in a better position than the author to grasp and describe 'the totality'.

Dilthey's understanding of lived experience

From its background in scriptural and other textual interpretation, hermeneutics came to be seen as the core discipline that provided a foundation for understanding all great expressions of human life, cultural and physical. The instigator of this transition was Dilthey (1833–1911), who referred to this range of concerns as the 'human studies' or the 'human sciences'. Dilthey argued that the study of human conduct should be based on the method of understanding (*verstehen*) to grasp the subjective consciousness of the participants, while the study of natural phenomena should seek causal explanation (*erklären*). He rejected the methods of the natural sciences as being appropriate to the human sciences, and addressed his work to the question of how objectivity is possible in the human sciences. He set out to demonstrate the methods, approaches and categories that he believed were applicable in all the human sciences, and that would guarantee objectivity and validity. Whether or not he succeeded is a matter of some debate. However, he is regarded by some as the most important philosopher in the second half of the nineteenth century.

In his early work, Dilthey thought that the foundation of the human sciences would be descriptive psychology, an empirical account of consciousness devoid of concerns with causal explanation. He believed that psychology could provide a foundation for the other social sciences, in the same way as mathematics underlies the natural sciences. All human products, including culture, were seen to be derived from mental life. However, he later came to realize the limits of this position, and turned to Husserl's phenomenology, particularly his doctrine of *intentionality* of consciousness. Subsequently, he became convinced that this did not go far or deep enough. He finally moved from a focus on the mental life of individuals to understanding based on socially produced systems of meaning. He came to stress the role of social context and what he called 'objective mind' – objectifications or externalizations of the human mind – the 'mind-created world' – that is sedimented in history, in what social scientists now call culture.

Dilthey now argued that phenomena must be situated in the larger wholes from which they derive their meaning; parts acquire significance from the whole, and the whole is given its meaning by the parts. 'The emphasis shifts from the empathetic penetration or reconstruction of other people's mental processes to the hermeneutic interpretation of cultural products and conceptual structures' (Outhwaite 1975: 26).

Dilthey insisted that the foundation for understanding human beings lies in life itself, not in rational speculation or metaphysical theories. Life, by which he meant the human world – social, historical reality – provides us with the concepts and categories we need to produce this understanding. He was critical of the approaches to human understanding of philosophers such as Locke, Hume and Kant, because there was 'no real blood flowing in the veins' of their human subjects, 'only the diluted juices of reason as mere mental activity'.

He considered the most fundamental form of human experience to be *lived experience*, first-hand, primordial, unreflective experience. Such experience is a series of acts in which willing, feeling, thinking, imaginative and creative human beings interact with the physical environment and with other human beings and, in the process, create their world. This lived experience can be understood only through its expressions – gestures, facial expressions, informal rules of behaviour, works of art, buildings, tools, literature, poetry, drama, laws, social institutions (such as religion and cultural systems) – which come to possess an independent existence of their own. These 'objectifications of life', or residues of our thoughts in cultural achievements and physical things, can be understood through an inner process of *verstehen*, of hermeneutic understanding.

The dual process of discovering taken-for-granted meanings in their external-ized products, and understanding the products in terms of the meanings on which they are based, is what Schleiermacher had earlier referred to as the *hermeneutic circle*. Dilthey continued to assert the view that objective understanding must be the ultimate aim of the human sciences, even if they use this circular method of understanding.

The capacity of another person, or a professional observer, to understand human products is, according to Dilthey, based on a belief that all human beings have something in common. However, he accepted the possibility that human 'expressions' of one group may be unintelligible to members of another group. On the other hand, they may be so familiar that they do not require interpretation.

Husserl's pure consciousness

Many scholars have contributed to the development of hermeneutics. Two other early writers are discussed here because of their methodological relevance: Husserl and Heidegger. Husserl (1859–1938) was instrumental in establishing a parallel intellectual tradition to hermeneutics known as *phenomenology* (Husserl 1964, 1967).

Phenomenology began as a reaction against the use of the methods of the natural sciences, particularly as advocated by Positivism, in psychology and in the social sciences. It was argued that by placing the emphasis on explaining human behaviour in terms of internal or external causes, such methods at best distort and at worst miss the way in which phenomena appear to us in our consciousness.

> The term 'phenomenon' refers to that which is given or indubitable in the perception or consciousness of the conscious individual; phenomenology thus comprises the attempts to describe the phenomena of consciousness and to show how they are con-stituted, although the descriptions and constitutive analysis of the various strands of the movement differ in the way they regard consciousness. (Phillipson 1972: 121)

Phenomenological philosophy can be traced back to the second half of the nine-teenth century in the writings of Brentano (1838–1917) (Brentano 1972). However, its foundations were laid by Husserl, one of Brentano's students, in the early part of the twentieth century, and it was continued in the 1960s, by Merleau-Ponty in particular (1962, 1964), and also Sartre (1968, 1969). Their concern was with the problem of consciousness, with the way in which human beings are con-scious of themselves and the world around them. However, the work of the two later writers presented a different version of phenomenology from that developed by Husserl. He presented a 'transcendental phenomenology', which may be regarded as a form of idealism, while they were interested in 'existential phenom-enology', which was more realist in its concerns (Phillipson 1972).

Brentano focused on the idea of intentional conscious activity, and was con-cerned with describing the mental acts of people. He argued that consciousness is an activity in which an active subject is conscious of some object. '[I]n the activ-ity of thinking, there is something thought about; in the activity of believing, there is something that is believed; in the activity of loving there is something loved, and so on for all forms of conscious activity' (Roche 1973: 2).

Brentano advocated the use of 'inner perception' as the way a person can describe their ongoing conscious activity. 'Inner perception is simply knowing what one is now doing, being able to put one's own conscious activity at any particular moment under some description such as, for instance, "daydreaming", "calculating", "lying", "missing the point", etc.' (Roche 1973: 3). However, Brentano argued that this phenomenological description of experience is not the sole concern of psychology; alongside it is a neurological psychology, whose concern is the explanation of the origin of experience in brain-cell activity. In this regard, he accepted the application of the methods of the natural sciences in this physiological aspect of psychology, but rejected these methods in the phenomenological aspect.

Brentano adopted a *realist* ontology with regard to the existence of persons as having physiological characteristics and having the capacity for consciousness. At the same time, he accepted an *idealist* position with regard to mental phenomena. While he asserted that the latter have a different kind of existence to physical phenomena, mental phenomena are nevertheless real. Hence, he rejected the view that only things that can be apprehended by the human senses are real, and was inclined to give primacy to mental over physical phenomena (Roche 1973: 5).

Husserl ended up rejecting much of his teacher's work by radically reformulating the idea of inner perception into an intuitive search for the essences of objects of consciousness. He regarded essences as the essential characteristics that enable an object to keep its identity.

In his early work, Husserl set himself the task of developing a method that would achieve pure understanding, liberated from the relativism of historical and social entanglements. This was the method of phenomenological reduction, in which consciousness is freed from presuppositions and thus is able to grasp meaning in its true essence. What Husserl wished to do was to be able to set aside the 'natural attitude' – the naïve attitude of everyday life in which the natural and social worlds are regarded as being real – in order to get at the essence of objects of consciousness. This involved abandoning all pre-judgements so that nothing is taken as pre-given (Phillipson 1972: 128). '[C]onsciousness liberated from the world will be capable of grasping the true meaning; not the contingent meaning, meaning as it happens to be seen – but meaning in its true, necessary essence' (Bauman 1978: 111).

Husserl was not interested in the 'real' world, only in 'describing the objects of consciousness (the noema), and showing how they are built up or constituted (the noesis)' (Phillipson 1972: 125). For Husserl, phenomenology 'is not empirical; the descriptions of phenomenology, undertaken through the reduction, are not concerned with real objects of existence but essences. . . . Essential descriptions deal not with real but with possibly imagined things' (Phillipson 1972: 131).

Husserl wished to establish truth independently of what people in socio-historical situations happen to think it is. He argued that in everyday life people naïvely accept their world as self-evident; they complacently refrain from questioning or doubting it. Only an exceptional person is able to break out of this natural attitude, to bracket absolutely everything that such an attitude requires us to assume. What is required is nothing less than transcendental *epochē*, the suspension of belief. What is left after this transcendental reduction has been undertaken is, according to Husserl, pure consciousness, freed from historical, cultural and social factors that influence the ways in which individuals understand their world. Hence, for Husserl, the path to truth is through pure consciousness.

The desire for this path, uncontaminated by taken-for-granted ideas, beliefs and prejudices, and unrestricted by the limits of personal knowledge and experience, is not new. What is new in Husserl is the belief that it is possible for a human being to exist in a state of pure consciousness. It is a state that can be imagined only in a negative way – as emptiness.

While it is possible to understand why Husserl wished to clear consciousness of contaminating external influences, it is hard to imagine a consciousness emptied of socio-historical content, uninfluenced by association with other people. As Bauman has pointed out, to bracket away the world and leave the empirical individual 'would be like installing burglar alarms on the door but leaving the thief inside the house' (1978: 121). Bauman was also critical of the elitism in Husserl's position, the claim that pure consciousness is a feat that only a few can accomplish.

Roche (1973: 34–5) has distilled the main characteristics of phenomenology (its essences!), much of which is attributable to Husserl.

- Human beings can be conscious that they possess consciousness. While rarely stated, this is a fundamental assumption of phenomenology.
- Consciousness is intentional. Every act of consciousness refers to a tangible or imaginary object of some kind. Consciousness is not a receptacle with contents that can be examined; it consists of mental activities that can be described as imagining, believing, calculating and desiring, that relate to some such object.
- Phenomenological description requires the study of that which individuals experience.
- This needs to be done in a presuppositionless manner by bracketing the *naïve realism* that ascribes real existence to all objects of consciousness.
- This *naïve realism* is characteristic of the natural attitude in which the existence of the everyday world is taken for granted.

While Husserl wished to eliminate the natural attitude in order to get at the essences of the objects of consciousness, in the existential phenomenology of Merleau-Ponty (1962) but, more particularly, in the social phenomenology of Schütz (see the section on Interpretivism), the natural attitude was the primary field of concern. Rather than bracketing it away, the aim is to understand it.

Heidegger's understanding as a mode of being

Heidegger (1889–1976) was influenced by Dilthey, but also by the phenomenological method of his own mentor, Husserl. Heidegger, in turn, has helped to lay the foundation for one branch of Contemporary Hermeneutics.

What Heidegger found attractive in Husserl's work was the notion of a pre-conceptual method of grasping phenomena. Like Dilthey, he also wanted to establish a method that would reveal life in terms of itself. However, Heidegger saw this new method differently from Husserl, and ended up turning Husserl's position on its head. Husserl had demanded that we must radically disengage ourselves from involvement in our everyday world, in order to free our consciousness to grasp the truth. Instead, for Heidegger, understanding must be grasped by ordinary people; it is the foundation of human existence. The difference in their views may be related to the fact that Husserl was trained in mathematics and Heidegger in theology.

The central idea in Heidegger's work is that understanding is a mode of being rather than a mode of knowledge, an ontological problem rather than an epistemological one. It is not about how we establish knowledge; it is about how human beings exist in the world. Understanding is the basis of being human. For Heidegger, understanding is embedded in the fabric of social relationships, and interpretation is simply making this understanding explicit in language. In the everyday world, the need for understanding occurs only when the world does not function properly, when something goes wrong. Therefore, understanding is an achievement within the reach of all human beings; it is 'our fate, against which we can fight, but from which we cannot escape' (Bauman 1978: 166).

The implication of Heidegger's position, which he clearly recognized, is that history is viewed, as it were, from the inside, not the outside; there is no understanding of history outside of history. As Heidegger has put it, 'Interpretation is never a presuppositionless grasping of something in advance.' To assume that what is 'really there' is self-evident is to fail to recognize the taken-for-granted presuppositions on which such assumed self-evidence rests. All understanding is temporal; it is not possible for any human being to step outside history or their social world. Hence, Heidegger moved away from both Dilthey and Husserl.

Summary

Classical Hermeneutics arose in order to overcome a lack of understanding of texts; the aim was to discover what a text means. Schleiermacher shifted the emphasis away from texts to an understanding of how members of one culture or historical period grasp the experiences of members of another culture or historical period. He argued for a method of psychological interpretation, of re-experiencing the mental processes of the author of a text or speaker in a dialogue. This involved the use of the *hermeneutic circle*, a process of grasping the unknown whole from the fragmented parts and using this in order to understand any part. Dilthey then shifted the emphasis again, to the establishment of a universal methodology for the human sciences, one that would be every bit as rigorous and objective as the methods of the natural sciences. He moved from mental states to the socially produced systems of meaning, from introspective psychology to sociological reflection, from the reconstruction of mental processes to the interpretation of externalized cultural products. Lived experience provides the concepts and categories for this understanding. Schleiermacher and Dilthey both argued that as an interpreter's prejudices inevitably distort his or her understanding, it is necessary to extricate oneself from entanglement in a socio-historical context.

Whereas Husserl wished to establish a path to pure consciousness, and hence to pure truth, by bracketing the natural attitude, Heidegger regarded understanding as being fundamental to human existence and, therefore, the task of ordinary people. He argued that there is no understanding outside history; human beings cannot step outside of their social world or the historical context in which they live. Pre-judgements shaped by our culture are the only tools we have (see Bauman 1978: 170).

A fundamental issue, which came to divide Classical Hermeneutics, concerned the possibility of producing 'objective' knowledge freed from the limitations of the social and historical location of the observer. The aspiration that human beings could exist in a state of pure consciousness gave way to a full-blown recognition that not only is this impossible, but also that it is undesirable. The social world should be understood on its own terms in the same manner as its participants understand it, from the inside as it were, not from some outside position occupied by an expert.

Interpretivism

Interpretivism had its origins in Hermeneutics and phenomenology. Various terms have been used to identify this RP, such as anti-naturalist or anti-positivist. Its central tenet is that there is a fundamental difference between the subject matters of the natural and the social sciences. The study of natural phenomena requires a scientist to invent concepts and theories for description and explanation; a scientist has to study nature from the 'outside'. Through the use of theories, a natural scientist makes choices about what is relevant to the problem under investigation. According to Interpretivism, the study of social phenomena requires an understanding of the social world that people have constructed and which they reproduce through their continuing activities. However, people are constantly involved in interpreting and reinterpreting their world – social situations, other people's actions, their own actions, and natural and humanly created objects. They develop meanings for their activities together, and they have ideas about what is relevant for making sense of these activities. In short, social worlds are already interpreted before social scientists arrive.

The contributors to Interpretivism who have been selected for consideration have their roots in German intellectual traditions and in British ordinary language philosophy: Weber, Schütz and Winch. While the publications of the last two spill over into the contemporary period, their work has been regarded as pioneering, and has become the inspiration for many contemporary writers.

Weber's rational models of meaningful social action

Although Weber (1864–1920) followed in the hermeneutic tradition, he was also highly critical of it. As he was concerned with establishing causal explanations, his work can be seen as a blend of Hermeneutics and Positivism. Weber's fundamental methodological concern was with the conditions of, and limits to, establishing the validity of interpretive understanding. Like Dilthey, he set himself the task of devising an objective way of understanding the essentially subjective subject matter of sociology, of establishing an objective science of the subjective. It was through the translation of his work that the term *verstehen* became known among English-speaking social scientists.

The core of Weber's position can be found in the passages in which he defined sociology and its methodological foundations (Weber 1962, 1964; Runciman 1977). Sociology is 'a science which attempts the interpretive understanding of social action in order thereby to arrive at a causal explanation of its course and effects' (Weber 1964: 88). This interpretive understanding is directed towards the subjective states of mind of social actors and the meanings that they use as they engage in particular social action. However, understanding for Weber 'is not the subtle intuitive sympathy which philosophers favour – but intellectual, analytical and predictive explanation of action' (Sahay 1971: 68).

Weber distinguished between *action* and *social action*. Action refers to 'all human behaviour when and in so far as the acting individual attaches a subjective meaning to it' (1964: 88). 'By "social" action is meant an action in which the meaning intended by the agent or agents involves a relation to *another* person's behaviour and in which that relation determines the way in which the action proceeds' (Runciman 1977: 7). Therefore, for action to be regarded as social, and to be of interest to the social scientist, the actor must give it meaning, and it must be directed towards the activities of other people. 'Social action, which includes both failure to act and passive acquiescence, may be oriented to the past, present, or expected future behaviour of others . . . The "others" may be individual persons, and may be known to the actor as such, or may constitute an indefinite plurality and may be entirely unknown as individuals' (Weber 1964: 112). In other words, social actors can act towards both known persons and categories or collectivities of people, such as 'the poor' or a particular crowd. This definition excludes from a social scientist's interest non-social overt action directed towards an inanimate object.[5]

According to Weber, subjective meanings may be of three kinds: they may refer to the actual intended meanings used by a social actor; they may refer to the average or approximate meanings used by a number of social actors; or they may be thought of as typical meanings attributed to a hypothetical social actor (1964: 96).

Drawing on Dilthey, Weber (1964) distinguished between four modes of understanding: two broad types – *rational* understanding and *empathetic* or appreciative understanding – and two versions of the rational type – *direct* and *motivational* understanding. 'In the sphere of action things are rationally evident chiefly when we attain a completely clear intellectual grasp of the action-elements in their intended context of meaning. Empathetic or appreciative accuracy is attained when, through sympathetic participation, we can adequately grasp the emotional context in which the action took place' (Weber 1964: 90–1). *Direct* understanding of a human expression or activity is like grasping the meaning of a sentence, a thought or a mathematical formula. It is an immediate, unambiguous, matter-of-fact kind of understanding that occurs in everyday situations and that does not require knowledge of a wider context. *Motivational* understanding of social action, on the other hand, is concerned with the choice of a means to achieve some goal.

It was with this motivational form of rational action that Weber was primarily concerned. He regarded human action that lacks this rational character as being unintelligible. The statistical patterns produced by quantitative data, such as the relationship between occupation and religion, are not understandable on their own. Not only must the relevant action that links the two components of the relationship be specified, but the meaning that is attached to this action must also be identified (Weber 1964: 100).

Weber's approach is clearly illustrated in his research on *The Protestant Ethic and the Spirit of Capitalism* (1958). He became fascinated by differences in the occupations of Protestants and Catholics. 'A glance at the occupational statistics of any country of mixed religious composition brings to light with remarkable frequency . . . the fact that business leaders and owners of capital, as well as the higher grades of skilled labour, and even more the higher technically and commercially trained personnel of modern enterprises, are overwhelmingly Protestant' (Weber 1958: 35).[6]

While Weber recognized that these differences might be due in part to historical circumstances, such as the advantages of inherited wealth and the educational opportunities it affords, he argued that the explanation must be sought in the intrinsic character of the religious beliefs of Protestants and Catholics. In looking for different kinds of motivation, he focused on differences in the meaning given to work. These differences, in turn, were seen to derive from differences in the dominant theologies of the two groups. In short, the Calvinist doctrine of predestination – that God has already determined who will go to heaven, and no amount of penitence or good works will alter this – created a problem for the believer in being able to find out whether he or she has been chosen. The ability to live a pure, honest, non-indulgent life was seen to be a clue, and this was accompanied by a view of work as a 'calling', as a way of serving – even worshipping – God. The result of hard work and frugality gave the early Protestants the motivation and resources to both stimulate and take advantage of the capitalist economic revolution. This approach to work came to be known as the *Protestant work ethic*. In Catholicism, by contrast, a 'calling' was to a specifically religious life, and work was regarded as necessary for survival, but not religious in character. According to Weber, all of the other major world religions lacked this meaning, and hence motivation, for work. Therefore, the explanation for the association between religion and occupation was to be found in the differences in religious beliefs, which resulted in different meanings being given to work.

Weber defined a motive as 'a complex of subjective meaning which seems to the actor himself or to the observer an adequate ground for the conduct in question' (Weber 1964: 98). He acknowledged that motives can be both rational and non-rational; they can be formulated to give action the character of being a means to some end, or they can be associated with emotional (affectual) states. Only in the case of rational motives did he consider that it was possible to formulate sociological explanations.

Weber regarded meaningful interpretations as plausible hypotheses that need to be tested. As experimentation is generally not available in the social sciences, he recommended the use of the comparative method, in which experimental conditions are sought in natural situations. If this is not possible, he suggested that the researcher resort to an 'imaginary experiment', 'which consists in thinking away certain elements of a chain of motivation and working out the course of action which would then probably ensue, thus arriving at a causal judgment' (Weber 1964: 97).

Although Weber's methodology is founded on meaningful social action, he was more particularly concerned with social relationships, 'the situation where two or more persons are engaged in conduct wherein each takes account of the behavior of the other in a meaningful way and is therefore oriented in these terms' (Weber 1962: 63). Nor was he primarily concerned with the actor's own subjective meaning but, rather, with the meaning of the situation for a constructed hypothetical actor.

While he was influenced by Hermeneutics, Weber dealt with different issues; he wished to understand and explain social action and social relationships, rather than engage in the interpretation of texts. Even though his own research dealt mainly with historical data, he adopted a sociological rather than a historical approach. He saw sociology as being concerned with general concepts and generalized uniformities, whereas he saw history as dealing with individual actions (Weber 1962: 51).

In developing his version of *verstehen*, he gradually disengaged himself from Hermeneutics by developing a view of understanding based on typical motives. He transformed the subjectivity of *verstehen* into understanding based on the construction of rational models of social action.

An aspect of Weber's approach which has caused later sociologists some difficulties was his willingness to treat as equivalent the meanings that the social actor attributes to his or her actions and the meanings that an observer regards as adequate. He was not particularly interested in the specific meanings that social actors give to their actions, but with approximations and abstractions. In any case, as he did not wish to confine himself to either contemporary or micro-situations, he was forced to deal with the observer's interpretations. Nevertheless, he regarded such interpretations only as hypotheses to be tested. For example, his work on the Protestant ethic dealt with the typical meaning given to work by the early Calvinists, not with the meaning given by John Calvin himself or any one of his followers.

Weber's desire to link statistical uniformities with *verstehen* has led to a variety of responses to his version of Interpretivism. Positivists who have paid attention to his work have tended to regard the *verstehen* component as simply a potential source of hypotheses, while Interpretivists have tended to ignore his concern with statistical uniformities and causal explanation. 'Neither of these positions does Weber justice and what is overlooked is that the whole argument about the two types of explanation is intended to lead into a discussion about truly sociological concepts (i.e. concepts which refer not merely to the meaning of action but to social relations and structures of social relations)' (Rex 1971: 24).

Schütz's methodology of typifications

As Weber never pursued methodological issues beyond the requirements of his own substantive work, he operated with many tacit assumptions, and some of his concepts were not well developed. These aspects of Weber's work have been taken up sympathetically by Schütz (1899–1959) (Schütz 1963a, 1963b, 1970,

1976), for whose work Weber and Husserl provided the foundations. Like Weber, he considered that 'the most serious question that the methodology of the social sciences has to answer is: How is it possible to form objective concepts and objectively verifiable theory of subjective meaning-structures?' (Schütz 1963a: 246). He regarded the meanings and interpretations that people give to their actions and situations as being the distinguishing feature of social phenomena. Social reality consists of the 'cultural objects and social institutions into which we all are born, within which we have to find our bearings, and with which we have to come to terms. From the outset, we, the actors on the social scene, experience the world we live in as a world both of nature and of culture, not as a private but as an intersubjective one . . .' (Schütz 1963a: 236).

This is a world of taken-for-granted meanings and interpretations that both facilitate and structure social relationships.

A consequence of holding this view of social reality is that interpretive social science requires a very different approach to that of the natural sciences.

> It is up to the natural scientist to determine which sector of the universe of nature, which facts and events therein, and which aspects of such facts and events are . . . relevant to their specific purpose . . . Relevance is not inherent in nature as such, it is the result of the selective and interpretive activity of man [sic] within nature or observing nature. The facts, the data, and events with which the natural scientist has to deal are just facts, data, and events within his observational field but this field does not 'mean' anything to the molecules, atoms, and electrons therein . . . But the facts, events, and data before the social scientist are an entirely different structure. His observational field, the social world, is not essentially structureless. It has a particular meaning and relevance structure for the human beings living, thinking, and acting therein. They have preselected and preinterpreted this world by a series of common-sense constructs of the reality of daily life, and it is these thought objects which determine their behavior, define the goal of their action, the means available for attaining them – in brief, which help them to find their bearings within their natural and socio-cultural environment and to come to terms with it. (Schütz 1963b: 305)

From the outset, Schütz's aim was to put Weber's sociology on a firm foundation. In pursuing this task, he not only elaborated the concept of action, but also offered a methodology of ideal types (1963a, 1963b). In assuming that the concept of the meaningful act is the basic and irreducible component of social phenomena, he argued that Weber failed, among other things, to distinguish between the meaning that a social actor *works with* while action is taking place, the meaning that a social actor *attributes to* a completed act or to some future act, and the meaning that a sociologist *attributes to* the action. In the first case, the meaning worked with during the act itself, and the context in which it occurs, are usually taken for granted. In the second case, the meaning attributed will be in terms of a social actor's goals. In the third case, the context of meaning will be that of an observer, not a social actor. Weber appeared to assume that the latter is an adequate basis for arriving at a social actor's attributed meaning, and that there would be no disputes between actors, or between actors and observers, about the meaning of a completed or future act.

Schütz has provided the foundation for a methodological bridge between the meaning that social actors attribute and the meaning that social scientists must attribute in order to produce an adequate theory. According to Schütz, social life is possible, in both face-to-face and more anonymous situations, to the extent that social actors use typifications of both persons and courses of action. The particular typifications used by social actors will be related to their biograph-ically and situationally determined system of interests and relevances, and are socially transmitted, constructed and refined by a process of trial and error (1963a: 243).

In intimate face-to-face situations it may be possible for social actors to grasp fragments of the subjective meaning that other actors bestow on their actions. However, according to Schütz, in these situations, and more particularly in anony-mous situations, subjective meanings – motives, goals, choices, plans – can be experienced only in their typicality (1963a: 244). He argued that it is from these typifications that social theories must be constructed.

> Now, this same social world which we immediately experience as meaningful is also meaningful from the standpoint of the social scientist. But the context of meaning in which he [*sic*] interprets this world is that of systematizing scrutiny rather than that of living experience. His data, however, are the already constituted meanings of active participants in the social world. It is to these already meaningful data that his scien-tific concepts must ultimately refer: to the meaningful acts of individual men and women, to their everyday experiences of one another, to their understanding of one another's meanings, and to their initiation of new meaningful behavior of their own. He will be concerned, furthermore, with the concepts people have of the meaning of their own and others' behavior and the concepts they have of the meaning of artefacts of all kinds. (Schütz 1976: 10)

Schütz has added to the discussion of the role of *verstehen* in the social sciences by distinguishing three uses of the concept. First, it refers to the epistemological problem of how understanding is possible (Gadamer's problem); second, it refers to a method peculiar to the social sciences (Dilthey's problem); but, thirdly, it refers to the experiential form in which social actors deal with the social world (Heidegger's problem). Schütz argued that *verstehen* is not 'subjective' in the sense that under-standing the motives of another person's action 'depends upon the private, uncon-trollable, and unverifiable intuition of the observer or refers to his [*sic*] private value system' (1963a: 240). Rather, it is 'subjective' because its aim is to discover what a social actor 'means' by his or her action in contrast to the meaning that this action has for other social actors in the situation or for an outside observer.

Winch's rule-following

Another tradition of Interpretive social science was developed in Britain by Winch (1958, 1964), under the influence of the later philosophy of Wittgenstein. Winch wanted to make a clear distinction between the natural and the social sciences, while at the same time arguing for an essential identity between the social sciences and philosophy. He was one of the first to draw on British ordinary language philosophy as a basis for explicating what is meant by 'social', and his arguments thus drew heavily on Wittgenstein's concepts of 'language-game' and 'form of life'.

At a time when Positivism and Critical Rationalism ruled supreme in the social sciences in the English-speaking world, Winch argued that basing social science on natural science was a mistake, because understanding society is both conceptually and logically different from understanding nature (Winch 1958: 72, 94, 119). The difference between society and nature is not just that the former is more complicated than the latter, as was claimed by Mill (1947). He rejected attempts to understand human activity based on physiological states, general dispositions or causal explanations, in favour of 'reasons' for acting in a particular way.[7]

While there is some debate about whether Winch accepted a positivist view of the natural sciences (see, e.g., Keat 1971; Stockman 1983), he certainly claimed that there is a radical difference between the natural and the social sciences. Winch followed Wittgenstein's view of language as rule-following within a 'form of life' or culture. Whereas the natural sciences are concerned with establishing causal sequences, the social sciences are concerned with understanding the meaning of human conduct in terms of rule-following. To understand what someone is doing, it is necessary to grasp the rule being followed. These rules are not private; they are shared and maintained by people in a social context, and are embodied in the behaviour of other people. A person's actions are intelligible to others to the extent that they follow accepted standards of what is appropriate in that social context. The presence of social regularities is used as evidence that some rule is operating, whether or not people are consciously aware of it. Rules provide both the reasons and the motives for the behaviour, and learning these rules 'belongs to the process of learning to live as a social being' (1958: 83). Hence, Winch linked the notion of meaningful action to rule-following.

Winch posed, and endeavoured to answer, a fundamental epistemological question: What is the relationship between 'the world' and the language in which we try to describe 'the world'? (1958: 120). He argued that language determines what will count as 'the world'.

> Our idea of what belongs to the realm of reality is given for us in the language that we use. The concepts we have settle for us the form of the experience we have of the world . . . [However] when we speak of the world we are speaking of what we in fact mean by the expression 'the world': there is no way of getting outside the concepts in terms of which we think of the world . . . The world *is* for us what is presented through those concepts. That is not to say that our concepts may not change; but when they do, that means that our concept of the world has changed too. (Winch 1958: 15)

This position led Winch to the view that language and social activity are inextricably bound together. Further, he argued that 'the social relations between men [*sic*] and the ideas which men's actions embody are really the same thing considered from different points of view' (1958: 121). In other words, the 'social reality' of social relationships is embedded in the concepts used by participants in social contexts to talk about their 'world'. He was determined to show 'that social relations really exist only in and through the ideas which are current in society; or alternatively, that social relations fall in the same logical category as do relations between ideas' (1958: 133).

Summary

Hermeneutics and phenomenology have provided the foundations for Interpretivism's view of the relationship between the natural and the social sciences. For Interpretivism, social reality is the product of its inhabitants; it is a world that is already interpreted by the meanings that participants produce and reproduce as a necessary part of their everyday activities together. Hence, because of this fundamental difference in the subject matters of the natural and the social sciences, different methods are required.

The founders of Interpretivism followed the branch of Classical Hermeneutics that sought to establish an objective science of the subjective, with the aim of producing verifiable knowledge of the meanings that constitute the social world. Attention focused on the nature of meaningful social action, its role in understanding patterns in social life, and how this meaning can be assessed. Rather than trying to establish the actual meaning that social actors give to a particular social action, these Interpretivists considered that it is necessary to work at a higher level of generality. Social regularities can be understood, perhaps explained, by constructing models of typical meanings used by typical social actors engaged in typical courses of action in typical situations. Such models constitute tentative hypotheses to be tested. Only social action that is rational in character, i.e. which is consciously selected as a means to some goal, is considered to be understandable.

The question of whose meanings are used to construct these ideal types has been a matter of some dispute. Can the observer's point of view be used to attribute likely meanings, or must they be taken from the social actor's point of view? The later contributors to Interpretivism raised the question of the relationship between social actors' concepts and meanings and the concepts and meanings used in social theories, and argued that the latter must be derived from the former. Language came to be seen as the medium of social interaction, and everyday concepts as structuring social reality. It is argued that it is social actors', not social investigators', points of view that are the basis of social scientific accounts of social life.

Chapter Summary

- The four major classical research paradigms – Positivism, Critical Rationalism, Classical Hermeneutics and Interpretivism – offer fundamentally different answers to the question of the relationship between the methods of the natural and the social sciences.
- In supporting the thesis of *naturalism*, Positivism argues for the same logic of enquiry in the natural and the social sciences under the common banner of *empiricism*.

- Critical Rationalism also accepts the use of a common logic, but rejects *empiricism* in favour of the critical method of conjecture and refutation.
- While not challenging either Positivism's or Critical Rationalism's conceptions of the methods of the natural sciences, Classical Hermeneutics and Interpretivism rejected them in favour of radically different methods for the social sciences.
- Classical Hermeneutics claims that the qualitative differences in their subject matters require the use of a science of understanding (*verstehen*) in the social sciences.
- Classical Hermeneutics has many strands, two of which are diametrically opposed: one is a search for a path to true (objective) understanding from a position outside and in spite of history; the other claims that there is no understanding outside of history, that interpretation is an essential part of everyday life, and that true understanding is unattainable.
- Interpretivism also rejects the methods of the natural sciences because of the differences in subject matters; hence, nature has to be studied from the 'outside', whereas social phenomena have to be studied from the 'inside'.
- Both Weber and Schütz, like Dilthey before them, were concerned with how to form objective concepts and objectively verifiable theory of subjective meaning-structures.
- Winch shifted the emphasis from meaningful social action to rule-following within a 'form of life'; he also argued that language and social activity are inextricably bound together, with the result that the social reality of social relationships is embedded in the concepts that are used by participants in social contexts to talk about their 'world'.
- While Interpretivists have been concerned primarily with understanding rather than explanation, some, such as Weber and Schütz, have adopted a middle ground.
- Positivism and Interpretivism have been regarded as mutually exclusive options, due, no doubt, to the desire of Interpretivists to assert the legitimacy of their position in the face of the overwhelming dominance of Positivism, especially in the 1960s and 1970s.

Further Reading

Anderson, R. J., J. A. Hughes and W. W. Sharrock. 1986. *Philosophy and the Human Sciences*.
Bauman, Z. 1978. *Hermeneutics and Social Science*.
Betanzos, R. J. 1988. 'Introduction'.
Bryant, C. G. A. 1985. *Positivism in Social Theory and Research*.
Chalmers, A. F. 1982. *What is this Thing Called Science?*
Giddens, A. 1974. *Positivism and Sociology*.
Halfpenny, P. 1982. *Positivism and Sociology*.
Keat, R. and J. Urry. 1982. *Social Theory as Science*, 2nd edn.
O'Hear, A. 1989. *An Introduction to the Philosophy of Science*.
Outhwaite, W. 1975. *Understanding Social Life*.
Palmer, R. E. 1969. *Hermeneutics*.

Phillipson, M. 1972. 'Phenomenological philosophy and sociology'.
Popper, K. R. 1959. *The Logic of Scientific Discovery.*
——1961. *The Poverty of Historicism.*
Roche, M. 1973. *Phenomenology, Language and the Social Sciences,* ch. 1.
Schütz, A. 1963a. 'Concept and theory formation in the social sciences'.
——1963b. 'Common-sense and scientific interpretation of human action'.
——1976. *The Phenomenology of the Social World.*
Smith, M. J. 1998. *Social Science in Question.*
Weber, M. 1964. *The Theory of Social and Economic Organization.*
Winch, P. 1958. *The Idea of Social Science and its Relation to Philosophy.*
——1964. 'Understanding a primitive society'.

5

Contemporary Research Paradigms

Introduction

The six contemporary research paradigms that are discussed in this chapter are critical of or entirely reject both Positivism and Critical Rationalism and, to varying degrees, use or build on Classical Hermeneutics and/or Interpretivism. They provide another range of responses to the key question, 'Can the methods of the natural sciences be used in the social sciences?'

The first of the contemporary RPs to be reviewed, Critical Theory, provides a 'Yes and No' response to the question; it argues for the use of a combination of methods in the social sciences, including some aspects of Positivism and Interpretivism, and adds a concern with human emancipation. The second RP, Ethnomethodology, provides a 'No' response. It not only regards the methods of the natural sciences as irrelevant but, while receiving inspiration from some phenomenologists, also rejects Hermeneutics and Interpretivism. The third RP, Social Realism, is another 'Yes and No' response. In recognizing the qualitative differences in subject matters between the natural and the social sciences, it also adopts aspects of Interpretivism, but argues for principles of enquiry different from those contained in any of the other responses, principles that are claimed to be common to both areas of science. The fourth RP, Contemporary Hermeneutics, is another definite 'No'; it develops the concerns of Classical Hermeneutics in directions that take it further away from Positivism and Critical Rationalism than any of the other responses. The fifth RP, Structuration Theory, is essentially a 'No' response; it provides a synthesis of aspects of many theoretical and philosophical traditions, with a strong foundation in Contemporary Hermeneutics, Interpretivism and Ethnomethodology. While its concerns are more ontological than epistemological, it transcends many of the deficiencies in earlier RPs. The last RP, and another 'No' response, is Feminism. It not only includes some issues absent in the other RPs – for example, a concern about the masculine nature of science and the consequences for knowledge of women being viewed as an oppressed class – but it also grapples with many of the same issues. It shares some features of Interpretivism, Critical Theory and Structuration Theory and, in its present developing state, includes a variety of views. It is worth noting that these contemporary RPs are much more complex than most of the classical ones, and also incorporate a high level of internal diversity.

Critical Theory

Critical Theory, established by the Frankfurt School in Germany in the 1930s, developed out of German intellectual traditions. Following the Second World War, during which its founders moved to the United States, the school became popular outside Germany, particularly in the late 1960s. It was founded on the idea that reason is the highest potentiality of human beings, and that through its use it is possible to criticize and challenge the nature of existing societies. The early Critical Theorists, particularly Horkheimer and Marcuse, saw human beings as free, autonomous agents who are able to create and control their own lives as long as their society lacks any form of alienation. They regarded capital-ist society as fundamentally irrational, in that it fails to satisfy existing wants and produces false wants and needs. Hence, the writings of the early Critical Theorists not only presented a particular view of human beings, but also offered a critique of capitalism.

At the same time, Critical Theorists were opposed to Positivism, particularly logical positivism, mainly because it denied the intelligibility of the concept of reason. According to the logical positivists, as reason is not derived from experi-ence, it falls outside the realm of scientific knowledge. Hence, for Critical Theorists, Positivism supports the *status quo* because it rules out the possibility of a society based on this critical capacity (Keat and Urry 1975: 220).

Habermas's three forms of knowledge

The views of Critical Theory on the relationship between the natural and the social sciences discussed here are restricted to those of its leading contemporary expo-nent, Jürgen Habermas. With his intellectual roots in Hermeneutics, Habermas claimed that the subject matters of the natural and social sciences are fundamen-tally different and use different modes of experience. The natural sciences use 'sense experience', and the social and cultural or hermeneutic sciences use 'com-municative experience' (Habermas 1970, 1972). The former is based on direct observation, and the latter on the understanding of meaning derived from com-munication with social actors.

Following Husserl, Habermas rejected the 'objectivist illusion' of Positivism, according to which the world is conceived as a universe of facts independent of 'observers', whose task it is to describe them, and he accepted the same premiss as Interpretivism: that social and cultural reality is already pre-interpreted by the par-ticipants as a cultural symbolic meaning system that can change over time. Therefore, the process for understanding this socially constructed reality is 'dia-logic'; it allows individuals to communicate their experiences within a shared framework of cultural meanings. By contrast, in the natural sciences the process is 'monologic', the technical manipulation by the researcher of some aspect of nature. In the latter, the researcher is a 'disengaged observer', whereas in the former, the researcher is a 'reflective partner' (Stockman 1983: 143–4, 152).

The 'objectivist illusion' involves regarding the objects that are 'perceived' by means of theoretical constructs as things that actually exist, that are real. There is a failure to recognize that knowledge of the seemingly objective world of facts is based on assumptions about the nature of reality that are embedded in the common-sense and frequently taken-for-granted thinking of everyday life. Hence, once this illusion is recognized, Habermas considered that it is possible to identify the fundamental interests that underpin the procedural rules of any science.

One of the central concepts in Habermas's understanding of knowledge is that of 'interest' or, more correctly translated, 'cognitive interests' or 'knowledge-constitutive interests'. These interests, he argued, determine what count as the objects of knowledge, the categories relevant to what is taken to be knowledge, as well as the procedures for discovering and justifying knowledge. Interests are fundamental, because they relate to the conditions that make the continuation of human life possible (Bernstein 1976: 192).

Habermas (1972: 301–17) classified the processes of scientific enquiry into three categories, each of which produces its own form of knowledge. They are distinguished according to their underlying interests, their anthropologically rooted strategies for interpreting life experiences, and their means of social organization. The first form of knowledge is derived from the *empirical-analytic* sciences (including the natural sciences and economics, sociology and political science), in which human social existence is seen to be based on work (the ways in which individuals control and manipulate their environment in order to survive). It is interested in technically exploitable knowledge, in prediction and control, and thus with increasing the possibility of human domination over nature and social relations. The second form of knowledge is derived from the *historical-hermeneutic* sciences, in which human social existence is seen to be based on interaction (ordinary language communication). It is concerned with the interpretive understanding of linguistic communication in everyday discourse, between individuals and within and between social groups, and with the understanding of traditions and their artistic and literary products. The third form of knowledge is derived from *critical theory*, in which human social existence is seen to be based on power (asymmetrical relations of constraint and dependency). It involves self-reflection, and is based on an emancipatory interest in achieving rational autonomy of action freed from domination (Habermas 1972).

This scheme can be summarized as follows (based on Giddens 1977b: 140).

Type of science	Underlying interests	Aspects of social existence
Empirical-analytic	Prediction and control	Work (instrumental action)
Historical-hermeneutic	Understanding	Interaction (language)
Critical theory	Emancipation	Power

The distinction between 'work' and 'interaction' is central. Individuals are seen to shape and determine themselves both through work and through communicative action and language. 'Work' refers to instrumental action and/or rational choice: instrumental action is governed by technical rules based on empirical

knowledge, and rational choice is governed by strategies based on analytic knowledge. 'Interaction', on the other hand, is communicative action, and is governed
by shared norms enforced through sanctions (Habermas 1971: 91–2). For
Habermas, it is not only important to recognize the need for both the *empirical-
analytic* sciences and the *historical-hermeneutic* sciences, but also to recognize the
differences between them.[1]

According to Habermas, the distinction between these two types of science is
not intended to correspond to differences in subject matter. Human beings can be
studied as part of nature, as in biology, or as social actors. Rather, the distinction
is concerned with the interests of the researcher and, hence, with the way in which
reality is viewed. The *empirical-analytic* sciences are concerned with bodies in
motion, with events and processes that can be explained causally, while the
historical-hermeneutic sciences deal with speaking and acting subjects whose
utterances and actions can be understood (McCarthy 1984: 70).

This distinction appears to run parallel to the long-established contrast in
German social thought between 'explanation' and 'understanding', the former
being associated with the natural sciences and the latter with the social and cultural sciences (Bottomore 1984: 57–8). However, Habermas argued that Critical
Theory involves all three forms of knowledge, and is therefore not identical with
self-reflection alone. It includes interpretive understanding of systems of belief and
modes of communication using the methods of *historical-hermeneutic* science, the
critical evaluation of these, and the investigation of their causes by the methods of
empirical-analytic science.

Within the social sciences, Habermas distinguished between the hermeneutic or
cultural sciences and the 'systematic' social sciences, such as sociology. The latter,
he argued, may have to draw on the methods of *empirical-analytic* science in order
to study relatively stable and widespread empirical regularities in social life, even
if these regularities are historically specific. They may have to draw on methods
other than hermeneutic ones. In addition, it may be necessary for *emancipatory*
science to draw on both the other two forms of knowledge.

In his later work, Habermas further developed his theory of cognitive interests. In order to provide a foundation for *emancipatory* science, he had to find a
way to establish the truth of the claims of a 'critical' theory. This was achieved
by developing a 'consensus theory of truth', as against Positivism's correspondence theory of truth. In brief, he argued that truth claims can ultimately be
decided only through critical discussion, through the achievement of a 'rational
consensus', not through an appeal to evidence gained by observation. For such
a consensus to be regarded as perfectly rational, it must be possible to demonstrate that any rational, competent person would come to the same conclusion
if they were free of all constraints or distorting influences, whether their source
was open domination, conscious strategic behaviour, or the more subtle barriers
to communication deriving from self-deception. Such a set of circumstances he
called 'an ideal speech situation'. Even if such a situation is impossible to achieve,
it is nevertheless assumed or anticipated in all discourse. All participants must
not only have the same chance to speak, but they must also be free to question
and refute claims of other speakers. Any such discourse is based on the assumption that what a speaker says is understandable and true, and that the claims

made are sincere and appropriate for the speaker to make. It is deviation from these assumptions that leads to 'distorted communication'. Hence, truth involves the promise of reaching a consensus.

Critical Theory is critical of the natural sciences because, as a result of their dependence on technical rationality (or instrumental reason) and their success in the domination of nature, they and technology have become an important new source of authority and power in society. In order to be emancipated from the domination of technical rationality, the social theorist must enable people to understand their situation in the social world, to help them become emancipated through being competent communicators.

The broad view of Positivism with which Critical Theorists have worked has made it possible for Habermas to accept some of the features of Positivism while at the same time rejecting others. For example, he rejected Positivism's ideas about causal laws as universal truths in favour of the view that they have a practical function. They can be the basis for action, the results of which can be assessed and fed back into their improvement (Stockman 1983: 67).

Fay's four theories of critical social science

A modified version of Critical Theory has been developed by Fay (1975) as an alternative to both Positivism and Interpretivism. He gave his version three main features. First, as it is based on the felt needs and sufferings of a group of people, it is necessary to understand the world from their point of view. Secondly, his Critical Theory recognizes that many of the actions that people perform are caused by conditions over which they have no control and which are not based on conscious knowledge and choice. Therefore, it is necessary to try to discover the 'quasi-causal and functional laws of social behaviour' that operate in particular contexts. Thirdly, there is recognition that social theory is interconnected with social practice, such that the truth or falsity of a theory is partially determined by whether it can be translated into action. Hence, if an adequate understanding has been achieved of people's felt needs and experienced privations, and of the structural conflicts and inherent contradictions that cause them, and this leads to action that overcomes them, then the theory must have some validity. This is usually referred to as the 'pragmatic view of truth'. Thus, not only is the theory grounded in the self-understanding of the social actors, but it must be possible to translate it into their language, in order for them to be able to change their self-understanding and act on the theory (Fay 1975: 109–10).

More recently, Fay (1987) has argued that a fully developed critical social science consists of a complex of four different theories, which comprise ten sub-theories.

I   A theory of false consciousness, which

    1 demonstrates the ways in which the self-understandings of a group of people are false, or incoherent, or both;

    2 explains how the members of this group came to have these self-understandings, and how they are maintained; and

3 contrasts them with an alternative self-understanding, showing how this alternative is superior.

II A theory of crisis, which

4 spells out what a social crisis is;
5 indicates how a particular society is in such a crisis; and
6 provides a historical account of the development of this crisis partly in terms of the false consciousness of the members of the group and partly in terms of the structural bases of the society.

III A theory of education, which

7 offers an account of the necessary and sufficient conditions for the sort of enlightenment envisioned by the theory; and
8 shows that, given the current social situation, these conditions are satisfied.

IV A theory of transformative action, which

9 isolates those aspects of a society that must be altered if the social crisis is to be resolved and the dissatisfactions of its members lessened; and
10 details a plan of action indicating the people who are to be the 'carriers' of the anticipated social transformation and at least some general idea of how they might do this. (Fay 1987: 31–2)

These theories must not only be consistent with one another, but must also be systematically related such that the elements of one theory or sub-theory are employed, where appropriate, in the other theories or sub-theories. Fay argued that Habermas's theory of late capitalism covers all the components of this scheme except for sub-theories 8 and 10. This gap in Habermas's work has been one of the most frequent criticisms: that is, that his theories are academic and utopian, and have little bearing on political life (Fay 1987: 33).

Summary

The Critical Theory of Habermas supports the view that, as the subject matters of the natural and the social sciences are fundamentally different, the use of a common logic of enquiry must be rejected. In common with Interpretivism and Structuration Theory, Habermas accepted the pre-interpreted nature of social reality and its methodological implications. He argued that the natural sciences can only use observation, but that the social sciences can use communication. However, he rejected the possibility of 'objective' observation in the natural sciences, arguing that the assumptions embedded in both theoretical constructs and common-sense thinking determine what will be regarded as reality, rather than producing knowledge of it directly; 'cognitive interests' can influence what is produced as knowledge, even in the natural sciences.

LIVERPOOL
JOHN MOORES UNIVERSITY
I.M. MARSH LRC
Tel: 0151 231 5216

For Habermas, scientific enquiry falls into three categories based on different interests: the *empirical-analytic* sciences, which are interested in technical control over nature and social relations; the *historical-hermeneutic* sciences, which are based on practical interests of communicative understanding; and *critical theory*, which has an emancipatory interest in human autonomy. While the first is characteristic of the natural sciences, it can also be applied to social life. In fact, Habermas argued that all three need to be used in the social sciences.

Critical Theory, then, rejects the interests of the *empirical-analytic* sciences, but not necessarily all its methods, and it uses *historical-hermeneutic* methods and rational criticism in the interest of human emancipation. The clarification and systematization of Critical Theory by Fay (1975, 1987) stresses the need for the social sciences to expose the nature and origins of false consciousness, to describe the nature and development of social crises, to identify what needs to be done to resolve such crises, and to provide a plan of action as to how people can effect the transformation of society.

Ethnomethodology

While Habermas was developing his version of Critical Theory in Europe, Howard Garfinkel was attacking the bastion of American sociology from the inside. His ideas emerged in the context of Parsonian orthodoxy that dominated sociology in the middle of last century.

Origins and aims

The inspiration for this RP can be traced back to work done by Garfinkel and Mendlovitz in the mid-1940s (Garfinkel 1974: 15), but it was not until more than twenty years later that Garfinkel (1967) set out its conceptual, theoretical and methodological foundations in papers he had written over a twelve-year period, and established its name. The term 'ethnomethodology' means the methods that people use to create and maintain a sense of order and intelligibility in their everyday lives. Hence, it is the study of everyday practical reasoning used by ordinary members of society to 'make sense of, find their way about in, and act on the circumstances in which they find themselves' (Heritage 1984: 4).

In order to pursue this aim, ethnomethodologists focus their attention on ordinary, everyday, practical activities, rather than on large-scale social events, institutions or processes, or on current social problems. In the process, they study the everyday talk or accounts that people present 'to describe the factual status of their experiences and activities' (Cicourel 1973: 99). In Garfinkel's own words:

> Ethnomethodological studies seek to treat practical activities, practical circumstances, and practical sociological reasoning as topics of empirical studies, and by paying to the most commonplace activities of daily life the attention usually accorded extraordinary events, seek to learn more about them as phenomena in their own right. (Garfinkel 1967: 1)[2]

He was concerned with the question of how social phenomena are constituted in these situated, practical activities.

Garfinkel drew considerable inspiration from the work of Schütz, Husserl and Heidegger. He adopted some of their ideas, including an interest in everyday activities, taken-for-granted knowledge and the bracketing of presuppositions, but rejected others. He was not interested in the constitution of individual consciousness or the kinds of social knowledge that social actors possess. Rather, his concern was with the 'socially shared procedures used to establish and maintain . . . an intelligible and accountable local social order' (ten Have 2004a: 16).

Critique of the orthodox consensus

As one of Parsons's Ph.D. students, Garfinkel set out to address the problem of order, 'with the conditions under which a person makes continued sense of the world around him [sic]' (Garfinkel 1952: 1). Much earlier, the philosopher Hobbes had discussed the question of how social order is possible when people, in pursuing egotistical goals, are potentially, if not constantly, in conflict with each other; life has the potential to be 'nasty, brutish and short'.

Whereas Parsons saw the answer to this question in shared, internalized values and norms, which constrain these order-threatening tendencies, Garfinkel saw social order as a practical accomplishment of daily social activity. He was interested in how people construct meaning, bring to or create norms and values in specific situations, and agree to apply them to their actions. Instead of norms and values being imposed on them 'by society', as Parsons would have it, Garfinkel focused on the processes by which people create or adopt and use them. In contrast to Parsons's consensus model of society, Garfinkel argued that members of society do not respond passively to social norms and pressures, but are active in producing social reality in interaction with others (Bergmann 2004: 73). Therefore, the problem of order ceases to be a theoretical one of concern to social scientists, and becomes a practical problem that social actors have to solve together in particular circumstances. In short, social order is not a reality in itself, but an accomplishment of social actors (Ritzer 1996: 256).

> The ethnomethodologist is *not* concerned with providing causal explanations of observably regular, patterned, repetitive actions by some kind of analysis of the actor's point of view. He [sic] *is* concerned with how members of society go about the task of *seeing*, *describing*, and *explaining* order in the world in which they live. (Zimmerman and Wieder 1971: 289)

In addition to his rejection of Parsons's ideas on the basis of social order, Garfinkel also denied the relevance of Durkheim's notion of 'social facts'. He agreed that social facts are the fundamental sociological phenomena, but he had a very different conception of them. For Durkheim, social facts provide the basis for explaining the actions of individuals. They are the norms, social structures and institutions that are external to, and coerce, members of a society. Such explanations, according to Garfinkel, treat social actors as 'judgemental dopes', as playing no role in determining their actions. In contrast, he was interested in how social facts are constituted and in their 'factuality'. Social facts are treated as accomplishments, as being produced by members[3] in and through their practical activities (Garfinkel 1967). 'While classical (Durkheimian) sociology is in the business of *explaining* social facts, the effort of ethnomethodology is directed towards an *explication* of their constitution' (ten Have 2004b: 151).

This point has been made by Zimmerman and Pollner (1971) in their claim that orthodox sociology is characterized by a confounding of *topic* and *resource*. They argued that 'the world of everyday life, while furnishing sociology with its favored topics of inquiry, is seldom a topic in its own right'. Ethnomethodology offers an alternative approach, in which common sense becomes a resource rather than a topic for research; lay constructions of reality, such as conceptions of 'objective' social structures, become topics for investigation. The major focus of research moves to understanding the activities whereby members create and sustain their continuing agreement on the 'objectivity' of such social structures.

It is important to note that ethnomethodologists also reject the concerns of Interpretivism in all its forms. They are not interested in motives, intentions, cognitive processes, emotions or other internal processes, just as they are not interested in the internalized norms and values of the Parsonian tradition. What they *are* interested in are the directly observable, overt activities of participants in social situations, and with the work that they do together to achieve order in their everyday lives.

Core concepts

Garfinkel developed a particular vocabulary to present his views on members' methods. The best-known concepts are: accounts, accountable, reflexivity, glossing practices, indexicality and indexical expressions, all of which are closely related.

An *account* is something that members produce that makes recognizable and understandable the meaning and order of a social event. It is in describing, criticizing and idealizing specific social events that members give accounts. However, this is not something that is reported after the event to an outside observer; it is an integral part of the event itself. When two people are speaking together, such as a customer in a shop and a sales assistant, their conversation will contain utterances that will confirm for each other the nature of their transaction, its purpose, the normal processes, the boundaries of their activities, etc. Order in the transaction comes from the accounts that are embedded in the transaction. The participants keep reinforcing for each other, through their accounts, the kind of transaction in which they are engaged.

While accounts create order in social events, they also obtain their meaning and intelligibility with reference to this social order; they possess a fundamental *reflexivity*. This is somewhat like the notion of the *hermeneutic circle* (see pp. 117–18). Accounts are intelligible only in the social context in which they originate, and the meaning and order of the context is dependent on such accounts.

The reflexive nature of social activities, both conversations and actions, is clearly evident in the shorthand, or *glossing practices*, that members use. Words or gestures used in a particular context will invariably take for granted not only activities that preceded or will follow the present occasion, but also the background knowledge of the participants. Take the simple example of a conversation where one person says, 'I had a flat tyre yesterday.' In this statement, the word 'I' does not refer to the speaker but to the speaker's car. Taken literally, the statement makes no sense, but in the context of a conversation, and according to conversational etiquette that the speakers assume, this glossing practice will make perfect sense to the hearer.

An aspect of this process is that all actions and utterances have an *indexical* character. They make sense only with reference to the context or situation in which they occur. As the context changes, so the meaning of actions and utterances also changes. For example, the statement 'I had a flat tyre yesterday' may be problematic in a conversation between train commuters who do not own cars. Hence, an *indexical expression* is one whose sense and meaning are derived from the occasion on which it is used (Benson and Hughes 1983: 100). The important consequence of this claim is that social activities can be understood only in context. According to Garfinkel, any attempt to produce abstract, 'objective', context-free knowledge is to deny the context-dependent quality of social activities. Recognizing the latter creates insuperable difficulties for traditional social science. Ethnomethodologists argue that attempts to replace indexical expressions with objective expressions lead to unreal expectations (Bergmann 2004: 75–6).

There is one other core characteristic of Ethnomethodology worth mentioning here, and that is *ethnomethodological indifference*. In the study of ethnomethods, the researcher maintains a posture of indifference as to the validity of these methods; no judgements are made about their appropriateness or correctness. Whatever their strengths or deficiencies, these practices and their products constitute everyday social reality, whether it be in the home, office, school, hospital or scientific laboratory (Pollner and Emerson 2001: 120). They have to be studied on their own terms, not in terms of extrinsic criteria of validity.

Methods for studying members' methods

A major problem for ethnomethodologists is how to reveal what members usually take for granted during social activities. Garfinkel devised some methods for doing this, and later practitioners have added others. The best-known ones are breaching experiments, becoming a member, and the use of audio-visual recordings.

Breaching experiments were used by Garfinkel in the early days of ethnomethodology mainly to demonstrate the existence of taken-for-granted expectations and assumptions present in social activities. 'I have found that they produce reflections through which the strangeness of an obstinately familiar world can be detected' (Garfinkel 1967: 38). Invariably, these experiments involved someone in an interaction situation saying something unusual or out of character, or behaving in an unexpected way. A few were conducted in laboratory settings, but most were field experiments, with students acting unpredictably. The students would then observe the reactions of others in the situation.

Garfinkel used as an example a conversation between two members of a car pool about an incident that happened the previous day. The subject of the experiment said to the experimenter, 'I had a flat tyre yesterday.'

> The experimenter responded: 'What do you mean, *you* had a flat tyre?' [The subject] appeared momentarily stunned. Then she answered in a hostile way: 'What do you mean, "What do you mean?" A flat tyre is a flat tyre. That is what I meant. Nothing special. What a crazy question!' (Garfinkel 1967: 42)

In this interchange, the experimenter had challenged an accepted glossing practice and, in the process, had disturbed a normal conversation. The subject, or 'victim', in such experiments would normally not be able to make sense of the breach in normal conversation or behaviour, and would try to restore some normality to the situation. However, if this was unsuccessful, they usually responded, as in this example, with a mixture of bewilderment and anger.

As an alternative to disturbing situations, ethnomethodologists have also adopted, or adapted, a commonly used ethnographic method of participant observation. The aim is to place oneself in unusual situations, such as those in which order is likely to be disturbed 'naturally' and where sense making becomes problematic for the members; where the researcher has to master the task of becoming a member; where members provide instructions on what is natural for them, but not the researcher (ten Have 2004a: 33). The researcher hopes to learn about the sense-making strategies used by members by experiencing them firsthand. The experiences of being 'a stranger' or 'a novice' (Schwartz and Jacobs 1979), and the pressures from the members to 'go native', are used as topics for investigation. In short, the researcher 'becomes the phenomenon' (Mehan and Wood 1975) rather than just observing and/or experiencing it. The researcher's presence in the situation, and the disturbances they 'naturally' cause, can become the research topic, rather than a problem to be solved. It is possible to reflect on how they and other members make sense of the researcher's presence in their everyday life.

The other major method used to study the ordinary practices of members in naturally occurring events is to make recordings using audio and/or video equipment. Transcriptions of the audio component can be used for a detailed analysis of the methods that members actually use to bring off these events, and to achieve, maintain and retrieve social order. It is possible to unearth details that may be difficult to identify when observing in real time (ten Have 2004b: 160). While this method can be used in conjunction with the others, it has spawned the specialized and now somewhat separate field of conversational analysis. 'The general idea lying behind these research practices is thus to evade as far as possible the unthinking and unnoticed use of common sense that seems to be inherent in empirical research practices in the social sciences at large' (ten Have 2004b: 155).

One of the ironies of ethnomethodological analysis is that it can be turned on the 'everyday' practices of the practitioners themselves, as well as on those in other fields of research specialization.

> No enquiries can be excluded no matter where or when they occur, no matter how vast or trivial their scope, organization, cost, duration, consequences, whatever their

successes, whatever their repute, their practitioners, their claims, their philosophies or philosophers. Procedures and results of water witching, divination, mathematics, sociology – whether done by lay persons or professionals – are addressed according to the policy that every feature of sense, of fact, of method, for every particular case of inquiry without exception, is the managed accomplishment of organized settings of practical actions, and that particular determinations in members' practices of consistency, planfulness, relevance, or reproducibility of their practices and results – from witchcraft to topology – are acquired and assured only through particular, located organizations of artful practices. (Garfinkel 1967: 32)

Summary

Ethnomethodology took as its rationale the study of the ways in which ordinary members of society achieve and maintain a sense of order in their everyday practical activities. The idea that social order is achieved by the passive acceptance of socialized norms and values was rejected in favour of a continuous process whereby members create or adopt norms and use them in their activities together. Maintaining order becomes a practical problem that members have to solve together in particular circumstances.

In addition to rejecting Parsons's solution to the problem of order, Garfinkel also rejected Durkheim's notion of 'social facts' as constituting external constraints that determine social behaviour. Instead, he regarded social facts as the creations of members in and through their practical activities, and their continuing facticity and relevance as an everyday accomplishment. Instead of using these social facts to explain social activity and individual actions, ethnomethodologists endeavour to explicate how they come into being, and how they are used by members to maintain order.

Because so much of what goes on in the dynamics of maintaining social order in everyday activities is taken for granted, ethnomethodologists have had to resort to the use of various techniques to help members become aware of their assumptions and the norms to which they are implicitly relating. Breaching experiments have been used to demonstrate the presence and relevance of what is being taken for granted, and participant observation and audio and video recording have been used as research methods. While these methods are widely used in various kinds of research, what gives this RP its particular character is their use in exposing what lies behind observable social practices.

Social Realism

At about the same time as American orthodox sociology, with its positivist foundations, was being challenged by Ethnomethodology for its misplaced approach to understanding social order, a British tradition began to emerge that attacked Positivism and Critical Rationalism on ontological grounds. Advocates of Social Realism believe that they have unearthed the only scientific principles capable of grasping the nature of reality. Science, they argue, is concerned with the ontological questions of what kinds of things there are and how these things behave. This RP has been referred to by a variety of labels: for example, 'scientific realism', 'transcendental realism', 'critical realism', 'theoretical realism' or just 'realism'. It is referred to here as Social Realism, in order to accommodate the diversity within the RP.[4]

Realist elements in philosophies of science are not new. What is relatively new is the elaboration of realist philosophies of social science that provide an alternative answer to the key question. The inspiration for the development of Realism in the social sciences came initially from Harré's writings in the philosophy of science (1961, 1970, 1972). Two of his students at Oxford, Keat and Bhaskar, elaborated his ideas (Keat and Urry 1975; Bhaskar 1978). Like Harré, Bhaskar's early work was concerned with the natural sciences, but both of them eventually turned their attention to the development of the realist scientific principles in the social sciences (Harré and Secord 1972; Harré 1974; Bhaskar 1979). In spite of considerable overlap in their ideas, the views of Harré and Bhaskar have diverged to the point where they now reject important elements of each other's position. They now support rather different versions of Realism in the social sciences.[5] While *critical realism* is now widely used to refer to Bhaskar's work, it is inappropriate for Harré's position. From the beginning, Bhaskar's work has had Marxist underpinnings, whereas Harré has moved from his earlier commitment to Realism towards a version of social constructionism. As we shall see, they now adopt rather different ontologies. In spite of Harré being in the field much earlier than Bhaskar, the latter's structuralist version will be discussed before the former's constructionist version.

Bhaskar's new naturalism

Bhaskar has sought a middle way between Positivism and Hermeneutics. He has argued for naturalistic explanations in the social sciences, while at the same time recognizing the fundamental difference between the natural and the social worlds. Even though he shares Positivism's desire to produce causal explanations, and Interpretivism's views on the nature of social reality, Bhaskar has argued for a view of science that is very different from either of these RPs. It has come to be known as *critical realism*, and it incorporates the *depth realist* ontology and the epistemology of *neo-realism*.

Bhaskar has rejected most of the arguments of *negativism*, and has insisted that social science is possible. However, he claimed that whereas the methods of the natural and the social sciences share common principles, their procedures differ because of the differences in their subject matters. '[T]he human sciences can be sciences in exactly the same sense, though not in exactly the same way, as the natural ones' (Bhaskar 1979: 203). He argued for a qualified anti-positivist naturalism. Social objects cannot be studied in the same way as natural objects, but they can be studied 'scientifically' as social objects (Bhaskar 1979: 26–7).

Bhaskar's (1978) aim was to provide a comprehensive alternative to Positivism, paying particular attention to its view of causal laws as constant conjunctions. He argued that there is a distinction between a causal law and a pattern of events.

A constant conjunction must be backed by a theory that provides an explanation of the link between the two events, a theory that provides a conception or picture of the mechanisms or structures at work. These structures and mechanisms are nothing more than the tendencies or powers that things have to act in a particular way in particular circumstances. Therefore, *critical realism* is ultimately a search for generative structures and mechanisms.

Bhaskar argued that it is necessary to assume that such mechanisms are independent of the events that they generate, such that they may be out of phase with the actual pattern of events. It is also necessary to assume that events can occur independently of them being experienced.

> The combined tendencies of these structures and mechanisms *may* generate events that in turn *may* be observed, but the events take place whether or not there is anyone around to observe them, and the tendencies of the underlying structures of reality remain the same even when they counteract each other in such a way as to produce no (directly or indirectly) observable change in reality. (Outhwaite 1983: 321–2)

Hence, Bhaskar proposed that experiences, events and mechanisms constitute three overlapping domains of reality; the domains of the *empirical*, the *actual* and the *real*. The *empirical* domain consists of events that can be observed; the *actual* domain consists of events whether or not they are observed; and the *real* domain consists of the structures and mechanisms that produce these events (see table 5.1). Bhaskar viewed *critical realism* as consisting of three phases.

> [W]e have in science a three-phase schema of development, in which in a continuing dialectic, science identifies a phenomenon (or range of phenomena), constructs explanations for it and empirically tests its explanations, leading to the identification of the generative mechanisms at work, which now becomes the phenomenon to be explained, and so on. On this view of science its essence lies in the move at any one level from manifest phenomena to the structures that generate them. (Bhaskar 1978: 4)

According to Outhwaite (1987: 45–6), Bhaskar's *critical realism* consists of five principles.

1 A distinction is made between transitive and intransitive objects of science. Transitive objects are the concepts, theories and models that scientists develop to understand and explain some aspects of reality; intransitive objects are the real entities and their relations that make up the natural and social worlds.

Table 5.1 Domains of reality

	Domain of empirical	*Domain of actual*	*Domain of real*
Experiences	✓		
Events		✓	
Mechanisms			✓

Source: adapted from Bhaskar 1978.

2 Reality is stratified into three levels or domains: the *empirical*, the *actual* and the *real*.
3 Causal relations are regarded as powers or tendencies of things that interact with other tendencies such that an observable event may or may not be produced, and may or may not be observed. Social laws need not be universal; they need only to represent recognized tendencies.
4 In the domain of the *real*, definitions of concepts are regarded as real definitions: i.e. statements about the basic nature of some entity or structure. They are neither summaries of what is observed nor stipulations that a term should be used in a particular way.
5 Explanatory mechanisms in the domain of the *real* are postulated, and the task of research is to try to demonstrate their existence.

Bhaskar (1983, 1986) has added an emancipatory component. He has argued that social science is non-neutral in a double sense: 'It consists of a *practical intervention* in social life, and it *logically entails* value judgments' (Bhaskar 1983: 275–6). He was critical of the view that social actors' interpretations or accounts must be regarded as not being open to correction by an outside expert, that these interpretations are all that is necessary for social knowledge, or that such knowledge is rooted in them. He argued that, in adopting such an interpretive (or hermeneutic) foundation for *critical realism*, it is necessary to distinguish between the meaning of an act or utterance and the actor's intention in performing it (Bhaskar 1983: 292). In this argument, Bhaskar has distinguished between meanings of actions that are necessarily social in character (presumably because they are intersubjective) and beliefs about, or reasons (motives) given, for actions, which are personal. He, like Giddens, considered it important to distinguish the knowledge (meanings) used in action from the beliefs (motives) that prompt or rationalize it. It follows from this that if a social scientist has an adequate theory showing that a particular belief is false (that it is illusory, inadequate or misleading), and why such a belief is believed, then it is possible to offer a critique of this belief, and mandatory to suggest action that might be rationally directed toward removing or transforming that false belief (Bhaskar 1983: 298). There is clearly some overlap between this position and the positions advocated by Habermas and Fay, and by Rex and Giddens, all of whom have sympathy with Marx's notion of false consciousness.

Bhaskar's *critical realism* contains heavy ontological furniture and, as a result, gives priority to ontology over epistemology. He wants to know what the structures of the world must be like for scientific knowledge to be possible. Bhaskar is committed to the reality of social structures, viewed as the relations between social agents in social positions. These structures have an influence on social activity, in that they both enable and constrain actions. However, it is only through the activities of social agents that social structures are reproduced – continue in existence – and may also be transformed (Benton and Craib 2001: 132). The scientist's task is to produce knowledge that reflects these structures, and this is done by gradually revealing more and more of the ontologically stratified reality (Kivinen and Piiroinen 2004). By distinguishing between transitive and intransitive things, Bhaskar is able to claim the existence of an external reality, to accept that knowledge of this reality is fallible, and to see the task of science as improving our interpretations of reality, rather than seeking definitive truth.

Harré's ethogeny

After many years attacking, and providing an alternative to, positivistic empiricism in the natural sciences (Harré 1970, 1972), Harré turned his attention to what he saw as deficiencies in the social sciences, in psychology in particular (see, e.g., Harré 1974, 1977, 1979, 1983, 1991). Throughout this period, he adhered to a realist ontology by arguing that what exists in the world cannot be reduced to what we know about it. 'We must separate the world from our knowledge of it' (Harré 1998: p. ii).

According to Harré, the first stage in the process of realist natural science is to produce, by 'exploration', critical descriptions of non-random patterns – to extend what is known by common observation – and, by 'experiment', to check critically the authenticity of what is thought to be known. In carrying out exploration, a scientist may have some idea about the direction in which to go, but no very clear idea of what to expect. This critical descriptive phase is referred to as *empirical studies*, and is followed by *theoretical studies*, the latter being concerned with producing an explanation of the non-random patterns found in empirical studies. This is achieved by identifying the causal or generative mechanisms that produce the patterns. It is possible, however, that phenomena that appear to have no pattern might be produced by a variety of different and unconnected mechanisms (Harré and Secord 1972: 69–71).

Harré has summarized his realist approach to the natural sciences as consisting of three key assumptions (Harré 1972: 91).

1 Some theoretical terms refer to hypothetical entities.
2 Some hypothetical entities are candidates for existence – some could be real things, qualities, and processes in the world.
3 Some candidates for existence are real – it can be demonstrated that they exist.

Hence, because causal mechanisms are, in general, different in kind from the phenomena that they explain, these mechanisms can become the subject for further scientific study. The explanation of their principles of operation requires the formulation of new models, and so on (Harré 1970: 261).

Harré has argued that creative model building, and the identification of powers and natures, should be an essential part of the methods of the social sciences, just as they are in the natural sciences. For him, it is the imitation of a false view of the natural sciences, the one presented by Positivism, which has led to disappointment in the progress of the human sciences (Harré and Secord 1972: 82).

Internal differences

Harré's and Bhaskar's philosophies of natural science have much in common. However, over the last twenty or thirty years they have agreed to disagree on the ontology of social life, particularly on the nature, status and origins of social structures.[6] For Bhaskar, social structures are central, and have a causal role to play; they exist independently of social actors and their activities. For Harré, social structures are intimately related to social activities, and have no causal efficacy.

Consistent with Giddens's notion of the *duality of structure*, *critical realism* regards social structure and human agency as being discursively related; people act within social structures and, in the process, reproduce or transform them.[7] However, according to Bhaskar, social structures do not emerge out of human activity; they have their origins in the past. Human agency acts on pre-existing structures; it does not create them from scratch. Social structures have to exist for human activity to be able to take place; they both enable and constrain this activity. While social structures are unobservable, their pre-existing and relatively autonomous status allow them to exert an influence on current human activity; they are known to exist because they produce effects. Hence, according to critical realists, social structures are real and are causally efficacious. Their role in the social sciences is analogous to the role of causal mechanisms in the natural sciences (Bhaskar 1986: 108).

Harré and his colleagues have challenged this view of social structure (see, e.g., Varela and Harré 1996; Harré 2002a, 2002b; Varela 2002). They claim that Bhaskar's social structures are reifications, abstractions that are assumed to exist. If they are only abstractions, they can hardly do things – cause things to happen. Harré has not denied the existence of social structures; he has just refused to accept that they cause anything to happen in the social world.

For Harré, social structures are generated from networks of relationships between people as they play roles and perform acts. 'Social structures, be they roles or acts, are secondary formations or products of the activity of people acting according to rules, customs and conventions' (Harré 2002a: 115). It is agents, individuals and collectivities, not social structures, which make things happen. 'People are the effective agents who are creating the social world, creating social structures in accordance with the rules and conventions that have come to them historically, and, for the most part, are immanent in social practices' (Harré 2002a: 119). Harré is at pains to point out that it is equally wrong to reify rules and conventions as having causal efficacy. They facilitate or constrain people to act in certain ways, but, according to Harré (2002b: 144), people are the centre of causal powers in the social world.

Others have entered this fray, either in defence of one or other position, or to propose modifications to overcome weaknesses (see, e.g., King 1999; Lewis 2000; Carter 2002; Varela 2002). We will return to more general criticisms of both branches of Social Realism in chapter 6.

Summary

The versions of Social Realism that have come to dominate contemporary philosophy of science are designed to replace both Positivism and Critical Rationalism with a view of science that, it is claimed, reflects what scientists actually do. The view of reality advocated by Positivism, based on what can be perceived by the senses, becomes, for Bhaskar, but one domain of reality. Reality consists not only of events that are experienced, but also of events that occur, whether experienced or not, and of the structures and mechanisms that produce these events. The aim of science is to discover these structures and mechanisms, some of which may be reasonably accessible by the use of instruments that extend the senses. However, inaccessible mechanisms require the building of hypothetical models of them and a search for evidence of their existence. Structures and mechanisms, as the causal powers or the essential nature of things, are independent of the events they produce; they exist at a 'deeper' level of reality, and may counteract each other to produce no observable event. Therefore, the constant conjunctions of Positivism are merely the observed regularities that need to be explained by establishing what links them.

However, the advocates of Social Realism disagree on the ontological status of social structures and mechanisms, and this has resulted in two versions of the RP, the *structuralist* and the *constructionist*.

Contemporary Hermeneutics

The review of Classical Hermeneutics in chapter 4 revealed two polarized positions that divide on the claim of whether or not objective interpretation is possible. One, based on the work of Schleiermacher and Dilthey, looks to hermeneutics for general methodological principles of interpretation. These two advocates endeavoured to establish an objective understanding of history and social life above and outside human existence. The other, based on the work of Heidegger, regards hermeneutics as a philosophical exploration of the nature and requirements for all understanding, and sees objectively valid interpretation as being impossible. It claimed that there is no understanding outside history and culture; understanding is an integral part of everyday human existence, and is therefore the task of ordinary people, not experts.

Two traditions continue

The two traditions established in Classical Hermeneutics have persisted. The one developed by Schleiermacher and Dilthey has been continued by Betti, and that developed by Heidegger has been extended by Gadamer and Ricoeur. Betti (1962), an Italian historian of law, argued that interpretation is a reconstruction of the meaning that the author intended. While he did not exclude subjectivity from human interpretation, he argued that the interpreter must be able to penetrate the foreign subjectivity that is embodied in the text being studied. The interpreter 'wants norms to distinguish right from wrong interpretations, one type of interpretation from another' (Palmer 1969: 59). Texts are regarded as having their own autonomy, and as having something to say to us that is independent of our act of understanding. The study of history should leave aside the present standpoint of the historian and return to objectivity.

By contrast, Gadamer regarded the search for objective historical knowledge as 'an illusion of objectifying thinking'. He regarded the search for 'objectively valid interpretations' as naïve, since this assumes that understanding is possible from some standpoint outside history (Palmer 1969: 46). In response to Betti's criticisms, Gadamer argued that he was interested in ontology, not epistemology, with establishing what all ways of understanding have in common rather than with problems of method. The basic issue that divides these two positions, of whether objectivity is possible, is particularly troublesome for social researchers, and has surfaced in the work of many contributors to Hermeneutics and Interpretivism.

Gadamer's fusion of horizons

Gadamer was not particularly interested in the further development of hermeneutic methods for the social sciences; nor was he specifically concerned with the interpretation of texts. Rather, his interest was in all human experience of the world and what is common to all modes of understanding. '[T]he way that we experience one another, the way that we experience historical traditions, the way that we experience the natural givenness of our existence and of our world, constitutes a truly hermeneutic universe' (Gadamer 1989: p. xiv). He wished to focus on the process of understanding itself, and did so by addressing three questions: How is 'understanding' possible? What kinds of knowledge can 'understanding' produce? What is the status of this knowledge? He regarded this agenda as philosophical, rather than methodological.

The key to understanding for Gadamer is the grasping of a 'historical tradition', a way of understanding and seeing the world at a particular time and in a particular place, within which, for example, a text is written. It involves adopting an attitude that allows a text to speak to us, while at the same time recognizing that the tradition in which the text is located may have to be 'discovered' from other sources. For Gadamer, hermeneutics goes beyond the analysis of a text on its own terms to the location of it in its historical context. The aim is to 'hear' beyond the mere words.

> Interpretation . . . does not refer to the sense intended, but to the sense that is hidden and has to be revealed. Thus every text not only presents an intelligible meaning but, in many respects, needs to be revealed. . . . [The historian] will always go back behind them and the meaning they express to enquire into the reality of which they are the involuntary expression . . . They, like everything else, need explication, i.e. to be understood not only in terms of what they say, but of what they bear witness to. (Gadamer 1989: 300–1)

When viewed in the context of disciplines such as anthropology and sociology, 'historical tradition' can be translated as 'culture' or 'worldview', and 'texts' as records of conversations, either between social participants or between them and a researcher. Gadamer's position requires us to look beyond what is said to what is being taken for granted while it is being said.

Another important feature of Gadamer's approach is the recognition that the process of understanding the products of other traditions or cultures cannot be detached from the culture in which the interpreter is located. He was critical of

Dilthey's attempt to produce an 'objective' interpretation of human conduct. Rather, the task of the interpreter is to engage a text (a historical or contemporary social event) in dialogue, with the aim of understanding the question to which it is an answer (Gadamer 1989: 334). However, to reconstruct the question, the interpreter needs to go beyond the original historical 'horizon' to include his or her own 'horizon'.

A text or historical act must be approached from within the interpreter's horizon of meaning, and this horizon will be broadened as it is fused with that of the act or text. According to Gadamer, the process of understanding involves a 'fusion of horizons', in which the interpreter's own horizon of meaning is altered as a result of the hermeneutical conversation with the other horizon, through the dialectic of question and answer. The interpreter engages the text in dialogue, a process that transforms both the text and the interpreter. The anticipation of an answer by the interpreter presumes that some historical consciousness has been achieved, as has an attitude of openness to the tradition entailed in the text. The interpreter is not trying to discover what the text 'really means', by approaching it with an unprejudiced open mind; she or he is not so much a knower as an experiencer to whom the other tradition opens itself.

For Gadamer, hermeneutics is about bridging the gap between our familiar world and the meaning that resides in an alien world. '*Understanding is not reconstruction but mediation . . .* [It] remains essentially a mediation or translation of the past meaning into the present situation . . . [It] is an event, a movement of history itself in which neither interpreter nor text can be thought of as autonomous parts' (Linge 1976: p. xvi). Collision with another horizon can make the interpreter aware of his or her own deep-seated assumptions, of her or his own prejudices or horizon of meaning, of which she or he may be unaware. Taken-for-granted assumptions can be brought to critical self-consciousness, and genuine understanding is possible. The interpreter does not simply read what is there in the text.

> Rather, all reading involves application, so that a person reading a text is himself [*sic*] part of the meaning he apprehends. He belongs to the text that he is reading . . . He can, indeed he must, accept the fact that future generations will understand differently what he has read in the text. And what is true for every reader is also true for the historian. The historian is concerned with the whole of historical tradition, which he has to combine with his own present existence if he wants to understand it and which in this way he keeps open for the future. (Gadamer 1989: 304)

Gadamer argued that understanding what another person says is not a matter of 'getting inside' his or her head and reliving her or his experiences. As language is the universal medium of understanding, understanding is about the translation of languages. However, 'every translation is at the same time an interpretation' (Gadamer 1989: 346). Every conversation presupposes that the two speakers speak the same language and understand what the other says. But the hermeneutic conversation is usually between different languages, ranging from what we normally regard as 'foreign' languages, through to differences due to changes in a language over time, or to variations in dialect. The hermeneutic task is not the correct mastery of another language, but the mediation between different

languages. Whether it is a conversation between two persons, or between an interpreter and a text, a common language must be created.

In the same way as people belong to groups, they also belong to language and
history; they participate in them. Language, after all, is the game of interpretation
that we are all engaged in every day. Thus, language allows us to understand not
only a particular experience, but also the world in which the experience occurs.
Gadamer argued that even from the world of our own language we can grasp the
world of another language.

Kilminster has summarized Gadamer's view of hermeneutics.

> For Gadamer, understanding is not a special method of *Verstehen* but an ontological
> condition of humankind. In the interpretation of texts written in different periods, it
> is impossible to eliminate the prejudices or preunderstandings that we bring to them,
> because we cannot escape the tradition from which we enter into the subject matter
> of the text. Both the interpreter and the tradition being investigated through the text
> contain their own 'horizon' in Gadamer's terms, so the task of hermeneutic inquiry is
> a circular one of integrating one's own horizon with that of the tradition concerned
> in a 'fusion of horizons'. This is an unending process whereby we test out our preun-
> derstandings, so changing our understanding of the past and ourselves in a continu-
> ous process. (Kilminster 1991: 104)

Ricoeur's decontextualized discourse

Ricoeur, a French philosopher who wrote mainly in the 1960s and 1970s, further
developed the hermeneutics of Heidegger and Gadamer. His contribution emerged
gradually during his career, and culminated in the formulation of a semantics of
discourse that provides the foundation for a general theory of interpretation
centred on the concept of the text. In addition to providing answers to several
philosophical problems, his theory of interpretation offers solutions to a number
of controversies in the methodology of the social sciences (Thompson 1981a: 70).

Like Weber, Ricoeur assumed that the central concern of the social sciences is
meaningful social action. He argued that such social action shares the essential features of texts, and can therefore be included within a general theory of interpretation. He defined a text as any discourse that is fixed in writing. While this
discourse could have been spoken, the written form takes the place of speech;
speech could have occurred in the situation that the text identifies. The reader
takes the place of the other person in the dialogue, just as writing takes the place
of speaking and the speaker. However, unlike Gadamer, Ricoeur argued that it is
not possible to say that reading is a dialogue with the author, as the relation of the
reader to the text is different from that between two speakers in a dialogue.

> Dialogue is an exchange of question and answer; there is no exchange of this sort
> between the writer and the reader. The writer does not respond to the reader. Rather,
> the book divides the act of writing and the act of reading into two sides, between
> which there is no communication. The reader is absent from the act of writing; the
> writer is absent from the act of reading. The text thus produces a double eclipse of the

reader and the writer. It thereby replaces the relation of dialogue, which directly con-
nects the voice of one to the hearing of the other. (Ricoeur 1981: 146–7)

Ricoeur argued that language has no subject – nobody speaks; it is outside time,
and it has no world. Discourse, on the other hand, is an event in time in which
something happens when someone speaks. In spoken discourse, the participants
are socially situated, and their dialogue is about something in *their* world.
However, in the case of a text, the author and the reader do not share a common
world. Therefore, this 'leaves the text, as it were, "in the air", outside or without
a world' (Ricoeur 1981: 148). It creates a distance from spoken discourse.

Ricoeur suggested a number of ways in which this distancing ('distanciation')
occurs. Putting discourse in writing severs the meaning of what is said from the
intentions of the speaking subject; the meaning of an utterance then stands in its
own right. In spoken discourse, the intention of the speaker and the meaning of
what is said frequently overlap; but the meaning of the text no longer coincides
with the meaning intended by the author. In spoken discourse, the speaker
addresses a hearer, while written discourse is addressed to an unknown audience
and to anyone who can read. 'The text thus "decontextualises" itself from its
socio-historical conditions of production, opening itself to an unlimited series of
readings' (Thompson 1981a: 52). Further, the text is not limited in terms of its
frame of reference, as is the case in spoken discourse.

A consequence of these distanciations is that several interpretations of a text are
possible, and, according to Ricoeur, they will not have equal status. If they are in
conflict, the problem is how to choose between them. Ricoeur concluded that the
problem of finding the right understanding cannot be solved by searching for the
alleged intention of the author; the author's intentions have no privileged role.
How, then, can the problem be resolved? By a rational process of argument and
debate (Thompson 1981a: 53).

For Ricoeur, to read is to join the discourse of the text with the discourse of the
reader. Because of its open character, a text is renewed in the process, and interpretation is achieved. This is accompanied by the self-interpretation of the reader
through 'appropriation', making one's own what was initially alien – the conver-
gence of the horizons of the writer and the reader. Appropriation is the process
whereby the revelation of new 'forms of life' (Wittgenstein), or 'modes of being'
(Heidegger), gives the reader new capacities for knowing herself or himself.

This view of the text allowed Ricoeur to develop an alternative view of the
opposition between explanation and understanding to that crystallized by Dilthey
and addressed by Weber. He rejected Dilthey's view of hermeneutics as the attempt
to reproduce the creative process that produced a text, and claimed that this view
was inconsistent with Dilthey's other concern to achieve an objective logic of interpretation. Instead, he argued that his distinction between speech and the text
allows for two possibilities: as readers, we can regard a text as having no author
and no world, and explain it in terms of its internal relations, its structure; or we
can treat the text as recorded speech and interpret it from that point of view. In
the first case, the text is regarded as language, and is treated according to the
explanatory rules of linguistics, while in the second case, it is treated as speech,
and is *interpreted*.

Ricoeur believed that this distinction provided a way of combining explanation and understanding. The analysis of the structure of language as a closed system provides a form of explanation, while in-depth interpretation of the text as speech provides understanding. He argued that understanding cannot be reduced to structural analysis; understanding requires a different attitude towards the text – one that is concerned not with what might be hidden in it, but rather with what it is pointing to.

Thompson regarded Ricoeur's proposal to conceive of action as a text as unsatisfactory. For example, he suggested that Ricoeur failed to provide a clear and convincing defence of the notion that the meaning of an action may be detached from the event of its performance. 'For the meaning of an action is linked to its description, and how one describes an action is deeply affected by circumstantial considerations' (Thompson 1981a: 127). He rejected Ricoeur's claim that participants (equivalent to authors) in social action have no particular privilege when it comes to interpreting their actions.

> For it is precisely because contemporaries do have a privileged position that there are methodological problems concerning the relation between the everyday descriptions of lay actors and the theoretical accounts of external observers, and concerning the relation between the latter accounts and the subsequent courses of action pursued by reflective and informed agents in the social world. (Thompson 1981a: 127)

While Ricoeur was aware of the limitations of a theory of action that ignored social structures, Thompson has argued that he failed to provide an adequate account of the relation between action and social structure. As in any philosophy of social science with an interpretive foundation or bias, Ricoeur tended to 'reduce the results of the empirical disciplines to diagnostic indications of hidden realms of subjectivity, rather than regarding them as evidence for the determination of objective social conditions' (Thompson 1981a: 129).

Summary

Contemporary Hermeneutics has further developed the two traditions of Classical Hermeneutics, but with most attention being given to the one founded by Heidegger. Instead of looking for what the author of a text intended, or the 'real' meaning, Gadamer argued that the text must be engaged in dialogue. Understanding involves the 'fusion of horizons' of the text and the interpreter, a process in which the interpreter's horizon is altered and the text is transformed; it is about mediation and the translation of languages. Different interpreters at different times are likely to produce different understandings.

Unlike his predecessors in the hermeneutic tradition, Gadamer was not concerned with methodological questions. Rather, he saw the task of his philosophical hermeneutics as being ontological, of addressing the fundamental conditions that underlie all modes of understanding, be they scientific or everyday. He was concerned not with the methods of gaining knowledge, but with the openness required of interpreters of literary or historical texts. Gadamer's hermeneutics takes as 'reality' the ever-changing world in which people are participants. He was concerned not with their individual, subjective meanings, but with the meanings they share with others. Neither was he interested in traditional views of 'objectivity' and 'truth'. For him, shared meanings are 'objective', and their 'truth' can be communicated. He was concerned 'to seek that experience of truth that transcends the sphere of the control of scientific method wherever it is found' (Gadamer 1989: p. xii).

Ricoeur distinguished between language and discourse, between the objective study of a text by structural linguistics and its interpretive study. He developed Gadamer's position by arguing that texts create a distance from spoken discourse. As texts have no social context and an unknown audience, and as no dialogue is possible between the reader and the author, they can be read in many ways. Interpretation is achieved by the reader recovering what the text points to and, in the process, achieving self-interpretation. Social action can also be decontextualized and can also have a variety of interpretations, inferior interpretations being eliminated by argumentation.

Structuration Theory

Structuration Theory is a contemporary approach to social theory and methodology developed by Anthony Giddens. It draws on Hermeneutics, phenomenology, Ethnomethodology and Interpretive social science, and in particular the work of Schütz, Garfinkel, Winch, Gadamer and Habermas. In terms of ontology and epistemology, Structuration Theory is based on an *idealist* ontology – although there are aspects that are consistent with a *subtle realist* ontology – and it definitely adopts an epistemology of *constructionism*.

'Structuration theory is not intended to be a theory "of" anything, in the sense of advancing generalizations about social reality' (Giddens 1991: 204). It is, rather, an attempt to reconstruct some of the basic premises of social analysis, particularly an ontological framework for the study of human social activities. For more than a decade, and culminating in *The Constitution of Society* (1984), Giddens attacked Positivism and its theoretical companion in the social sciences, Parsonian structural functionalism, and proposed an alternative ontological framework.

In his numerous publications, Giddens has identified what he believed to be the two most critical theoretical dilemmas in the social sciences today, and has proposed ways of moving beyond them. The first dilemma is the underlying theme in this and the previous chapter: the relation between the natural and the social sciences. The second dilemma concerns the relation between the individual and society, between 'agency' (or action) and 'structure', between deterministic and voluntarist theories of human behaviour.

Replacing the orthodox consensus

On the first dilemma, Giddens has presented arguments for the development of a 'hermeneutically informed social theory' to fill the gap created by the dissolution of the orthodox consensus that dominated sociology in the 1950s and 1960s. The intellectual strands of this consensus can be traced back into the nineteenth century and culminated in the positivistic view of the natural and the social sciences and a functionalist view of social theory. He has pointed out that the collapse of the orthodox consensus has highlighted the common theoretical concerns of a whole range of social sciences, as well as other disciplines, ranging from literary criticism to the philosophy of science.

As background to his views on the way in which social science needs to be redesigned, Giddens made a number of points about the relationship between the natural and the social sciences, and between Positivism and Interpretivism. Against the view that sociology is an immature natural science (see Merton 1957), he argued that social science 'is as old as natural science is; both can be dated back to the post-Renaissance period in Europe, as recognisably "modern" in form' (Giddens 1979: 241). While their developments have been uneven, the social sciences are not at a rudimentary stage along the path already successfully travelled by the natural sciences. '[S]ocial science is not a battered tramp steamer chugging along vainly in the wake of the sleek cruiser of the natural sciences. In large degree the two simply sail on different oceans, however much they might share certain common navigational procedures' (Giddens 1987: 18).

Giddens's critique of the orthodox consensus dealt with the nature of social laws, the role of ordinary language, the relationship between revelatory and critical views of social science, the distinction between description and explanation, and the need for an adequate theory of action. First, the issue of the differences between laws in the natural and the social sciences: it is now well established that no amount of accumulated data will determine which of two competing theories is accepted or rejected – known as the principle of the underdetermination of theories by facts. The level of underdetermination in most social sciences is likely to be higher than in most natural sciences. The reasons for this include 'difficulties of replication of observations, the relative lack of possibilities for experimentation, and the paucity of "cases" for comparative analysis with regard to theories concerned with total societies' (Giddens 1979: 243). Then there is the fundamental difference in the logical form of the laws in the natural and the social sciences. According to Giddens, in the natural sciences, laws are usually regarded as being immutable, given the operation of certain boundary conditions. This is not the case in the social sciences, where generalizations are restricted by time and space. This is because the 'boundary conditions involved with laws in the social sciences include as a basic element the knowledge that actors, in a given institutional context, have about the circumstances of their actions' (Giddens 1979: 244). This knowledge can change, including under the influence of knowledge of the laws themselves. The orthodox consensus had sociology pursuing laws of the same logical form as those assumed to apply in the natural sciences.

Secondly, the orthodox consensus also accepted the traditional view of language as a medium for describing the world. In this view, the basic features of language have a one-to-one relationship with objects in the real world; language is regarded as providing pictures of corresponding aspects of reality. However, description is only one of the things that language can do; it is also a medium of social life, and is therefore a central element in all the activities in which social actors engage. In the traditional view, the precision believed to be possible in a discipline-based language is preferred to the vague, imprecise language of everyday life. However, according to Giddens, the relationship between lay language and technical language is a central problem in the social sciences. Giddens's position is that all social science is parasitic upon lay concepts (1987: 19).

The third feature of the orthodox consensus was its reliance on a revelatory view of science, in which it is seen to demystify common-sense beliefs about the natural world by offering more profound explanations than are available in everyday knowledge. Social science based on this principle has frequently been criticized by lay people as 'only using more pretentious words to describe what they already know' (Berger 1963: 34). Giddens has rejected this revelatory view of social science, and has taken the lay critique of social science seriously.

Fourthly, Giddens (1987: 18) also rejected the opposition between explanation (*erklären*) and understanding (*verstehen*), which has been used to differentiate the natural and social sciences. Rather, he considered that the process of rethinking social theory in terms of a different view of the character of human social activity must be accompanied by a rethinking of the logical form of natural science. It is no longer appropriate to advocate a hermeneutic foundation for the social sciences and still retain a positivistic view of the natural sciences as, he claimed, Dilthey, Winch and Habermas have done. The natural and the social sciences

> *are not entirely separate endeavours, but feed from a pool of common problems.* For just as it has become apparent that hermeneutic questions are integral to a philosophical understanding of natural science, so the limitations of conceptions of the social sciences that exclude causal analysis have become equally evident. We cannot treat the natural and social sciences as *two independently constituted forms of intellectual endeavour*, whose characteristics can be separately determined, and which then subsequently can be brought together and compared. (Giddens 1979: 259)[8]

Duality of structure

In his reconstruction of social theory and methodology, Giddens has drawn heavily on Gadamer's version of hermeneutics, particularly the idea of understanding being based on the 'fusion of horizons'. But, unlike Gadamer, he has viewed hermeneutics as providing a basis for explanation and has been anxious to avoid problems of relativism. Although he argued that various branches of Hermeneutics and Interpretivism have made useful contributions to the clarification of the logic and method of the social sciences, he identified three problems that have to be resolved in order to transcend the limitations of Interpretivism: the concept of 'action' and the corresponding notions of intention, reason and motive need to be clarified; the theory of action needs to be connected to the analysis of the properties of institutional structures; and an appropriate logic of social scientific method needs to be developed. In addition, one of the strengths of the orthodox consensus, its primary concern with the unanticipated conditions and the unintended consequences of this social action, needs to be incorporated.

What distinguishes Giddens's theory from the orthodox consensus, and aligns him with Ethnomethodology, is his insistence that the production and reproduction of society is a skilled accomplishment of social actors. It is 'brought about by the active constituting skills of its members'; 'but they do so as historically located actors, and not under conditions of their own choosing'. This production of society by its members 'draws upon resources, and depends upon conditions, of which they are unaware or which they perceive only dimly' (Giddens 1976a: 157, 161). Therefore, it is necessary to 'complement the idea of the production of social life with that of the *social reproduction* of structures' (1976a: 126–7).

Out of these complementary ideas Giddens developed the central theorem of Structuration Theory, the *duality of structure*. 'By the *duality of structure* I mean that social structures are both constituted *by* human agency, and yet at the same time are the very *medium* of this constitution' (1976a: 121).

> One way to illustrate this idea is by taking an example from language. The structural properties of language, as qualities of a community of language speakers (e.g. syntactical rules) are drawn upon by a speaker in the production of a sentence. But the very act of speaking that sentence contributes to the reproduction of those syntactical rules as enduring properties of the language. The concept of the duality of structure, I believe, is basic to any account of social reproduction, and has no functionalist overtones at all. (Giddens 1981: 19)

From Giddens's point of view, social structures are both the conditions and the consequences of social interaction; they are the rules and resources that social actors draw on as they engage each other in interaction, not patterns of social relationships. They are not external to social actors; they exist in memory traces and are embodied in social practices. This view is very different from that adopted by the structuralist traditions of social science. 'Giddens's key conceptual innovation in this regard is to argue that we should cease to conceive of "structure" as a kind of framework, like girders of a building or the skeleton of a body, and that we should conceptualize it instead as the "rules and resources" which are implemented in interaction' (Held and Thompson 1989: 3).

Reasons and motives for action

Giddens regarded social actors as being both capable and knowledgeable. The former refers to the fact that social actors, in any phase in a given sequence of conduct, could have acted differently, even though they may generally act out of habit. The latter refers to what social actors know about their social situation and the conditions of their activity within it. Social actors are viewed as having the capacity reflexively to monitor interaction as it happens as well as the setting within which it occurs. At the same time, they can give reasons for (or rationalize) their actions. However, these accounts may not correspond to the mutual knowledge tacitly employed by them in the production of social encounters. They may not be able to articulate this knowledge, and they may have other unconscious motives (Giddens 1979: 56–9).

Giddens has distinguished between the reasons given for an action and the motives which may have produced it. 'Motivation refers to potential for action rather than to the mode in which action is chronically carried on by the agent . . . Much of our day-to-day conduct is not directly motivated' (Giddens 1984: 6). This is due to the fact that motives tend to be unconscious. Giddens has proposed four layers to consciousness and action: reflexive monitoring (using discursive consciousness); rationalization of action (giving reasons); practical consciousness (which may be tacit and cannot be readily articulated); and unconscious motivation (repressed semiotic impulses of which the social actor is usually not aware).

Giddens also stressed the need to acknowledge, as social theory had not done previously, that social existence occurs in time and space. 'The basic domain of study of the social sciences, according to the theory of structuration, is neither the experience of the individual actor, nor the existence of any form of societal totality, but social practices ordered across space and time' (Giddens 1984: 2).

Structuration Theory and social research

There are numerous implications of Structuration Theory for the conduct of social research. Giddens has proposed that social research can occur at four related levels:

1 Hermeneutic elucidation of frames of meaning.
2 Investigation of context and form of practical consciousness.
3 Identification of bounds of knowledgeability.
4 Specification of institutional orders.

In Schütz's terms, level 1 involves the description of first-order constructs and the generation of second-order constructs from them. At level 2, various investigations at level 1 across a variety of contexts, within a society or between societies, can be compared, and generalizations established about common elements of a range of types of practical consciousness, including efforts to probe unconscious meanings. Level 3 focuses on the limits of social actors' knowledgeability in the shifting context of space and time. This includes the study of unintended consequences and unacknowledged conditions of action. Level 4 deals with the conditions of social and system integration through the identification of the main institutional components of social systems, be they total societies or other smaller or larger systems (Giddens 1984: 328–9).

Giddens has suggested that levels 1 and 2 are usually associated with qualitative methods, and levels 3 and 4 with quantitative methods, reflecting also the division between 'micro' and 'macro' analysis. However, he argued that this division is a methodological residue of the dualism of structure and action, and can be overcome by recognizing the *duality of structure*. These levels of research are intended to reinforce the significance of the *duality of structure*. It is possible to focus research attention at one extreme largely to the exclusion of the other, but this must be regarded simply as a methodological device.

Finally, Giddens has provided some guidelines for orienting social research. First, all social research is necessarily 'anthropological' or ethnographic, due to the *double hermeneutic*. As a result, literary style is important for ethnographic descriptions that aim to describe a social world to those who are unfamiliar with it. Social scientists are communicators who mediate between frames of meaning using the same sources of description (mutual knowledge) as novelists or other fiction writers. 'Thick description' may be necessary in some types of research, especially of the ethnographic kind; but it is not necessary 'where the activities studied have generalized characteristics familiar to those to whom the "findings" are made available, and where the main concern of the research is with institutional analysis, in which actors are treated in large aggregates or as "typical" in certain respects' (Giddens 1984: 285).

Secondly, social research must be 'sensitive to the complex skills that actors have in co-ordinating the contexts of their day-to-day behaviour. In institutional analysis these skills may be more or less bracketed out, but it is essential to remember that such bracketing is wholly methodological' (Giddens 1984: 285). The usual mistake in this latter analysis is to allow a methodological device to determine the way in which reality is regarded. To the extent that social life is predictable, this predictability is made to happen by social actors. 'If the study of unintended consequences and unacknowledged conditions of action is a major part of social research, we should nevertheless stress that such consequences and conditions are always to be interpreted within the flow of intentional conduct' (Giddens 1984: 285).

Thirdly, the social researcher needs to be sensitive to the time–space constitution of social life. This means that it is no longer appropriate to 'let historians be specialists in time and geographers specialists in space . . . Analysing the time–space co-ordination of social activities means studying the contextual features of locales through which actors move in their daily paths and the regionalization of locales stretching away across time–space' (Giddens 1984: 286).

Critical humanism

Although Giddens regarded social theory as inevitably critical theory, he did not wish to defend a version of Marxism, or to align himself with Critical Theory. Rather, he adopted a humanistic position similar to that advocated by Berger (1963) that sociology has the potential to unmask the pretensions and propaganda whereby people cloak their relations with each other and can, thereby, empower people to take charge of their own lives. Giddens regarded sociology as an inherently critical discipline in its capacity to undermine ideology and the capacity of dominant groups to have their view of the world accepted as reality. The capacity of the theories and findings of the social sciences to be of value to policy makers is limited by the fact that, unlike natural science, the social sciences are involved in a subject–subject relation to their objects of study. While natural scientists and technologists can use their theories and findings to alter the reality they study, they normally do so at the time and in the manner of their choosing. However, once social scientific knowledge is made public, it has the capacity to have an influence on social life through being filtered by social actors into their day-to-day activities.

Summary

Structuration Theory is an attempt to establish a bridge between the concerns of some traditions of social theory with the experiences of social actors and the concerns of other traditions with the existence of forms of social totalities, between 'agency' and 'structure'. It requires a theory of the human agent, an account of the conditions and consequences of social action, and an interpretation of 'structure' as dealing with both conditions and consequences (Giddens 1979: 49). It dispenses with the notion of 'function' as used in the orthodox consensus, and is based on the view that dualities such as 'subject' and 'object', or 'action' and 'structure', need to be reconceptualized under the concept of *duality of structure*.

This key concept recognizes that social actors are engaged in both producing and reproducing their social world. Therefore, in addition to arguing that social actors are knowledgeable and capable of acting differently, have the capacity reflexively to monitor their continuing actions and to rationalize their actions, and can have unconscious motives, Giddens has recognized, unlike Interpretivists, that these actions occur within a framework of unacknowledged conditions and unintended consequences.

Giddens's idea of the *double hermeneutic* is in sympathy with Gadamer's notion of the 'fusion of horizons', and his argument that the language of social science is parasitic on lay language accepts key elements from both Schütz and Winch. However, he wished to differentiate between 'mutual knowledge' used as a basis for everyday activity and 'common sense' (social actors' justifications for what they 'know'). Social scientists must respect the authenticity of the former, but are free to critique the latter.

Giddens not only rejected the positivist view of the natural sciences; he also argued that 'explanation' and 'understanding' are relevant to both the natural and the social sciences. Nevertheless, he rejected the possibility of universal laws in the social sciences in favour of generalizations limited by time and space. The latter is a consequence of the pre-interpreted nature of social reality and the fact that a basic element in all social contexts is the knowledge that social actors have about their actions. As this knowledge can change, so too can generalizations produced by social scientists about social actors' actions.

Giddens has insisted that all social research is necessarily anthropological; it requires immersion in a form of life and a process in which the social scientist explicates and mediates divergent forms of life within the metalanguage of social science. These activities are ultimately critical in nature, in that they can expose and undermine the capacity of dominant groups to maintain and impose their view of reality. In contrast to Critical Theory, Giddens's form of critique is incidental to, rather than an integral part of, his scheme.

Feminism

While Feminism's answer to the key question is negative, many feminists seem not to wish to renounce the aims of science to 'describe, explain, and understand the regularities, underlying causal tendencies, and meanings of the natural and social worlds' (Harding 1986: 10). However, they have been critical of the view of the natural and social worlds and of the methods of the dominant approaches adopted in the natural and social sciences. Science is seen to be based on a masculine way of viewing the world and, thereby, omits or distorts women's experiences (Oakley 1974; C. Smart 1976; Stanley and Wise 1983). In short, it is androcentric. The argument has been presented as follows.

> What counts as knowledge must be grounded on experience. Human experience differs according to the kinds of activities and social relations in which humans engage. Women's experience systematically differs from the male experience upon which knowledge claims have been grounded. Thus the experience on which the prevailing claims to social and natural knowledge are founded is, first of all, only partial human experience only partially understood: namely, masculine experience as understood by men. However, when this experience is presumed to be gender-free – when the male experience is taken to be the human experience – the resulting theories, concepts, methodologies, inquiry goals and knowledge claims distort human social life and human thought. (Harding and Hintikka 1983b: p. x)

Critiques of natural science

Feminist critiques of androcentric science have ranged from liberal to radical (Keller 1987; Harding 1986). At the liberal end of the continuum, the charge concerns unfair employment practices that have led to more men than women in science and to men dominating the positions of leadership and power in scientific organizations. The next, slightly more radical criticism concerns the bias in the choice and definition of research problems; it is claimed that male definitions of problems and male forms of explanation have dominated allegedly value-neutral, objective science. This is particularly the case in the health sciences, where, it is argued, biological technologies have been used in the service of sexist (as well as racist, homophobic and classist) social projects. It is also claimed that there is bias in the design and interpretation of experiments. An example cited is that rats used in animal learning experiments are always male.[9] Claims are made that the interpretation of observations and experiments can be biased, particularly in the social sciences. Another more radical criticism relates to a series of rigid dualisms (such as objective/subjective, reason/emotion, mind/body, fact/value, public/private, individual/collective, self/other) that have been perpetuated and used to distinguish between 'fundamental' masculine and feminine characteristics. And, finally, the most radical criticism is to question the assumptions of objectivity and rationality that underlie traditional science.

Rose (1983) and Keller (1985) have argued that the androcentric character of science is not inevitable. Rather than rejecting science entirely, or trying to achieve the hopeless task of neutralizing it, women can reconstitute it. According to Rose, it is the division of labour that has been responsible for the distortion of science; the alienating effects of the division between mental and manual labour in the production of things has led to a concern to unite hand and brain (Rose 1983: 90).

Over the past thirty years, Feminism has challenged the notion of neutrality in science by addressing the areas of psychiatry and mental health, childbirth, contraception and abortion. These arguments have included concerns that women lack access to the benefits of science, that research does not take women's problems seriously, and that science has contributed to women's oppression. It is argued that medical knowledge serves male interests and legitimates inequalities between the sexes. By exposing the ideological nature of medical science, as misrepresenting the reality of women's health and illness and as serving the interests of the medical profession, feminists have sought to reclaim control of their bodies from the profession (Dugdale 1990).

It has been suggested that the preconditions of a feminist science would be the elimination of the boundary that separates the subject of knowledge, the knower, from the object of that knowledge. The scientist should not be seen

> as an impersonal authority standing outside and above nature and human concerns, but simply a person whose thoughts and feelings, logical capacities, and intuitions are all relevant and involved in the process of discovery. Such scientists would actively seek ways of negotiating the distances now established between knowledge and its uses, between thought and feeling, between objectivity and subjectivity, between expert and nonexpert, and would seek to use knowledge as a tool of liberation rather than domination. (Fee 1986: 47)

Keller (1978, 1987) has suggested that concerns with rationality, objectivity and technical tinkering, characteristic of the dominant view of science, are a consequence of the precariousness experienced by male infants in developing their identity as they distance themselves from their mothers. She regarded these masculine traits as potentially pathological. It is therefore necessary to reconceptualize objectivity as a dialectical process that breaks down the objectivity/subjectivity dualism; it also requires the application of critical reflection to scientific activities.

Critiques of social science

Millman and Kanter (1975) have presented (and Harding (1986) has reviewed) an early feminist critique of the social sciences, which has identified problematic assumptions that have directed sociological research.

1 Important areas of social enquiry have been overlooked. For example, by emphasizing a Weberian means–end model of motivation, the role of emotion in social life has largely been ignored.
2 Sociology has focused on the visible, dramatic, public and official spheres of social life, largely to the exclusion of the invisible, less dramatic, private and informal spheres. This tends to make invisible the ways in which women have gained informal power and has hidden the informal systems of sponsorship and patronage that facilitate career paths for men.
3 There is a tendency to assume a 'single society' and to ignore the possibility that men and women may inhabit different social worlds, in spite of living in the

same physical location (Bernard 1973). Women are likely to have different and broader views about what constitutes social interaction, and to regard much of what men count as nature as being part of culture.

4 In several areas of research, gender is not taken into account and analysed as a possible explanatory variable.

5 Social science frequently explains the *status quo*, rather than exploring alternatives for a more just and humane society.

6 The use of certain methods, particularly quantitative, can prevent the discovery of information that may be crucial for understanding the phenomenon under consideration. The preference for dealing with variables – as is the case with quantitative methods – rather than people – as in qualitative methods – may be related to a masculine need to manipulate and control, and an inability to relate to all types of people in an empathetic way, particularly in relatively unstructured and ambiguous natural situations.[10]

Characteristics of feminist social science

Rather than trying to create a feminist method for the social sciences, Harding (1987b: 7–9) has argued that the best feminist analysis has three distinctive characteristics. First, to counter the fact that social science has traditionally dealt with questions that are problematic within the social experiences characteristic of men, feminist researchers have insisted that their research must be based on women's experiences as a source of research problems, hypotheses and evidence. Secondly, as traditional social research has been for men, feminist research must be designed for women, to deal with what they regard as problematic from their experiences. Thirdly, in recognition that the cultural background of the researcher is part of the evidence that enters into the results of the research, the researcher must place herself or himself in the same critical plane as the subject matter. This feature of good feminist research avoids the 'objectivist' stance that attempts to have the researcher appear as an invisible, autonomous voice of authority. 'Introducing this "subjective" element into the analysis in fact increases the objectivity of the research and decreases the "objectivism" which hides this kind of evidence from the public' (Harding 1987b: 9; see also Harding 1993).

Feminist epistemology

Feminist epistemology identifies an uneasy alliance between Feminism and the philosophy of science. As we saw in chapter 2, traditional epistemology has dealt with a range of vexed problems, including the nature of knowledge, objectivity and the justification of knowledge claims. The history of feminist epistemology has been a clash between, on the one hand, the struggles of women to have their understandings of the world legitimated and, on the other hand, commitment to RPs, such as Positivism and Critical Rationalism, which have failed to allow such understandings to emerge (Alcoff and Potter 1993: 1–2).

Recognition of the androcentric features of science has led feminists to search for an appropriate epistemology for both the natural and the social sciences. Harding (1987c: 182–4) initially identified two main responses to this problem: *feminist empiricism* and the *feminist standpoint*.[11] A third response, *feminist post-modernism*, has challenged these positions as well as established epistemologies of *empiricism*, *falsificationism* and *neo-realism*.

Feminist empiricism

Feminist empiricism claims that the deficiencies in the existing dominant forms of science – the masculine bias in problem formulation, concepts, theories, methods of enquiry and interpretation of results – is the result of insufficient rigour in applying the rules of (this kind of) scientific method; it is 'bad science' that is responsible for these biases in research. Hence, feminist empiricism accepts the traditional views of science, and aims to eliminate the deficiencies in its practice; it challenges the incomplete ways in which science has been practised, not the norms of science themselves (Harding 1990: 92). Harding goes on to argue that feminist empiricists are ambivalent about placing faith in the traditional scientific method of *empiricism*.

> On the one hand, they [feminist empiricists] claim simply to be following the principles of inquiry even more rigorously than their androcentric predecessors who failed to control for gender bias in the process in numerous ways. On the other hand, they point out that without the challenge of feminism, scientific method couldn't detect or eliminate sexist and androcentric biases. (Harding 1990: 94)

Unfortunately, while feminist empiricism is critical of the practice of traditional science, it appears to be internally inconsistent. As Feminism is a political movement, feminist researchers clearly have strong commitments to bring about a particular kind of society. Traditional science, however, is supposed to be value-neutral and dispassionate; the norms of science are intended to eliminate or at least control the goals, interests and values of the researcher. The fact that feminist empiricism has argued that women (or feminists, either men or women) as a group are more likely to produce objective results than men (or non-feminists) as a group tends to undermine the central claim that adherence to scientific rules is the solution. Ultimately, the problem with this solution is that it is left with the inherent deficiencies of these historically dominant forms of natural science and the orthodox consensus in the social sciences. Feminist empiricism does not address the limitations of these traditional views of science.

In order to accommodate a later variant of feminist empiricism, Harding has labelled the version just reviewed as 'spontaneous feminist empiricism', and the newer version as 'philosophical feminist empiricism' (Harding 1993: 51–2). The latter comes from the work of Longino (1990) and Nelson (1990), and opposes not only traditional empiricism but also aspects of feminist empiricism and feminist standpoint. Both Longino and Nelson have rejected the view of the researcher as a neutral observer, and have focused on scientific communities as not only the creators of knowledge but also the arbiters of the rules of objectivity and what counts as evidence. They have both rejected relativism by appealing to socially constructed rules and standards (Hekman 1997: 357).

Feminist standpoint

The origins of *feminist standpoint* can be traced back to the 1970s in Dorothy Smith's critiques of the then male-dominated orthodox consensus in sociology. However, it was the influential work of Nancy Hartsock (1983a, 1983b) and Sandra Harding (1986) that laid the foundations. The idea of 'standpoint' can be traced to the work of Hegel, who suggested that what can be known about the master–slave relationship is different when viewed from the point of view of the master versus that of the slave. Marx and Engels later developed this into the 'standpoint of the proletariat' on which Marxist class theory is based (Harding 1993: 53–4). 'Standpoint' refers to the common experiences and, hence, shared worldviews of groups with shared histories based on their location in hierarchical power relations (Collins 1997: 376–7).

Feminist standpoint offers a different approach to dealing with androcentric science by developing some of the more implicit ideas in feminist empiricism, but then taking these in directions that neither empiricism nor feminist empiricism would accept. Rather than trying to improve the application of the rules and methods of traditional science, it has argued that these rules and methods are too weak to eliminate the influence of the social position, interests and agendas of the practitioners. It aims to produce stronger standards that will produce more objective results (Harding 1993: 52). 'The new paradigm of knowledge of which feminist standpoint is a part involves rejecting the definition of knowledge and truth as either universal or relative in favour of a conception of all knowledge as situated and discursive' (Hekman 1997: 356–7).

The foundation of feminist standpoint epistemology is that a person's social location both enables and sets limits to what that person can know. It has been argued that those who occupy dominant positions in stratified societies, whether based on class, race, ethnicity or gender, have a more limited understanding because of their inability to question critically the dominant beliefs. In contrast, the experiences of those who are marginalized in such hierarchies give them a much clearer understanding of problems that need to be addressed by research. 'They may know different things, or know some things better than those who are comparatively privileged (socially, politically), by virtue of what they typically experience and how they understand their experience' (Wylie 2004: 339). Marginalized lives can provide the research problems and questions, but not the solutions.

Hence, in feminist standpoint, knowledge is supposed to be grounded in experience. However, this is not the experience of the point-of-viewless observation of empiricist researchers. Rather, it is the social experiences of women. Women's lives 'provide the starting point for asking new, critical questions about not only those women's lives but also about men's lives and, most importantly, the causal relations between them' (Harding 1993: 55). But starting with women's experiences does not guarantee that a researcher can maximize objectivity; it is a necessary, but not a sufficient, condition.

Feminist standpoint epistemology focuses on the consequences of the experiences of women in the division of labour, including production and reproduction, and the differential experiences of boys and girls in their relationships to their mothers in the sexual division of labour in child rearing (D. E. Smith 1974, 1979; Flax 1983; Hartsock 1983b; Rose 1983).[12] 'Women and men . . . grow up with personalities affected by different boundary experiences, differently constructed and experienced inner and outer worlds, and preoccupations with different relational issues' (Hartsock 1983b: 295). It is argued that 'men's dominant position in social life results in partial and perverse understandings, whereas women's subjugated position provides the possibility of more complete and less perverse understandings' (Harding 1986: 26). In the same way in which Marx argued that the proletariat potentially has a superior capacity to know the world, derived from their particular subjugated experiences, feminists have argued that there is a feminine standpoint on the world that is 'a morally and scientifically preferable grounding for our interpretations and explanations of nature and social life' (Harding 1986: 26).

Weaknesses and some solutions

While standpoint feminism may avoid the problems of feminist empiricism, it has been attacked from both within and without Feminism. According to Dugdale (1990), it leaves uncontested the dualisms that structure sexual differences and current scientific practices. Rose (1986) has acknowledged that this continues to be a problem, but has suggested that the tensions within these dualisms can provide a creative framework for struggle. However, Harding has argued that it is not possible to establish a feminist method, as women's social experiences are cross-cut by class, race and culture. A single standpoint could be achieved only by the undesirable dominance of a group with one combination of these experiences. Therefore, as it is not possible to transcend the boundaries of class, race and culture, there must be many feminisms. Perhaps, as Fee has suggested, a truly feminist science will be possible only when society is fully transformed by the feminist project (Fee 1986: 54).

After occupying a prominent place in discussions of feminist epistemology from the late 1980s until the early 1990s, Hekman (1997) has argued that the criticisms of feminist standpoint have resulted in it having less prominence by the late 1990s.[13] In addition to the decline of Marxism as a theoretical perspective, on which the epistemology is based, the growing interest in *postmodernism* and poststructuralism may have undermined feminist standpoint. However, Harding has argued that in spite of the controversies, standpoint theory has not only survived but has also flourished. 'Disturbing though virtually everyone may find some or other of its claims and projects, standpoint theory apparently is destined to persist at least for a while as a seductively volatile site for reflection and debate about persistent contemporary dilemmas' (2004: 292).

Redefining truth and objectivity

A critical issue in feminist standpoint has been the need to find a way to establish the truth of claims made from such a standpoint if it is to assert that women have been and are oppressed. Such claims are essential to the politics of setting about rectifying this situation. The question that has to be answered is, 'How can knowledge be situated and also true?' To give up on the quest for truth would be to jeopardize feminist politics. To argue that knowledge is situated rather than general, local rather than universal, is to raise the spectre of relativism and undermine the search for truth.

This issue is exacerbated by the recognition that women are not a unified category, as was assumed by early feminist standpoint writers. If there is a plurality of different standpoints, based on race, class and geographic location, which are supposed to have privileged knowledge, where does the truth lie? If there are multiple feminist standpoints, then there must be multiple truths and multiple realities.

One attempt to deal with this issue has been to redefine the notion of objectivity as a basis for defending the truth of feminist knowledge. An early move in this direction was to define objectivity as 'the pursuit of a maximally authentic, and hence maximally reliable, understanding of the world around oneself' (Keller 1985: 116), and then to distinguish between two types of objectivity, 'dynamic' and 'static'.

> Dynamic objectivity aims at a form of knowledge that grants to the world around us its independent integrity but does so in a way that remains cognizant of, indeed relies on, our connectivity with that world. In this, dynamic objectivity is not unlike empathy, a form of knowledge of other persons that draws explicitly on the commonality of feelings and experiences in order to enrich one's understanding of another in his or her own right. By contrast, I call static objectivity the pursuit of knowledge that begins with the severance of subject from object rather than aiming at the disentanglement of one from the other. For both static and dynamic objectivity, the ambition appears the same, but the starting assumptions one makes about the nature of the pursuit bear critically on the outcome . . . Dynamic objectivity is thus a pursuit of knowledge that makes use of subjective experience . . . in the interests of a more effective objectivity. (Keller 1985: 117)

Harding (1993) has taken Keller's idea of dynamic objectivity a step further by arguing for 'strong objectivity'. This requires that the researcher (the subject of knowledge) and the researched (the objects of knowledge) be placed at the same level. Rather than aiming for detachment and value neutrality, researchers must also be part of the objects of knowledge. The objects of knowledge need to be able to reflect on the subjects of knowledge, not just the other way around.

Strong objectivity recognizes the plurality of feminist standpoints and that knowledge is socially situated. While Harding has rejected the idea of absolute truth, she has argued that some truths are less false – less partial and less distorted – than others. The more oppressed a group is, the more objective will be their knowledge (Harding 1991: 179–80).

Hekman (1997) has been critical of 'strong objectivity' on two grounds. First, she has claimed that Harding has offered no argument for why level of oppression is associated with level of privileged knowledge, although Harding (1997: 388) has rejected this. Second, Hekman has argued that there are no shared standards of judgement that could support such claims. Her solution lies in a different direction.

In presenting another attempt to deal with the issue of truth status, Hekman (1997) has reiterated the critical problem facing feminist theory today.

> [G]iven multiple standpoints, the social construction of 'reality,' and the necessity of an engaged political position, how can we talk about 'better accounts of the world,' 'less false stories'? . . . How do we select the perspectives and standpoints that are useful to us, that will help us achieve our theoretical and political goals, or are we condemned to the 'absolute relativism' that some critics fear? (Hekman 1997: 358–9)

Her solution was to return to Weber's notion of the *ideal type*, about which she has written extensively (Hekman 1983). 'An ideal type is formed by the one-sided *accentuation* of one or more points of view and by the synthesis of a great many diffuse, discrete, more or less present and occasionally absent *concrete individual phenomena*, which are arranged according to one-sidedly emphasized viewpoints into a unified analytic construct' (Weber 1949: 90).

Weber's notion of the ideal type provides an analytical accentuation of particular but typical characteristics of some phenomena; it is not a description of reality; it is not a synthesis of traits common to numerous individual cases; it is not an average based on statistical analysis; and it is not derived from reality, and may never be found in reality. Rather, it is a kind of measuring rod, created by the researcher, to assess the similarities and differences between actual social phenomena. 'It serves as a harbour until one has learned to navigate safely in the vast sea of empirical facts' (Weber 1949: 104).

Hekman has suggested that Weber's notion of ideal type is consistent with the idea that knowledge is partial and located, and that the subject of any analysis is determined by the interest of the researcher. In addition, she claims that the ideal type is developed on the assumption that social reality is socially constructed and that, while it does not solve all epistemological and methodological problems of feminist theory, it is very appropriate for some problems that have evolved out of feminist standpoint theory.

Of all the authors who have commented on Hekman's article on 'Truth and Method' (1997), only D. E. Smith has referred to the proposal to use ideal types, and she has rejected this solution. Because Weber's ideal types are always constructed from the point of view of the investigator, Smith has argued that

> ideal type methodology creates no commitments to how things are experienced by those who live them. It creates no openness towards those it studies. . . . Despite Weber's commitment to an interpretive sociology, his specification of Verstehen as a method in social science clearly privileges the standpoint of the external observer. . . . The system of sociological principles that Weber developed and on which his 'ideal type' methodology is based is incompatible with a sociology for women, or for people. (D. E. Smith 1997: 396–7)

Given the recognition of the limitations of Weber's ideal type methodology, particularly by Schütz, it is surprising that Hekman has adopted an unreconstructed Weberian approach. The starting point in Schütz's use of ideal types, the establishment of first-order constructs based on lay language and meanings, is compatible with Smith's commitments, but moving from first-order to second-order constructs may not appeal to Smith (see Interpretivism, pp. 127–9).

Ramazanoğlu and Holland (2002: 50–2) have also been critical of Harding's proposal of 'strong objectivity'. For a start, they have claimed that Harding does not give a clear definition of what she means by 'strong objectivity' except to say that it produces less partial and less distorted knowledge than male-centred knowledge. They have argued that Harding wants to find a defensible way of connecting knowledge with reality, without resorting to conventional notions of 'objectivity', but that she provides no clear criteria for establishing this connection. The result is that attempts to claim validity for feminist knowledge are left in confusion.

In taking up Harding's point that the more oppressed a group is, the more objective will be its knowledge, Wylie (2004) has taken a middle path by arguing that some standpoints, particularly disadvantaged ones, make a difference to what we know and how well we know it. This involves four aspects. First, there is access to evidence: 'those who negotiate social, legal, and economic institutions from a position of marginality may quite literally see a side of society that can be ignored by those who are comparatively privileged and that is systematically obscured (or inverted) by dominant world-views that legitimate entrenched hierarchies of privilege' (Wylie 2004: 347). The recurrent theme in feminist standpoint literature, domestic labour, is a relevant illustration. Second, there is the skill required to discern patterns and connections in this evidence. Third, while marginalization and oppression may restrict access to certain kinds of information and the analytic skills acquired through formal education, and may inhibit an understanding of the origins and maintenance of oppression, and the purposes it serves, the oppressed can have local knowledge that is inaccessible to their oppressors. These three aspects can lead to a fourth: the 'critical dissociation from the authoritative forms of knowledge that constitute a dominant world-view' (Wylie 2004: 348). Researchers who tap into these resources can achieve explanatory advantages. Wylie does not argue for the epistemic superiority of marginalized standpoints, but just for differential advantages such that 'objectivity can sometimes be improved and partiality reduced when inquiry is approached from these standpoints' (2004: 349).

The problem of multiple standpoints

It is evident from Hekman's article (1997) that feminist standpoint is far from a unified approach and, according to D. E. Smith, never was united. There are contributions from Marxists (Hartsock), Weberians (Hekman), ethnomethodologists/phenomenologists (D. E. Smith), race theorists (Collins) and Kuhnian philosophers of science (Harding), with backgrounds in sociology, political science and philosophy. There are differences in theoretical, methodological and political commitments, and disagreements over many issues. There are also variations as to where writers position themselves along the positivist–postmodern continuum. While all reject the extremes, there are differences in the extent to which they relate to either one. In short, there are multiple standpoints on feminist standpoint

(Harding 1997: 389). All this is a normal part of academic life. What is impressive is that the quality of the contributions to the debates about feminist epistemology places these writers at the forefront of the wider debates and controversies in the philosophy and methodology of the social sciences. Key issues in ontology and epistemology are all present, and are worked out in the context of practical attempts to improve women's lives.

Feminist research and postmodernism

One outcome of the methodological debates that have raged amongst feminist theorists and researchers over the past three decades has been a growing sympathy for a postmodernist position. However, there has also been a great deal of scepticism, even hostility, towards it.

In many ways, *postmodernism* provides feminist researchers with solutions to the deficiencies they have identified in traditional social science, but such a move has been vigorously resisted by standpoint feminists such as Hartsock (1983b, 1987). In claiming, as Hartsock has done, that the worldview of the ruling group is partial, perverse and ideological, and that that of the oppressed exposes the real relations between people, standpoint feminism has exposed itself to a central postmodern argument that all worldviews are 'partial and perverse'. Everyone speaks from some location, and none of these positions is closer to 'reality' than any other.

While modernists may reject the idea that there are no absolute truths, they wish to retain standards that distinguish between truth and falsity, and between rationality and irrationality. Postmodernists, on the other hand, reject the opposition between absolute and relative knowledge, arguing that all knowledge is contextual and historical. They deny that there are any standards for establishing truth and falsity, and argue that there are no absolute foundations for knowledge.

Feminists have had to steer their way through these minefields in their attempts to arrive at an epistemology that will serve their political purposes. Most, including feminist empiricists and standpoint feminists, have clung to modernist assumptions about knowledge. Hartsock (1997), for example, wanted to retain an epistemology that distinguishes between subjects and objects – something that *postmodernism* rejects – in order for women to be seen as subjects. This, she claimed, is essential for recognizing women's marginal status. She has also argued that *postmodernism* not only denies the possibility for the creation of knowledge, but also makes it difficult for feminism to maintain a defensible political position.

In contrast to these arguments, Hekman (1992) has claimed that there are striking similarities between feminism and *postmodernism*.

The two movements are by no means identical. They spring from different theoretical and political sources and, at present, regard each other with suspicion. The similarities between the two movements, however, are striking. Feminism and postmodernism are the only contemporary theories that present a truly radical critique of the Enlightenment legacy of modernism. No other approaches on the contemporary intellectual scene offer a means of displacing and transforming the masculinist epistemology of modernity. This fact alone creates a bond between the two approaches. (Hekman 1992: 189)

She goes on to argue that the two movements could benefit from a closer association.

The discourse theory of knowledge advanced by postmodernism can serve as a means of correcting some of the essentialist tendencies of contemporary feminism. Further, the postmoderns' emphasis on the constitutive powers of discourse can continue to remind feminists that women are made, not born. On the other hand, a feminist perspective can contribute a needed gender sensitivity to postmodern thought. (Hekman 1992: 189)

Feminist research methods

While this book is not about research methods *per se*, to round off this discussion let us take a side-trip into the field of research methods. Running alongside the discussion of epistemological issues, such as objectivity and truth, there have been debates within Feminism about the appropriateness of research methods.

An outcome of the feminist critique of androcentric science has been a rejection of quantitative research methods, on the following grounds: 'that the choice of topic often implicitly supports sexist values; female subjects are excluded or marginalised; relations between researcher and researched are intrinsically exploitative; the resulting data are superficial and overgeneralised; and quantitative research is generally not used to overcome social problems' (Oakley 1998: 709). The preference for working with variables in quantitative methods, rather than with people, was considered to restrict the ability of researchers to relate to and understand people and to facilitate manipulation and control. Quantitative researchers were seen, at best, as misunderstanding women and, at worst, as misrepresenting them. Hence, these mainstream/malestream methods were regarded as being detrimental to feminist theory and practice.

The preferred alternative was to use qualitative methods in feminist research, and in-depth interviews in particular (Oakley 1981). Such interviews, it is argued, allowed for a participatory approach to research, with the possibility of non-hierarchical, non-manipulative and non-exploitative relationships between the researcher and the researched (Reinharz 1983). These methods are seen to allow women's voices to be heard and the worlds in which they live to be revealed. The use of any methods other than in-depth interviewing was soon regarded as a betrayal of Feminism.

One of the early concerns about this dramatic rejection of quantitative methods, both within and outside Feminism, was the ability of researchers to produce valid results; truth/objectivity concerns were raised and had to be dealt with. As we have seen, various proposals have been made to resolve this, but the discourses continue.

More recently, there has been a move to free up adherence to the strict quantitative/qualitative dichotomy, not only to see methods as lying along a continuum, but also to judge methods on their appropriateness to the research topic and aims (Oakley 1998). The myth that feminist researchers 'only do interviews' has been attacked, and the legitimacy of other methods promoted. 'Feminism's interest in an emancipatory social science suggests a need for a range of methods within which "quantitative" methods would have an accepted and respected place' (Oakley 1998: 723). Oakley goes as far as to encourage the use of experimental research designs. 'Clearly . . . it is not necessary for a feminist researcher to engage in qualitative research to prove her feminist credentials' (Letherby 2004: 180). As Harding has noted, the distinctive features of feminist research are not located in the research methods used (1987b: 3). The fundamental issue has become 'the relationship between the process and the product – i.e. how what we do and how we do it affects what we get' (Letherby 2004: 194).

Oakley has been the major advocate of 'methodological pacifism' (Letherby 2004: 192) as far as the debates over the use of quantitative or qualitative methods are concerned. In her book *Experiments in Knowing*, she has argued that 'in the methodological literature today, the "quantitative/qualitative" dichotomy functions chiefly as a gendered ideological representation; that within this gendering of methodology, experimental methods are seen as the most "quantitative" and therefore as the most masculine' (Oakley 2000: 3). What is much more important, she has argued, is to recognize

> that the goal of an emancipatory (social) science calls us to abandon sterile word-games and concentrate on the business in hand, which is how to develop the most reliable and democratic ways of knowing, both in order to bridge the gap between ourselves and others, and to ensure that those who intervene in other people's lives do so with the most benefit and the least harm. (Oakley 2000: 3)

Summary

The foundation of feminist methodology is a critique of the natural and social sciences as being androcentric. It is argued that research questions, theories, concepts, methodologies and knowledge claims, which are supposed to be gender-free, in fact provide a distorted understanding of both nature and social life, and omit or distort women's experiences. In the social sciences, this has meant that important areas of social enquiry have been overlooked.

Feminist methodologists have received support from the debates that have raged in the philosophy of science during the second half of the twentieth century. This has resulted in three major traditions developing within feminist science: *feminist empiricism, feminist standpoint* and *feminist postmodernism*.

Feminist empiricism represents an attempt to reform traditional science rather than replace it. This position has been difficult to maintain in the face of the devastating criticisms of empiricism as practised within the Positivist RP. A partial solution has been presented in 'philosophical feminist empiricism' in which the notion of universal norms of science is replaced by the recognition that scientific communities are the creators of knowledge and the arbiters of rules regarding such things as what counts as objectivity and evidence.

Feminist standpoint methodology rejects the legitimacy of traditional scientific norms and practices and recognizes that the background and location of the researcher has a critical bearing on research outcomes. Initially, it was argued that members of oppressed groups have a clearer understanding of the problems that need to be investigated, and have had experiences that provide a more appropriate foundation for knowledge, than those of dominant groups. Hence, basing knowledge on women's experiences was regarded as providing more reliable knowledge on which to base political action.

A major difficulty with this approach was to find a criterion that would make such knowledge defensible in the face of opposition. This was further exacerbated when it was recognized that women have diverse experiences related to race, class and geographic location and, hence, have a plurality of standpoints. This recognition forced feminist methodologists to re-examine the notion of objectivity. 'Dynamic objectivity' (Keller 1985) and 'strong objectivity' (Harding 1993) have been proposed as solutions.

These attempts at reforming traditional science, and revising the notions of objectivity and truth, have been rejected by feminists of a postmodern persuasion as unsatisfactory. They recognize that knowledge is local and situated, contextual and historical, rather than universal, and that as there are no criteria for establishing truth and falsity, there are no absolute foundations for knowledge. They have raised serious questions about attempts to establish a feminist science, and are sceptical about the possibility of establishing any kind of science that can avoid replicating undesirable forms of human existence.

Chapter Summary

- The six contemporary research paradigms present more complex responses to the question of the relationship between the methods of the natural and the social sciences than do the classical paradigms.
- Five of these research paradigms – Critical Theory, Ethnomethodology, Social Realism, Structuration Theory and Feminism – have built on or adapted Classical Hermeneutics and/or Interpretivism.
- The sixth, Contemporary Hermeneutics, extends the two anti-positivist traditions that were developed in Classical Hermeneutics.
- Ethnomethodology, Contemporary Hermeneutics, Structuration Theory and Feminism all reject the use of the methods of the natural sciences in the social sciences.
- Critical Theory and Social Realism both give a 'Yes and No' response to this issue, the former accepting a variety of methods for different fields of research, and the latter allowing the use of different methods for description, in the domain of the empirical, and explanation, in the domain of the real.

Further Reading

Alcoff, L. and E. Potter (eds). 1993. *Feminist Epistemologies.*
Archer, M. et al. 1998. *Critical Realism: Essential Readings.*
Bhaskar, R. 1979. *The Possibility of Naturalism.*

——1986. *Scientific Realism and Human Emancipation.*
Carter, B. and C. New (eds). 2004. *Making Realism Work.*
Collier, A. 1994. *Critical Realism.*
Gadamer, H.-G. 1989. *Truth and Method.*
Garfinkel, H. 1967. *Studies in Ethnomethodology.*
Giddens, A. 1979. *Central Problems in Social Theory.*
——1984. *The Constitution of Society.*
Habermas, J. 1972. *Knowledge and Human Interests.*
Harding, S. 1986. *The Science Question in Feminism.*
——(ed.). 1987a. *Feminism and Methodology.*
——(ed.). 2004. *Feminist Standpoint Theory Reader.*
Harré, R. 1972. *The Philosophy of Science.*
——1986. *Varieties of Realism.*
——and R. F. Secord. 1972. *The Explanation of Social Behaviour.*
Keat, R. and J. Urry. 1975, 1982. *Social Theory as Science.*
Nicholson, L. J. (ed.). 1990. *Feminism/Postmodernism.*
Outhwaite, W. 1987. *New Philosophies of Social Science.*
Palmer, R. E. 1969. *Hermeneutics.*
Ramazanoğlu, C. and J. Holland. 2002. *Feminist Methodology.*
Sayer, A. 2000. *Realism and Social Science.*
Signs: Journal of Women in Culture and Society 22 (1997): 341–402.
Smith, D. E. 1974. 'Women's perspective as a radical critique of sociology'.
——1979. 'A sociology for women'.
Thompson, J. B. 1981a. *Critical Hermeneutics.*
——1981b. *Paul Ricoeur.*

6

Review and Critique of the Research Paradigms

Introduction

In the way in which the ten research paradigms were presented in chapters 4 and 5, it was difficult to discuss the linkages and differences between them. This is facilitated by revisiting and critiquing them here. Critiques of each RP are offered mainly by adherents to competing RPs. As this review must be selective, it will not be possible to pursue the dialogue between critics and protagonists. The selection of criticisms has been determined by what is considered to be helpful background for researchers faced with a choice between RPs and RSs. Some aspects of the critiques have been encountered in the previous chapters, as the advocates of later RPs presented their views on the deficiencies in earlier ones.

The chapter also includes a brief summary of the dominant ontological and epistemological assumptions of each RP and a review of the dilemmas that were introduced in chapter 2. They are examined in terms of the positions adopted in each of the RPs.

Research Paradigms Revisited: Ontology and Epistemology

Before undertaking a critique of the RPs, the ontological and epistemological assumptions with which each one works will be reviewed, as the various answers to the key question about the use of the methods of the natural sciences in the social sciences are largely derived from these assumptions. For some RPs, such as Positivism and Critical Rationalism, the assumptions are clear and straightforward. For most of the other RPs, there are some internal variations.

Positivism incorporates the *shallow realist* ontology, the epistemology of *empiricism*, and the thesis of *naturalism*. Social reality is viewed as a complex of causal relations between events that are depicted as a patchwork of relationships between variables. The causes of human behaviour are regarded as being external to the individual. Knowledge is seen to be derived from sensory experience by means of experimental or comparative analysis, and concepts and generalizations are shorthand summaries of particular observations. It is claimed that what can be observed with the senses is what is real. Scientific laws are identical with empirical regularities.

Critical Rationalism entails a *cautious realist* ontology and the epistemology of *falsificationism*. While this ontology has much in common with the *shallow realist* position adopted by Positivism, it differs in important ways. The existence of an independent external reality is assumed, but our ability to know it directly is impeded by the limitations of the human senses and the interpretive nature of observation. The distinguishing feature of this ontology is that we cannot be sure what reality is like. Hence, this ontology is imbued with its accompanying epistemological assumptions, and it is the latter that distinguish it from the *shallow realist* ontology. The emphasis is on causal explanation, which is achieved by means of a set of related and satisfactorily tested hypotheses.

The contributors to Classical Hermeneutics were searching for ways to understand social life that do not adopt the methods of causal explanation characteristic of the natural sciences. In spite of the differences in their epistemologies, they all share some kind of *idealist* ontology. Schleiermacher assumed the independent existence of an author's or an actor's original intended meaning, while he no doubt regarded meaning as a human construction. Dilthey assumed the existence of shared cultural meanings within which individual actions occur. Brentano was a realist as far as the physiological existence of people was concerned, and also assumed the existence of mental phenomena. Husserl was an *agnostic idealist* as far as the existence of a 'real' world was concerned, and assumed the existence of the 'natural attitude' in everyday life and 'pure consciousness' for the expert few. Heidegger argued that understanding is an ontological, not an epistemological, problem. Humans have to be able to understand to exist. In all these positions, the ability of (at least some) human beings to be able to give meaning to, and understand, their world is assumed. In so far as social reality exists, it is the consequence of the operation of these abilities and capacities.

The common epistemological thread running through the representatives of Classical Hermeneutics is *constructionism*. However, their ways of understanding differ considerably. Schleiermacher's concern was to retrieve the meaning the author intended (or social actor used) by means of the hermeneutic circle. Dilthey proposed the use of *verstehen*, initially, to grasp the subjective consciousness – the mental processes – of individuals. Later, he focused on 'lived experience' and, by discovering taken-for-granted meanings from externalized cultural products, was able to understand these products in terms of the meanings on which they were based. Husserl was concerned with the intuitive search for the core of certain knowledge by bracketing everyday understanding in order to achieve pure consciousness. Heidegger argued that, as understanding is essential to human existence in the world, it is a mode of being, rather than a mode of knowledge. All knowledge of social life is temporal; it is bound by time and space, to the context to which it relates. The journey through the ideas of these thinkers has taken us from the use of dialogue between parts and the whole, to the use of empathy, intuition and interpretation.

The various branches of Interpretivism adopt some version of an *idealist* ontology and the epistemology of *constructionism*. The extent to which the existence of an external world is acknowledged, and, if so, whether or not it has an influence on the ideas that people have about the nature of the social world, vary between the different branches. Radical Interpretivism either denies the existence or relevance of an external world (*atheistic idealists*), or has an open mind about its existence and assumes that it has no relevance (*agnostic idealists*). The more common versions of Interpretivism accept that an external world exists, but regard differing views of reality as perspectives on this world (*perspective idealists*) and/or acknowledge that this places constraints on the ways in which social realities are constructed (*constrained idealists*).

As with ontological assumptions, Interpretive epistemological assumptions come in various forms. The core feature is that researchers have to learn about any social world from the social actors who inhabit it. Social reality has to be discovered from the 'inside' rather than being filtered or distorted through some 'outside' expert's theory; the process is 'bottom up' rather than 'top down'.

In Habermas's version of Critical Theory, both natural and social realities are seen to be socially constructed, although these realities are regarded as being fundamentally different. Cognitive interests – strategies for interpreting life experiences – determine the objects of reality. The world is not a universe of facts that exist independently of the observer; theoretical statements do not describe reality, they depend on assumptions embedded in theoretical constructs and common-sense thinking. Hence, objective observation is considered to be impossible in both the natural and the social sciences due to the interests and assumptions held by the observer. Three types of interests lead to three types of knowledge: causal explanation, interpretive understanding and human emancipation. The pursuit of the latter may require the use of one or both of the two other forms of knowledge. Causal laws are not regarded as universal truths, but have a practical function as the basis for action. Truth is based not on the evidence but on the consensus that could be expected in an ideal speech situation.

The result is that Habermas's Critical Theory entails a rather complex combination of ontological and epistemological assumptions. While there is a dominant strand of *idealist* ontology, the use of three diverse types of knowledge-generating epistemologies suggests that some other types of ontological assumptions may be lurking in the background. There is certainly a strong adherence to the epistemology of *constructionism*, but elements of *conventionalism*, *empiricism* and *rationalism* are also present. *Conventionalism* is evident in the ways in which theories are viewed, *empiricism* in the use of *empirical-analytic* methods, and *rationalism* in the way in which the ideal speech situation leads to a consensus view of truth.

There is no doubt that the ontology implied by Ethnomethodology is *idealist*, and possibly *agnostic idealist*. Ethnomethodologists deny the existence of 'social facts' as constituting objective reality, but do not deny that members of a collectivity may experience reality in this way. So, instead of researchers regarding social reality as being objective and external, the latter is regarded as something which members accomplish for themselves through their everyday activities.

When ethnomethodologists conduct their research, they assume that members already inhabit a social reality. They are not particularly concerned with how social realities come into being or with their content. Rather, they are aware that in normal, everyday situations, much of what constitutes social reality will be taken for granted. Such social realities are precarious and potentially fluid.

Of the six epistemologies discussed in chapter 1, Ethnomethodology fits best within *constructionism*. However, whereas constructionism focuses on the collective generation and transmission of meaning, Ethnomethodology is more concerned with activities that restore meaning and order. Garfinkel believed that 'one should not assume that the members of a setting share meanings or common understandings, but should study the methodical ways people claim (or "account for") these common meanings and understandings' (Johnson 1977: 160).

The *critical realism* version of Social Realism adopts the *depth realist* ontology and the epistemology of *neo-realism*. These ontological and epistemological assumptions distinguish it from all other RPs discussed here. In *critical realism*, the ultimate objects of scientific enquiry are considered to exist and act independently of scientists and their activity. A distinction is made between the domains of the empirical, the actual and the real. Social reality is viewed as a socially constructed world in which either social episodes are the products of the cognitive resources that social actors bring to them (Harré) or social arrangements are the products of material but unobservable structures of relations (Bhaskar).

The aim of Social Realism is to explain observable phenomena by reference to underlying structures and mechanisms. This involves building hypothetical models of structures and/or mechanisms such that, if they were to exist and act in the postulated way, they would account for the phenomenon being examined.

Just as with Classical Hermeneutics, Contemporary Hermeneutics includes a diversity of ontological and epistemological assumptions, but with common elements. Like some contributors to Classical Hermeneutics, Betti, Gadamer and Ricoeur were not concerned with the nature of social reality as such. Rather, their focus was on the statuses, roles and relationships between the author of a text, the reader and the text itself. When this is transposed into social scientific concerns, the focus is directed towards the characteristics, actions and interpretations of social actors, the records of these, and their interpretations by the social scientist. These latter concerns are clearly exemplified in Giddens's Structuration Theory.

In assuming that the meaning contained in texts is independent of the act of understanding them, Betti's ontological assumptions verge on the *shallow realist*. He claimed that texts have an autonomous reality; they contain meaning that is there to be discovered. This view contrasts with that of Gadamer, for whom texts have no fixed, independent reality. There are only different interpretations, different understandings of them, which depend to a considerable extent on the location of the interpreter in time and space. For Ricoeur too, the meaning a reader derives from a text is not necessarily what the author intended. When transposed into equivalent social scientific ontological assumptions, Gadamer's and Ricoeur's positions would have to be classified as *idealist*.

Betti's epistemology takes us back to Schleiermacher and Dilthey. From a social science point of view, this means that a researcher searches for truth from a detached standpoint. However, for Gadamer, understanding is about mediation between languages. To understand a text, it is necessary for the reader to grasp the historical tradition, the time and place, within which that text was written. This is done from the point of view of the reader's location in time and space. The task of the reader is to go 'behind' the text to reveal the meaning that resides in, and is derived from, the context in which it was written, something that the author would have taken for granted. The outcome will be a fusion of that tradition with the author's. Again, transposing this into social scientific discourse, the researcher has somehow to discover what social actors take for granted while they are acting. This cannot be obtained in 'pure' form, but will be fused with the assumptions that a researcher brings to the task. Researchers' and social actors' understandings are likely to be altered by this process. Betti adopted an epistemology of *empiricism*, whereas the views of Gadamer and Ricoeur fit clearly within *constructionism*.

Structuration Theory is based on an *idealist* ontology. Social reality is seen to be produced and reproduced by the skilled activities of social actors, but not necessarily under the conditions of their own choosing. Social structures are constituted by human agency and, at the same time, are the medium of this constitution. As the conditions and consequences of social interaction, they form the *duality of structure*.

Although Structuration Theory does not present a predetermined set of epistemological principles, it nevertheless provides the grounds for gaining knowledge of the social world. Social scientists must use the skills that social actors use to produce and reproduce their social world to penetrate the frames of meaning that actors draw upon in these activities. In order to grasp this world, it is necessary to get to know what social actors already know, and need to know, to go about their daily activities, through a process of immersion in that world. The resulting descriptions of this world have to be translated into technical concepts that can then be used to mediate the lay frames of meaning. In short, Structuration Theory advocates the use of the Abductive RS and, as such, clearly adopts the epistemology of *constructionism*.

Differences and changes in ontological and epistemological assumptions have emerged as Feminism has developed. The following summary, while not comprehensive, attempts to identify the dominant elements, giving greater weight to later positions. The ontological assumptions of Feminism are essentially *idealist*. Feminists claim that both the natural and the social worlds are social constructions, and that these worlds are constructed differently by people who, in different social locations, have had different life experiences (e.g. men and women). Hence, multiple realities are possible. It is argued that it is necessary to counter the fact that the dominant forms of science have constructed these worlds from a male point of view, by focusing on women's constructions of the world.

Feminism adopts the epistemology of *constructionism*. This substitutes women's experiences for men's experiences as the basis for knowledge. Traditional views of objectivity and rationality are rejected, and are replaced with notions of objectivity as drawing on the commonality of feelings and experiences, as a dialogical process located in a political context. Feminism is committed to change, to producing a better world for women and, hence, for men.

While it is possible to identify some of the dominant ontological and epistemological assumptions adopted by feminist researchers, it is important to acknowledge that they do not speak with a unified voice. As feminist researchers have faced difficulties in overcoming the androcentric character of traditional science, in giving voices to women in their everyday lives, in recognizing that women's experiences are diverse and different, in basing knowledge on these experiences,

and in producing knowledge that can be defended as a reliable basis for programmes of emancipatory change, they have arrived at different solutions.

Critique of the Research Paradigms

The critiques of each of the RPs have been made from the point of view of another
RP, rather than on logical or other rational grounds. The disputes that have gone
on between RPs can be traced back to differences in their ontological and epistemological assumptions.

Positivism

As a philosophy of science, Positivism has been subjected to devastating criticisms.
Some of the main points of dispute are:

- that experience is a sound basis for scientific knowledge;
- that science should deal only with observable phenomena, and not with abstract
  or hypothetical entities;
- that it is possible to distinguish between an atheoretical observation language
  and a theoretical language;
- that theoretical concepts have a 1:1 correspondence with 'reality' as it is
  observed;
- that scientific laws are based on constant conjunctions between events in the
  world; and
- that 'facts' and 'values' can be separated.

It is not possible to review these criticisms in detail here.[1] Some comments, related
to claims about the appropriate logic to be used in the development and testing of
theories, were made in chapter 3.

Positivism has been attacked from the points of view of Interpretivism, Critical
Rationalism, Critical Theory, Social Realism and Feminism, as well as from the
position labelled *conventionalism*, which is derived largely from the work of Kuhn
(1970a). The Interpretive critique has focused on what is regarded as Positivism's
inadequate view of the nature of social reality – its inadequate ontology. Positivism
simply takes for granted the socially constructed world that Interpretivism regards
as social reality. Positivism cannot account for the ways in which social reality is
constructed and maintained, or how people interpret their own actions and the
actions of others. Therefore, according to Schütz, positivists, as well as critical
rationalists, construct fictitious social worlds out of the meaning that the world
has for *them*, and neglect what it means to social actors. Instead, he argued that
the 'subjective' point of view of the social actors, as against the so-called objective
point of view of the social scientist, has to take precedence. 'The safeguarding of
the subjective point of view is the only but sufficient guarantee that the world of
social reality will not be replaced by a fictional non-existing world constructed by
the scientific observer' (Schütz 1970: 271).

The central feature of Critical Rationalism's critique of Positivism is its process for 'discovering' knowledge and its basis for justifying this knowledge. First, because it regards experience as an inadequate source of knowledge, and as all observation involves interpretation, the argument of Critical Rationalism is that it is not possible to distinguish between observational statements and theoretical statements; all statements about the world are theoretical to at least some degree.[2] Secondly, it is argued that experience is an inadequate basis for justifying knowledge, because it leads to a circular argument. On what basis can experience be established as a justification for knowledge except by reference to experience?

Positivism's claim that reality can be perceived directly by the use of the human senses has been thoroughly discredited. Even if it is assumed that a single, unique, physical world exists independently of observers – and this assumption is not universally accepted – the process of observing it involves both conscious and unconscious interpretation. Observations are 'theory-laden'; 'there is more to seeing than meets the eyeball' (Hanson 1958).[3] The processes that human beings use to observe the world around them, be it in everyday life or for scientific purposes, are not analogous to taking photographs. In 'reading' what impinges on our senses, we have to engage in a complex process that entails both the use of concepts peculiar to the language of a particular culture, and expectations about what is 'there'. Furthermore, we do not observe as isolated individuals, but as members of cultural or subcultural groups that provide us with ontological assumptions. Therefore, observers are active agents, not passive recipients. And the particular baggage of experience, knowledge, expectations and language that an observer brings to research will influence what is observed. It can be argued that we are able to see only those things for which we have concepts in our language. When two observers use very different languages, they are likely to see different things. Critical Rationalism claims to have overcome these deficiencies in Positivism with its criteria of falsification rather than verification, and its tentative view of the truth of theories.

The solution of Social Realism to the theory-laden nature of observation and description is to draw a distinction between the transitive and intransitive objects of science. While our descriptions of the *empirical* domain may be theory-dependent, the structures and mechanisms of the *real* domain exist independently of our descriptions of them. Reality is not there to be observed, as in Positivism; nor is it constructed, as in Interpretivism; it is just there. Therefore, the relative success of competing theories to represent this reality can be settled, according to the Social Realists, as a matter of rational judgement (Outhwaite 1983: 323).

As well as accusing Positivism of having an inadequate ontology, Social Realism also attacked the positivist method of explanation in terms of constant conjunctions between events. Even if two kinds of phenomena can be shown to occur together regularly, there is still the question of why this is the case. According to Social Realism, establishing regularities between observed events is only the starting point in the process of scientific discovery (Harré 1977).

According to Bhaskar (1978), constant conjunctions of events occur only in closed systems, those produced by experimental conditions. In open systems characteristic of both nature and society, a large number of generative mechanisms will be exercising their powers to cause effects at the same time. What is observed as an 'empirical' conjunction may, therefore, not reflect the complexity of the mechanisms that are operating. The interaction of mechanisms in open systems may cancel each other out and produce no observable outcomes. Bhaskar argued that Positivism and Critical Rationalism treat the world of nature as a closed system. Hence, because it conflates the domains of the empirical and the real, and the transitive and the intransitive, Positivism is not an adequate philosophy of science.

In their various publications between 1937 and 1969, the founders of Critical Theory worked with a rather broad and imprecise view of Positivism. Their criticism of it had three aspects (Bottomore 1984: 28):

- that it is an inadequate and misleading philosophy that is unable to attain an adequate understanding of social life;
- by focusing on what exists, it condones the present social order; and
- that it is a major contributor to a new form of domination: technocratic-bureaucratic domination.

This critique 'is motivated, not by a deep interest in the logic of the natural sciences, but by concern for the consequences of positivism's universalization of that logic for the human and social sciences' (Stockman 1983: 43).

Since this period, the critique of Positivism has continued in the work of Habermas. According to Habermas (1972), Positivism suffers from an 'objectivist illusion' in believing that all knowledge is derived from 'objective facts' that are obtained free of the interests of the researcher. Positivists believe that they obtain knowledge of 'reality', and fail to recognize that they have an implicit standpoint in their interest in technical control. By denying the possibility of universal laws in the hermeneutic sciences, Habermas opened up the possibility of other realms of knowledge with different interests.

Critical Rationalism

Popper argued that falsification, rather than justification, should be regarded as embodying the appropriate methodological rules for both the natural and the social sciences, and that this is most likely to facilitate the processes of gaining scientific knowledge. However, according to Stockman (1983: 126), Popper lapsed into a positivistic justification for these rules, by regarding them as correct descriptions of the scientific method, rather than a matter of agreement.

The central requirement of Critical Rationalism is that hypotheses are compared with observation statements in order to eliminate those that do not coincide with reality. However, Hindess (1977: 182–7) has argued that rejecting the idea of a theoretically neutral observation language removes any possible rational foundation for testing a theory against the facts of observation. If the possibility of establishing correspondence between observations and reality is problematic, then theories cannot be rejected conclusively. If reality cannot be observed directly, because observations are contaminated by interpretation, then theory testing cannot be a purely rational process. 'To maintain, as Popper does, both the rationality of testing, and the thesis that observation is an interpretation in the light of theory, is to collapse into a manifest and absurd contradiction. Popper's theory of science is therefore strictly incoherent' (Hindess 1977: 186).

The matter is further complicated by the fact that the process of testing theories advocated by Popper is not as simple as he suggested. There are many elements in a theory: general statements which describe relationships between phenomena; other statements which specify conditions under which these general statements will hold; and logic of some form. If the test fails, the theory is supposed to be refuted. But a judgement has to be made as to which element must be rejected. Hindess (1977) has argued that refutation is always a matter of decision. Communities of scientists will develop their own rules for making these judgements, and these rules will have no independent scientific basis (Habermas 1976: 204).[4]

The most influential challenge to the Critical Rationalist view of scientific progress comes from the seminal work of Thomas Kuhn, *The Structure of Scientific Revolutions* (1970a), first published in 1962. As a scientist, and later a historian of science, Kuhn came to the conclusion that traditional accounts of science did not reflect the historical evidence. As an alternative to both the Positivist and the Critical Rationalist views of scientific progress, either as the accumulation of observations or as a process of trial and error, Kuhn argued for a psychological and sociological view, rather than a logical one.

For Kuhn, scientific progress is achieved by scientific revolutions that change the ways in which scientific communities view the world, and define and go about solving puzzles. The critical tests that Popper saw as sifting out false hypotheses, Kuhn regarded as 'extraordinary science', rare events that may be associated with the advent or development of a scientific revolution. In addition, Popper's distinction between science and pseudo-science, based on the criterion of the testability of theories, is replaced by the criterion of puzzle solving; sciences have puzzles, and non-sciences do not; astronomy has puzzles, but astrology does not (Kuhn 1970b: 7–10).

This difference between Kuhn and Popper hinges on whether science is regarded as the pursuit of absolute truths about the world. Popper claimed it was, although he recognized that we never know when we have arrived, while Kuhn can be interpreted as being agnostic on this point. He was more concerned with the values that scientists invoke to make choices between competing theories and paradigms. For Kuhn, a paradigm is not true or false, only useful in solving the puzzles *it* defines, using criteria that *it* specifies. Truth becomes a matter of community consensus. These views constitute a shift from criticism to commitment, from logic to community loyalty, from falsification to conversion.

Kuhn argued that, as proponents of rival paradigms 'live in different worlds', their paradigms are incommensurable. This issue relates to his claim that, as the concepts and propositions of theories produced by a community of scientists depend on the assumptions and beliefs in their paradigm for their particular meaning, and that, as paradigms embody different and incompatible worldviews (including ontological and epistemological assumptions), it will be difficult for members of different scientific communities to communicate effectively, and it will be impossible to adjudicate between competing theories. There is no neutral language of observation, no common vocabulary, and no neutral ground from which to settle claims.

Popper vigorously rejected the relativistic implications of Kuhn's thesis, which he called 'the myth of the framework'. He accepted that we are inevitably caught up in the framework of our theories, but argued that it is possible to break out of such frameworks at any time (Popper 1970: 56). He was unwilling to acknowledge that a critical comparison of competing theories is impossible, and he rejected Kuhn's idea that sociology, psychology or history can be of assistance in understanding the nature of scientific activity.

Kuhn's work has spawned a vast literature, and has received detailed criticism by philosophers and historians of science. Nevertheless, his view of science has had a great influence on the philosophy of the natural and the social sciences, and has also provided a framework for some other disciplines to understand their crises and revolutions. His ideas were taken up enthusiastically by many social scientists in the 1960s and 1970s (see, e.g., Friedrichs 1970).

Another well-known but more sympathetic critique of Critical Rationalism has been made by Lakatos (1970). In order to overcome the piecemeal nature of the Critical Rationalist view of science, Lakatos argued that the growth of science is characterized by continuity that evolves from the existence of *research programmes*. 'The programme consists of methodological rules: some tell us what paths of research to avoid (*negative heuristic*); and others what paths to pursue (*positive heuristic*)' (1970: 132). A research programme is regarded as *progressive* if it predicts novel phenomena and *degenerating* if it fails to do so. Scientists will persist in developing the theory, even despite disconfirming evidence, as long as it continues to be progressive. However, a research programme may eventually be discarded if it degenerates, even if its theories have not been refuted; theories are not overthrown by crucial experiments, they are just neglected. They may even be revived at a later stage. Lakatos argued that as the history of science is characterized by research programmes, so the advancement of scientific knowledge becomes an orderly and efficient process. Scientists are provided with both a relatively secure context in which to operate and some directions for their work.

Classical Hermeneutics

(See Contemporary Hermeneutics.)

Interpretivism

The critics of Interpretivism come from within as well as without the paradigm. Giddens and Rex considered themselves to be within the tradition, drawing heavily on Gadamer's hermeneutics and Weber's interpretive sociology, respectively. Bhaskar, on the other hand, adopted some elements in his *critical realism*, but was nevertheless critical of other elements. Similarly, Habermas has incorporated Interpretivism as an aspect of his overall scheme, but is aware of its limitations. As these critiques overlap at a number of points, they will be dealt with in an integrated way.

1 Giddens argued that the central concepts of Interpretivism, 'intention', 'reason' and 'motives', are all potentially misleading, in that they imply that competent social actors engage in a continuous monitoring of their conduct and are thus aware of both their intentions and the reasons for their actions. However, it is usually only when actors either carry out retrospective enquiries into their own conduct, or when their actions are queried by others, that this reflection occurs. Following Ethnomethodology, it might be added that reflection is required when action breaks down and/or when social situations are disturbed, such that they cannot continue in a taken-for-granted manner. However, most of the time action proceeds without reflexive monitoring. 'Routine . . . is the predominant form of day-to-day social activity. Most daily practices are not directly motivated' (Giddens 1984: 282).

2 Rex and others have argued that the social scientist should be able to give a different, competing account of social actors' actions from the actors' own accounts. His comments were made in the context of a position held by many Interpretivists that they should not meddle with, seek to alter, or criticize social actors' accounts of their actions. Bhaskar referred to this as the *linguistic fallacy*, which is based on a failure to recognize that there is more to reality than is expressed in the language of social actors. Social actors' constructions of reality are only one element in Social Realism, not its entire concern.

3 Interpretivism fails to acknowledge the role of institutional structures, particularly divisions of interest and relations of power. Giddens argued that the production and reproduction of the social world requires social actors to draw upon resources, and to depend on conditions, of which they are either completely or partly unaware. These structures are both the condition and the consequence of the production of interaction. Rex was also critical of Interpretive social scientists for dissociating themselves from any form of structural analysis, and argued that it was important for them to be interested 'in actual historical structures as they appear to the sociologist and not merely the structures that actors believe to exist, or believe that they make, in the process of thinking them to exist' (Rex 1974: 50).[5]

4 From the point of view of Social Realism, Bhaskar and Outhwaite have argued that Interpretivism also commits the *epistemic fallacy*. Although 'interpretive processes are a significant part of what goes on in the social world, and . . . our access to the social world is necessarily via our understanding of these interpretive processes, it does not follow that this is all that exists, or can be known to exist' (Outhwaite 1987: 76). Social realists, of course, want to specify a domain of the 'real' that not only exists independently of the observer, but that includes intransitive structures and mechanisms about which social actors may be unaware and which, unlike the structures referred to by Rex, may not be obvious to the social scientist.

5 Fay (1975) considered that Interpretivism is not able to deal with the conditions that give rise to meanings and interpretations, actions, rules and beliefs. '[I]t does not provide a means whereby one can study the relationships between the structural elements of a social order and the possible forms of behaviour and beliefs which such elements engender' (Fay 1975: 83–4). Focusing on people's intentions prevents Interpretivism from explaining the pattern of unintended consequences of actions (a point also made by Giddens).

6 Fay regarded Interpretivism as being implicitly conservative, in that it ignores the possible structures of conflict in a society and, hence, the possible sources of social change. It is also unable to give an account of historical change – of why a specific institution or social order came to be what it is and why it changed in particular ways. However, Fay did not see these last two criticisms as undermining the basic foundations of Interpretivism. Rather, they indicate that there are some areas of interest to the social scientist with which Interpretivism cannot deal.

Critical Theory

The critique of Critical Theory that follows is confined to some specific methodological issues in Habermas's work.[6] According to Held, critical theorists have exposed major flaws in traditional RPs, but they have left unresolved a range of epistemological issues that they intended to solve (Held 1980: 399).

Some critics have accused Habermas of adopting a misleading differentiation between the natural and the social sciences based on the distinction between causal explanation and interpretation. It was noted earlier that an interest in prediction and control is not specific to the natural sciences; it can also be a concern of social science based on Positivism and Critical Rationalism. However, in adopting his view of the *empirical-analytic* sciences, which includes some social sciences, Habermas failed to address Positivism's many well-accepted deficiencies (Keat and Urry 1975: 227; Giddens 1976a: 68; 1977b: 148–51; Stockman 1983: 105).

While Keat and Urry considered Habermas to be correct in distinguishing between the forms of knowledge involved in the *empirical-analytic* and *historical-hermeneutic* sciences, they considered that there is a danger that Critical Theory could be split between these two approaches, between research that does not involve an examination of the social actors' interpretations and research that concentrates on interpretive understanding. In the context of their support for *critical realism*, they argued that both traditions of research must be combined (Keat and Urry 1975: 227).

Giddens has argued that Habermas's classification of disciplines into the *empirical-analytic* and the *historical-hermeneutic* is unsatisfactory. First, hermeneutic problems are not confined to the human studies; an interest in meaningful understanding is more integral to science than Habermas allowed. As Kuhn (1970a) and Gadamer (1989) have pointed out in their own ways, with respect to 'paradigms' and 'traditions', 'all knowledge, whether in science, literature, or art, is achieved within and by means of frames of meaning rooted in natural-language communities' (Giddens 1977b: 150). Second, an interest in prediction and control, which Habermas associated with the *empirical-analytic* sciences, is not logically tied to concerns with causal explanation. 'On the contrary, they are of primary significance in interaction itself, and are manifestly crucial to the constitution of that form of knowledge . . . whereby the understanding of others is achieved' (Giddens 1977b: 151).

In a somewhat similar vein, Bernstein (1976: 221) has suggested that Habermas's attempt to introduce categorical distinctions between forms of knowledge and enquiry has been unsuccessful. While it is difficult to deny that technical cognitive interests have played a major role in shaping the history and form of the *empirical-analytic* sciences, and that technical interests have come to dominate forms of knowledge, this does not mean that the *empirical-analytic* sciences are guided by technical interests that determine their form of knowledge.

Bernstein also argued that there is a qualitative difference between the disciplines guided by technical and practical interests and those guided by an emancipatory interest. In the case of the first two categories of science, Habermas specified the formal conditions that are required to produce the particular types of knowledge, the 'objects' that they study, the methods they employ, and the criteria used to evaluate competing interpretations. But the disciplines guided by an emancipatory interest appear to be different; it is not possible to specify formal procedures for such activity. In spite of Habermas's appeal to reason as a means of self-reflection, critique is a normative activity (Bernstein 1976: 209).

The problem faced by all members of the Critical Theory school was how to adopt an independent critical position while still being located in a particular cultural and historical context (Held 1980: 398–9). Is a solution to this problem possible? Habermas attempted to deal with it in terms of a consensus theory of truth. A major difficulty with this theory is that its own justification is based on the same process, thus leading to an infinite regress. However, depending on one's point of view, this can be viewed as either a reasonable method for dealing with the insoluble problem of the relativity of all knowledge, or an inadequate attempt to overcome the problem of relativism.

Ethnomethodology

In mounting its attack on sociological orthodoxy in the United States, especially during the 1970s and 1980s, ethnomethodologists came to be regarded as the lunatic fringe of sociology. Their concerns with everyday life and what were regarded as trivial activities, and their use of unconventional and unfamiliar jargon, meant that they were relegated to the margins. Gouldner (1971: 394) referred to the writings of the early ethnomethodologists as 'dense and elephantine formulations'.

Ethnomethodology became a term of abuse amongst mainstream sociologists and, from that point of view, its work was regarded as having no practical use. While it is still regarded this way by social scientists who try to defend orthodox principles and practices, Ethnomethodology, along with other sociologies of everyday life, has gained and maintained a considerable following, and has had some influence on contemporary approaches to social enquiry (P. Atkinson 1988: 442).

The initial and continuing critique of Ethnomethodology has focused on a range of issues, including choice of research topics, its use of a 'private' language, its hostility towards general theorizing, and its lack of interest in any kind of structural analysis. Such critiques are typical of paradigmatic disputes in which the adherents of one RP denigrate another on the basis of their own ontological and epistemological preferences. I do not wish to dwell any further on these critiques here. Instead, attention will be given to the way in which Ethnomethodology has developed and diverged and, in the process, how it has come both to neglect its foundation principles and to drift back to more empiricist types of research.

One branch of Ethnomethodology has been concerned with detailed, real-world descriptions of sequences within and between activities. This has been justified as being equivalent to the precise observations conducted by scientists in the nineteenth century. However, this concern with recapitulating observable detail runs the risk of simply producing descriptive reports of little significance and devoid of meaning. By concentrating on the activities of members, this branch has also lost interest in the phenomenological and interpretive origins. It has become the study of the ways in which everyday activities are organized, and the role of meaning is restricted to the location of activities in concrete situations. The original concern with social order has become the study of sequential activities, the order in which things take place, such as turn taking in conversations and queuing behaviour (P. Atkinson 1988: 446–7).

This trend is most apparent in the branch of Ethnomethodology known as *conversation analysis*, in which sequence is the primary concern. Whereas the intentions and motives that were so central to Schütz were recognized by Garfinkel as being relevant, they have been all but eliminated in conversation analysis. The original hermeneutic-interpretivist character has been overshadowed by more empiricist tendencies. 'If the model actor is not quite the Parsonian ignoramus, then at least he or she is frequently represented as a mere exponent of sequenced activities' (P. Atkinson 1988: 450). However, there have been a number of attempts to counter these trends (see, particularly, Cicourel 1973; Coulter 1983a; and P. Atkinson 1988).

Atkinson has attacked the limited view of 'context' inherent in conversation analysis. The focus on sequence in activities underplays the need for members to engage in practical reasoning, and limits the temporal framework within which members' meaning-giving is located. According to Schütz, the understanding that people have of the present is influenced by the way they view the past and anticipate the future. This time consciousness, which is an important element in the way in which members experience everyday life, is written out of one-dimensional sequential analysis. In addition, so much of the order in conversations has little to do with the context and a great deal to do with conventional rules that are relevant across many contexts (Coulter 1983b).

As Ethnomethodology has become more accepted by the now more diverse sociological mainstream, and some branches of the latter have moved more in that direction, there has been a lament in some quarters that it has lost its original radical reflexivity (Pollner 1991). Reflexivity involves recognition that all social activities, including the activities of ethnomethodologists, are skilled accomplishments. This makes it possible to do an ethnomethodological study of an ethnomethodological study, and so on, thus fostering a self-critical attitude within this type of research. The self-analytical characteristic of early Ethnomethodology appears to have been neglected by some ethnomethodologists with the risk that it is 'settling down in the suburbs of sociology' (Pollner 1991: 370) and becoming just another speciality within the discipline (Ritzer 1996: 257).

It is interesting to note that a major mainstream concern about ethnomethodological research was that its findings were seen to be context-specific. The idea of typologizing, generalizing, theorizing or applying knowledge produced in one context to other contexts was rejected by Garfinkel. In some ways, Ethnomethodology pioneered this point of view in North American sociology. Today, however, such arguments for context-specific knowledge can be found in a number of traditions, and such knowledge is a key platform of *postmodernism*.

Social Realism

A systematic critique of the early form of 'scientific realism' in the natural sciences has been presented by van Fraassen (1980) from a position that he has described as *constructive empiricism*.[7] He was critical of a central feature of scientific realism – the search for 'a true description of unobservable processes that explain observable ones' (van Fraassen 1980: 3). Instead, he argued for a view of science in which theories are regarded as giving an account of what is observable. To the extent that these theories postulate unobservable entities or processes, they do so to facilitate the description of what can be observed, and these unobservables need not themselves exist, or be true, 'except in what they say about what is actual and empirically testable' (1980: 3).

Van Fraassen's emphasis was on the empirical adequacy of a theory, such that 'what it says about the observable things and events in this world, is true' (1980: 12). However, as theories usually describe much more than what is observable, what matters, according to van Fraassen, is empirical adequacy, and not the truth or falsity of how theories go beyond observable phenomena (1980: 64). It is possible for the scientist to accept a theory as empirically adequate without believing it to be true. In adopting this position, van Fraassen seems to have failed to recognize the full implications of the theory dependence of observations used in theory testing.

Van Fraassen's ideas about constructive empiricism challenged a group of eminent realist philosophers from around the world to engage him in debate (see Churchland and Hooker 1985). They indicated that they were severely disturbed by his arguments, but claimed that they had managed to maintain their views (see, e.g., Churchland 1985 and Musgrave 1985). These criticisms of realism were not directed towards Harré and Bhaskar. Social Realism has other critics.

We have already encountered the family squabble between Harré and Bhaskar about the ontological status of social structures. Bhaskar recognized that social structures are different from natural structures, because the former are both produced by social activity and reproduce that activity (Bhaskar 1979: 48). However, he argued that 'social structures' and 'society', like the objects of natural scientific enquiry, are theoretical and unobservable, and can also be known only by their effects. Stockman (1983) has argued that, in spite of his recognition of this important difference, Bhaskar overlooks the dialogic nature of social research.

By not recognizing the kind of distinction that Habermas made between sensory experience and communicative experience, the difference in accessibility of mechanisms in the natural and the social sciences is not, according to Stockman, fully appreciated. In the natural sciences, the effects of unobservable mechanisms may be detected by scientific instruments. However, in the social sciences, the notion of unobservability is more complex. 'For structures of social relations are not "unobservable" in the same sense as elementary particles or black holes; . . . that they are only accessible to a form of experience which goes beyond sensory experience, namely communicative experience' (Stockman 1983: 207). In other words, natural scientists can only observe their subject matter, whereas social scientists can converse with theirs.

Keat and Urry (1975, 1982) have also argued that social structures are theoretical entities that cannot be perceived by direct observation. They claim, instead, that they are abstracted from such observations. According to Stockman, this argument also ignores the claim of Critical Theory that access to structures of social relations has to be achieved by communicative experience. Therefore, in spite of the acceptance by some Social Realists that the social world is pre-interpreted, there is a failure to recognize that this has a bearing on the manner in which the social world is studied (Stockman 1983: 209). This point could also be made by Interpretivists. However, this criticism does not apply to Harré's constructivist version of realist social science.

Benton (1981) has argued that the objective of Social Realism, and Bhaskar's version in particular, is to transcend the polar opposition between Positivism and Interpretivism. However, he claimed that Bhaskar has not achieved this, because his position tends to support the differences between the natural and the social sciences rather than presenting a qualified naturalism. By holding firm to Interpretive views about the nature of social reality, as existing only in and through the activities of human agents, problems are created for the transitive/intransitive distinction and for an understanding of the nature of power. At the same time, controlled experiments, prediction and decisive tests of theory are considered by Bhaskar to be impossible in the social sciences because of the open nature of social systems and the lack of opportunity in the social sciences to create closed systems artificially. Benton suggested that this latter argument indicates a residue of positivistic conceptions of experiment/prediction/testing thinking. Some natural sciences (e.g. evolutionary biology) have to operate in open systems in which a plurality of mechanisms may be present. Hence, he argued that a critique of the 'constant conjunction' conception of causal laws is insufficiently radical, as it retains the view that experimental closure is possible in all the natural sciences. According to Benton, Bhaskar has made a series of concessions to Interpretivism that are quite unnecessary, 'such that his position would be better described as a form of anti-naturalism, rather than as a naturalism, however qualified' (Benton 1981: 19). In other words, Bhaskar is not naturalistic enough.

Layder (1985b) and Fay (1990) have also offered critiques of Bhaskar's *critical realism*. Layder's main point is that the strong emphasis on ontology borders on dogmatic rather than theoretical claims about reality. 'Bhaskar is implicitly claiming there is an extra-theoretical givenness to the structures of reality which, as a result, determines our knowledge of them' (Layder 1985b: 268). Knowledge has to mirror the features of this a-theoretical reality. While Bhaskar accepted that knowledge is transient, whereas reality is intransient, Layder claimed that our ontological claims must also be transient because they are theoretical. Even though we may believe in a real, external world, we have no direct access to it; we can only theorize about it, and our theories may not be accurate. Fay has made similar claims by arguing that Bhaskar's *critical realism* is a form of essentialism. The idea of an underlying causal structure at work behind surface phenomena suggests that reality is unitary and invariant. This 'encourages the belief that there is only One True Picture which corresponds with this pre-existing, pre-formed reality' (1990: 38).

King (1999) has taken some of these criticisms a bit further, and has brought us back to the disputes between Harré and Bhaskar. He focused on Bhaskar's dualistic social ontology, which, he argues, entails two antinomies. Bhaskar has argued, first, for the existence of prior social structures *and* for meaning-giving individuals who re-create and transform these social structures, and, second, for social action to be regarded as intentional *and* as having non-intentional material features. 'In maintaining the existence of intransitive structure which is irreducible to individuals, Bhaskar paradoxically argues that society is dependent on individuals and yet also independent of them and that social action is both intentional and unintentional or objective' (King 1999: 269).

Bhaskar's solution to the first paradox was to argue that society, or social structures, consist not just of individuals but of emergent structural properties: society has features that cannot be predicted from the properties of individuals. Bhaskar used the notion of 'emergence' to explain the fact that social reality, which precedes and is definitely more than the individuals involved, is, nevertheless, simultaneously only the result of individual action (King 1999: 270).[8] King has argued that this appeal to emergence disguises a relapse into sociological reification, 'which fails to recognise that the properties of networks of interacting individuals, while certainly more than any individual in them, cohere exactly with those networks. What Bhaskar has regarded as emergent, is nothing more than "the activities of individuals interacting with each other, often in other times and other places"' (King 1999: 283). Hence, 'society consists only of individuals in complex networks of interaction with other individuals stretching across time and space which do give rise to distinctive social realities but which realities are always reducible to all those individuals who produced them together' (King 1999: 284). This is an argument from the hermeneutic tradition, which insists that 'individual action, even of the most personal sort, is only explicable in the context of the existence of a wider network of social relations through which each individual is constituted as a social agent' (King 1999: 274). Individuals acting together constitute a different phenomenon from individuals acting alone. Hence, King takes us back to the kind of arguments that Harré used against Bhaskar's position (see chapter 5).

The second paradox is an extension of the first. Bhaskar has argued that social action is always intentional – individuals must interpret their actions and social relations – *and* that social action can be understood with reference to pre-existing, external, material structures. King has responded to this paradox by arguing that the reality which confronts people in the present is the product of a myriad of other individuals acting meaningfully in the past. While this reality confronts people in the present as real, and involves a material aspect that influences the kind of life we can lead, and it is independent of *my* interpretation of it, it is the result of other individuals interacting meaningfully with each other (King 1999: 282). King has claimed that hermeneutics does not deny 'the actuality and materiality of social relations; it simply maintains that those social phenomena which involve material reality are inevitably meaningful' (1999: 284). They do not constitute an independent reality that can be interpreted; they are the result of past and present interpretations. Hence, King has confronted what he has regarded as Bhaskar's paradoxes, and claims to have resolved them from a hermeneutic point of view.[9]

Contemporary Hermeneutics

Classical and Contemporary Hermeneutics have their critics and supporters amongst the other RPs. They are anathema to adherents of Positivism and Critical Rationalism as, for the most part, they do not accept the notions of objectivity and truth that these versions of science espouse. There is, of course, a close affinity between Hermeneutics and Interpretivism, Ethnomethodology and Structuration Theory. As Habermas's version of Critical Theory had its foundation in Hermeneutics, and identified the *historical-hermeneutic* sciences as being concerned with understanding, it is not going to be attacked from that direction. Similarly, Social Realism's concerns are primarily with the deficiencies of Positivism and Critical Rationalism, and it has affinities with Interpretivism. However, as we have seen, there are tensions between *critical realism* and Hermeneutics. As Structuration Theory owes a considerable debt to Hermeneutics and its derivatives, Interpretivism and Ethnomethodology, its only reaction has to do with the versions of Hermeneutics from which it has drawn. While none of the branches of Feminism lay claim to Hermeneutics as a foundation, those with a postmodern sympathy are unlikely to regard at least some parts of Hermeneutics as a problem. Rather, it is possible to find affinities with its epistemology. Therefore, Hermeneutics has not been a focus of critical attention from the more recent RPs. Reactions to Gadamer's and Ricoeur's versions of Contemporary Hermeneutics appear to be rather muted.

As with Interpretivism and Feminism, much of the debate about Hermeneutics has come from within the tradition. Successive contributors have endeavoured to correct or improve on the ideas of their forerunners, and, of course, there has been considerable critical dialogue between the supporters of its two traditions. In so far as Hermeneutics has contributed to the development of other RPs, it is open to some of the criticisms that have been levelled at them.

Structuration Theory

The magnitude of the task that Giddens has attempted in rethinking modern social theory, the range of the territory traversed, and the ontological position adopted have created abundant scope for critics of various theoretical and philosophical persuasions to find something to debate. It is neither possible nor necessary to attempt to review the extensive range of Giddens's work; there is already a thriving industry working on this. In addition to the numerous reviews of his many books, more recent contributions include I. J. Cohen 1989; Held and Thompson 1989; Clark et al. 1990; Bryant and Jary 1991; Craib 1992; and Meštrović 1998.

The discussion here will be confined mainly to points that have a direct bearing on methodological issues.

Many authors have argued that the central concepts in Giddens's scheme – *structure, structuration* and *duality of structure* – are ambivalent and inadequately developed (Dallmayr 1982); that they are abstract and lack empirical examples (Layder 1981); that the notion of rules and resources as the basis of structure generates confusion and obscures important issues (Thompson 1984, 1989); that there is no allowance for negotiation of rules, which still imply an external force acting on people (Bauman 1989); that emphasis on the enabling character of structure has underplayed the role of structural constraints (Thompson 1984, 1989); that the relation between action and structure is one of tension rather than duality; and that the conceptualization of time and space is inadequate (Gregory 1989). Furthermore, it is argued that the theory does not come to terms with the fact that structural constraints derive from prior, relatively enduring inequalities of power within groups to which individuals belong, and this determines their relative bargaining or negotiating strengths (Layder 1985a); it under-rates the role of domination as a prior structure (Clegg 1979).

In spite of the extent to which Giddens's work has been reviewed, few authors have specifically addressed the issue of the relation between Structuration Theory and social research (see, e.g., Thrift 1985; I. J. Cohen 1989; Gregson 1989). Perhaps this is not surprising, considering that Giddens devoted comparatively little attention to it himself. In addition, those who have reviewed his work have been interested primarily in theoretical and philosophical issues. Some authors, however, have considered its practical implications. Bryant (1991) has discussed the broader issue of its relevance to applied or policy-oriented sociology, and others have considered the extent to which it can be considered a critical theory (see, e.g., I. J. Cohen 1989; Gregson 1989; Kilminster 1991).

Gregson (1989) has argued that the issue of the relevance of Structuration Theory to empirical research is important on two grounds: first, if it is unable to illuminate and explain social life, it will have failed to fulfil the main objective of social science; and, secondly, given Giddens's commitment to a critical social science, in order for it to offer a process of social transformation, it must be able to relate to what happens 'out there'. She has taken issue with Giddens's insistence that Structuration Theory has something to offer the social researcher other than an ontological framework.

She went on to argue that Structuration Theory should be regarded as second-order theory (or meta-theory), as its concerns are with conceptualizing the general constituents of human society rather than theorizing the unique. Therefore, it would be unrealistic to expect Structuration Theory to have any direct relevance to social research. However, Giddens did not accept this distinction between first-order and second-order theory, though he did acknowledge a distinction between 'theory' as a generic category and 'theories' as explanatory generalizations. In short, Giddens has accepted that Structuration Theory is a 'theoretical perspective' (RP), but he considered 'theory' (RPs) to be as important as 'theories' in social science (Giddens 1989: 295).

In spite of his insistence on the relevance of Structuration Theory to social research, Giddens has argued that there is no obligation on the social researcher to use the concepts of his theory in preference to those of ordinary language. Its concepts are to be regarded as sensitizing devices to be used in a selective way in thinking about or interpreting research findings (Giddens 1989: 296). He went even further in proposing that it is not necessary to 'bother with cumbersome notions like "structuration" and the rest if first-rate social research can be done without them' (1984: 326). Thrift (1985) has expressed his disappointment in this 'take it or leave it' argument.

As a result of the criticisms of the usefulness of Structuration Theory for social research, Giddens has proposed what a structurationist programme of research might look like. First, 'it would concentrate on the orderings of institutions across time and space, rather than taking as its object the study of "human societies"'. Secondly, it would analyse the regularities in social practices, i.e. social institutions, and the ways in which they change through time. Thirdly, it 'would be continuously sensitive to the reflexive intrusions of knowledge into the conditions of social reproduction'. And, finally, it 'would be oriented to the impact of its own research upon the social practices and forms of social organization it analyses' (Giddens 1989: 300).

Another area of criticism concerns the extent to which Structuration Theory can be regarded in any sense as critical theory. Giddens has argued that social research is closely tied to social critique, and that 'structuration theory is intrinsically incomplete if not linked to a conception of social science as critical theory' (1984: 287).[10] However, Giddens's claims about the critical nature of Structuration Theory have been disputed by a number of authors (see, e.g., Gregson 1989 and Bernstein 1989).

Feminism

Feminism has been the arena in which some of the liveliest and best-informed discussions of contemporary issues in the philosophy of science and social science have been conducted.[11] Feminist researchers in the social sciences have been leading the way in putting into practice the implications of these debates and in moving feminist research totally or partially in a postmodern direction.

The initial attack by feminist scientists on male-dominated natural and social sciences tended to alienate orthodox male researchers. More recent developments in feminist methodology have further exacerbated the relationship with mainstream social scientists. However, at least in the areas of the world in which I have worked, mainstream social science, or at least sociology, is now dominated by women, most of whom are feminists of some kind, together with some 'reconstructed' males. Feminism is gradually becoming the mainstream in many academic sociology departments, or is at least accepted as a legitimate specialization in the discipline.

It was inevitable that the responses of orthodox social scientists to early Feminism tended to be defensive. As the methodological commitments of Feminism have become more clearly articulated, and as the debates with traditional views of science have become more sophisticated, reactions to it have been along similar lines to those RPs that share similar views. Topics such as objectivity, truth, value freedom and the relationship between researcher and researched are relevant to debates between most RPs.

As sufficient space has already been devoted to these issues, and as the methodological debates within Feminism were reviewed in chapter 5, they will not be rehearsed again here.

Review of Some Major Dilemmas

Another way of reviewing and comparing the ten RPs is to return to some of the dilemmas that were introduced in chapter 2. Six closely related issues are discussed.

Lay language and social science discourse

A central question for the practitioner, and particularly for one who adopts an Interpretive approach, is what position to adopt on the relationship between lay language (concepts, meanings and accounts) and social science discourse (concepts and theories). Positivism and Critical Rationalism both explicitly reject any role for lay language in either description or explanation. On the other hand, Social Realism (in its interpretive foundations), Interpretivism and Structuration Theory place great emphasis on its importance. However, within the broad spectrum of positions included within Interpretivism, there are disagreements about the status of lay language and how it is to be used.

The positivist position is well illustrated in Durkheim's (1964) injunction that the sociologist should formulate new concepts at the outset and not rely on lay notions. In his quest to establish social facts as the subject matter of sociology, and to achieve what he regarded as objective methods, Durkheim argued that it was necessary to leave aside any reference to the ways in which social actors conceptualize their world. For him, everyday concepts include fallacious ideas, and merely express the 'confused impressions of the mob'.

One view of language is as a medium for describing the world. It is assumed that the metalanguage of science can improve upon and correct the inadequacies of lay language. Science is seen to demystify common-sense beliefs about the natural world by offering more profound explanations than are available in everyday knowledge. An alternative view states that description is only one of the things that language is capable of; it is also the medium of social life, and is therefore a central element in all the activities in which social actors engage. As a result, it is necessary for social scientists to build their accounts of social life on lay language. Giddens has argued that all social science 'is parasitic upon lay concepts' (Giddens 1987: 19).

It is evident from the discussion of the Abductive RS that this relationship has been approached from many directions. For some writers, ordinary language, concepts and meanings are all there is; even the language of science is just another ordinary language. However, those who accept a role for lay language in the construction of social theory differ in a number of important ways: on the issue of retaining the integrity of the phenomenon; on the extent to which they are prepared to generalize from and thus decontextualize sociological accounts; on the extent to which explanation is the aim; and on whether it is appropriate to correct or interpret lay accounts in the light of sociological theory. It is to these issues that we now turn.

Retaining the integrity of the phenomenon

Schütz, Winch, Douglas, Rex and Giddens are in basic agreement about the importance of, and the 'logic' for, generating technical language from lay language; that it is necessary for social scientists to first grasp lay concepts, to penetrate hermeneutically the particular form of life; and that social theories need to be built on everyday concepts. But they appear to take rather different positions on the critical issue of whether these theories can also incorporate concepts that are not derived from lay concepts: that is, the extent to which 'foreign' concepts and theoretical ideas can be imported into the social scientists' account before it ceases to be authentic and useful. Schütz and Douglas wished to anchor sociological discourse to lay discourse by insisting that social actors should be able to recognize themselves and others in sociological accounts, thus retaining the integrity of the phenomenon. However, this was not seen to inhibit their desire to produce decontextualized social theories. Winch also wished to keep the two languages tied together, but was prepared to allow the use of technical concepts that are not derived directly from lay concepts. His main restriction was that such concepts must at least be based on a previous understanding of lay concepts. The interest of both Rex and Giddens in social contexts and structures, which are beyond the direct experience or even awareness of social actors, requires the use of at least some elements of technical language that are independent of lay language.

Schütz's postulate of adequacy appears to have been interpreted in different ways. Douglas (1971) preferred to use it as a rule of thumb, and Pawson (1989) regarded it as requiring a one-to-one translation of lay concepts into sociological concepts. Giddens has accepted that 'there is necessarily a reciprocal relation between the concepts employed by members of society and those used by sociological observers' (Giddens 1976a: 153), but he suggested (incorrectly, I contend) that Schütz has this relationship the wrong way around. Giddens has interpreted Schütz's postulate as meaning that 'the technical concepts of social science have to be in some way capable of being reduced to lay notions of everyday action' (1976a: 158), a position similar to that adopted by Pawson. Instead, and in fact consistent with Schütz, Giddens argued that 'the observing social scientist has to be able first to grasp those lay concepts, i.e. penetrate hermeneutically the form of life whose features he [*sic*] wishes to analyse or explain' (Giddens 1976a: 158–9).[12] At the same time, it is not necessary for these social actors to grasp the concepts that social scientists use (Giddens 1982: 13).

Decontextualizing, generalizing and explaining

Within Interpretivism, Ethnomethodology and Structuration Theory there are a variety of views as to whether it is legitimate to try to go beyond description of social actors' accounts to some kind of explanation. At one extreme,

Ethnomethodology insists that both lay accounts and sociological accounts must be considered in the contexts in which they are used. It has no interest in or need for general propositions, except in the sense of the ontological claims made about the reality of interest to it. Ethnomethodology is not interested in developing causal explanations of observed patterns of social activity. It is the manner in which social actors describe the order in their situation that is of interest.

Other writers are willing to accept some degree of decontextualizing. Winch implied an interest in such a process, and Weber, Schütz, Douglas, Rex and Giddens all explicitly aimed to achieve it. Schütz expressed this as a process of moving from the 'subjective' contexts of everyday life to the 'objective' contexts of social science. Douglas argued that while it is essential to ground our understanding of everyday life on the situations in which it occurs, it is important to recognize that there is considerable variability in the degree to which everyday knowledge is contextually determined. He argued that just as there is a tension between situational and trans-situational aspects of human existence, so there is a similar tension between the need to retain the integrity of the phenomenon and the need to produce useful knowledge about everyday life. As it is not possible to completely decontextualize this knowledge, Douglas recognized that it constitutes only partial truths.

If it is accepted that lay language can be decontextualized and generalized, at least to some degree, and particularly by the development of ideal types, then it is a small step to the development of explanations, even if these are limited in time and space. Weber, Schütz and Rex all agreed that ideal types can provide the foundation for testable propositions.

Corrigibility of lay accounts

Garfinkel regarded any attempt to correct or pass judgement on social actors' accounts as being completely inappropriate. Rex, on the other hand, argued that the social scientist should be able to give a different, competing account of social life from that offered by social actors. However, Giddens drew a distinction between 'mutual knowledge' and 'common sense', and argued that only the latter is open to correction. The largely tacit mutual knowledge upon which social actors draw to make sense of what each other says and does, and on which the social scientist draws to generate descriptions of their conduct, must be regarded as authentic and not open to correction by the social scientist. On the other hand, common sense – that is, everyday justifications and explanations – is correctable in terms of the findings of the natural and the social sciences. In any case, the relationship between this everyday knowledge and the accounts of it produced by social scientists is a shifting one. Just as social scientists adopt everyday concepts and use them in a specialized sense, 'so lay actors tend to take over the concepts and theories of the social sciences and embody them as constitutive elements in the rationalization of their own conduct' (Giddens 1976a: 159) – the *double hermeneutic*.

Bhaskar has described as the *linguistic fallacy* the claim by many Interpretivists that social actors' concepts cannot be corrected. He saw this fallacy as a failure to recognize that there is more to reality than is expressed in the language of social actors. Social actors' constructions of reality are only one element in a *critical realist* social science, rather than being its entire concern (Bhaskar 1979: 199).

Explicitly or implicitly, the researcher takes a stand on this complex issue; the choice is likely to be influenced by pragmatic, personal and contextual factors. It is important to be aware of the nature of the issue and the consequences of a particular choice.

The researcher and the researched

The RPs and their associated RSs entail different views of the relationship between social scientists and social actors, ranging from the position of detached observer to that of fully engaged participant. In the name of achieving their conception of objectivity, Positivism and Critical Rationalism adopt the extreme, detached position. Research is conducted from the 'outside', and the research methods used are standardized. The social actors' concepts and meanings are either ignored or intentionally rejected, and any hint of 'subjective' involvement on the part of the researcher is deplored.

From its initial concern with the interpretation of ancient texts, Hermeneutics has provided the foundation for the other extreme. One version has taken *verstehen* to mean that the investigator places himself or herself in the shoes of the author or social actor (Dilthey), while another version has viewed the relationship as involving the investigator in the mediation of languages (Gadamer). These alternatives are reflected within Interpretivism.

Critical Theory views the researcher and the researched as engaged in dialogic communication. The researcher is a reflective partner – a co-participant whose task is to facilitate the emancipation of the victims of social, political and economic circumstances, to help people to transform their situations and hence meet their needs and rectify deprivations.

Feminism has adopted the most extreme position on this issue, in a manifesto that provides a useful summary of the 'involved' alternative. It argues that social scientists should not be detached and impersonal, but should make use of their thoughts, feelings and intuitions as part of the research process. Social research should mediate the experiences of the researcher and the researched; it should facilitate understanding and change in their lives and situations. This manifesto also relates to the emancipatory aspects of Critical Theory and Bhaskar's *critical realism*, and places stress on participatory action research (see, e.g., Whyte 1991).

The position of Feminism on this issue has been expressed by Mies: 'The postulate of *value free research*, of neutrality and indifference towards the research objects, has to be replaced by *conscious partiality*, which is achieved through partial identification with the research objects' (1983: 122). Conscious partiality recognizes the larger social context and the researcher's place in this. It is different from mere subjectivity or empathy, as it involves a critical distance between the researcher and the researched.

Again, this fundamental issue cannot be glossed over lightly. As it has ethical and political as well as methodological components, it needs to be considered independently of other issues, and may, therefore, influence the choice of RP and RS.

Objectivity and truth

The RPs adopt different positions on this issue. The extreme absolutist position is taken by Positivism in its claim that objective knowledge can be achieved through the use of pure observation, uncontaminated by theoretical notions, and accompanied by the separation of 'facts' and 'values'. It is argued that the truth of generalizations from such observations is the result of the 1:1 correspondence between observation statements and 'reality'. Critical Rationalism also adopts this *correspondence theory of truth*, and argues that objectivity is achieved by the use of logical (deductive) reasoning to criticize false theories. While it aims to produce truths about the world, it accepts the theory dependence of observations, and it believes in the superiority of the logic of falsification. This leads to the position that scientists can never know when a theory is true, only when it is false (although even this latter claim has been challenged).

Some versions of Hermeneutics and Interpretivism provide the alternative relativistic extreme. One branch of Hermeneutics has argued that there is no objectively valid interpretation of a text or social situation; it is not possible for a researcher to stand outside history or become detached from culture. All that is possible is culturally and historically situated accounts that lead to an unlimited number of interpretations. However, when meanings in any social situation are shared by the participants, they may be regarded as being objective in the sense of being *their* reality, and *their* truth can be communicated.

By separating the transitive and intransitive objects of science, the tools for explaining reality from reality itself, *critical realism* has tried to avoid the problems of objectivity. It accepts that if a mechanism hypothesized in a model can be shown to exist and act in the manner postulated, then it must be real. But theories provide imperfect accounts of reality and can change.

Critical Theory has rejected the *objectivist illusion* that the world is made up of facts independent of the observer. Truth is not a matter of evidence from observations, but is achieved in an 'ideal speech situation' through open and equitable critical discussion. This *consensus view of truth* is founded on reason; competent people, freed from constraints and distorting influences, can be expected to achieve consensus. This capacity for rational criticism is used in the interests of human emancipation. However, some latter-day Critical Theorists (e.g. Fay) have adopted a *pragmatic view of truth*; if a theory leads to action that meets the felt needs and overcomes the privations caused by structural conflicts and contradiction, then it must be true.

Giddens addressed the issue of truth in the context of notions such as 'multiple realities' (Schütz), 'alternate realities' (Castañeda) and 'competing paradigms' (Kuhn). He distinguished between *relativism on the level of meaning*, the view that forms of life have mutually exclusive constructions of reality such that translation between these frames of meaning is logically impossible, and *judgemental rela-tivism*, which views these different realities as being distinct and logically equiva-lent, and not open to rational comparison and evaluation. While he was concerned to go beyond lay accounts in producing explanations, he accepted time and space limitations on all social theories (Giddens 1976a). The consequence of this view is that ultimate truths are impossible in social science.

The standpoint branch of Feminism has much in common with the relativistic branch of Hermeneutics, and it is in this approach that a great deal of the con-temporary debate about objectivity has taken place. Some feminists see a concern with achieving objectivity and overcoming subjectivity in science as reflecting the dualistic way in which males view the world. Instead, it has been argued that dynamic objectivity can be achieved through the use of subjective processes by which other people can be understood. This knowledge is seen to be gained from shared feelings and experiences; the use of subjectivity increases objectivity and decreases the false claims of objectivism.

Dilemmas in, and possible solutions to, this issue can be illustrated by review-ing the radical views of a biologist, Haraway (1986), in her analysis of primatol-ogy. She regarded all scientific knowledge claims as social constructions, and the concepts, theories, methods and results as historically and culturally specific. For Haraway, facts are laced with values. '[L]ife and social sciences in general, and primatology in particular, are story-laden; these sciences are composed through complex, historically specific storytelling practices. Facts are theory-laden; theo-ries are value-laden; values are story-laden. Therefore, facts are meaningful within stories' (Haraway 1986: 79). A good story is one that fits with available visions of these possible worlds. On the basis of different histories, experiences and worldviews, feminist scientists have reconstructed existing stories. The result is that the structure of a field of study like primatology can be changed radically; it is not a case of replacing false stories but of creating new ones. Haraway argued that 'feminist science is about changing possibilities, not about having a special route to the truth about what it means to be human – or animal' (1986: 81).

These aspects of Feminism have produced some contradictions; feminists want a new kind of science while at the same time recognizing the historically situated character of knowledge. While this could be seen to lead to a form of relativism, Haraway (1986: 80–1) rejected such implications in her work; one account of monkeys and apes is not as good as another; some stories are better than others. The problem is that what will count as a more accurate, fuller, more coherent story is part of the craft of constructing good stories. And all stories are related to matters of power, race, sex and class, and the struggles people have in telling each other how we might live together.

Dugdale (1990) has argued against drawing a relativist conclusion from Haraway's social constructivist position. 'Certainly social constructionism leaves no value-free or neutral position from which to make knowledge-claims. But in recognising the stakes involved in the conversion of knowledge-claims to facts, social constructivism leaves no innocent positions. It undermines the universalist perspective usually attributed to science and opens science up as a field of politi-cal struggle' (Dugdale 1990: 61).

Association between Research Strategies and Research Paradigms

The extent to which a RS shares ontological and epistemological assumptions with a RP determines the extent to which they can be used together (see table 6.1). Some RSs and RPs are very clearly associated: Positivism with the Inductive RS; Critical Rationalism with the Deductive RS; Social Realism with the Retroductive RS; and versions of Interpretivism, together with Structuration Theory, with the Abductive RS. This association is not surprising, as the division between RPs and RSs is somewhat artificial. Some RPs, such as Critical Theory, make use of a combination of RSs. In this case, it depends on whether emphasis is being given to *empirical-analytic* or *historical-hermeneutic* research. This leaves Classical and Contemporary Hermeneutics, Ethnomethodology and Feminism unaccounted for. In so far as it engages in description, Feminism uses either the Inductive or the Abductive RS. When Feminists seek to understand some social phenomenon, some form of the Abductive RS is likely to be used, particularly in Dorothy Smith's version. Because of their predominant focus on the analysis of texts, and their internal diversity, the classification of Classical and Contemporary Hermeneutics is not straightforward. However, their closest affinity is with the Abductive RS. Ethnomethodology can use only the Inductive RS.

In practice, of course, it is the researcher who decides the combination of RP and RS. The only requirement is that there should be compatibility in their ontological and epistemological assumptions.

Chapter Summary

As we have seen, none of the RPs has escaped criticism. It is not surprising that these criticisms come from proponents of other RPs, as there is no neutral ground from which it is possible to make 'objective' or independent evaluations (see, e.g., Gadamer 1989 and Kuhn 1970a). It has been argued that there are incommensurable differences between some of these RPs (see, e.g., Kuhn 1970a, and, for the

Table 6.1 Research paradigms and research strategies

Research Paradigm	Research Strategy			
	Inductive	Deductive	Retroductive	Abductive
Positivism	✓			
Critical Rationalism		✓		
Classical Hermeneutics				?
Interpretivism				✓
Critical Theory	✓	✓		✓
Social Realism			✓	✓
Contemporary Hermeneutics				?
Ethnomethodology	✓			
Structuration Theory				✓
Feminism	✓			✓

most part, this is due to their incompatible ontological and epistemological assumptions. Therefore, when a social researcher makes a choice about which RP(s) to adopt, a judgement will have to be made about the veracity of these criticisms.

Many of the criticisms discussed earlier in this chapter centre on the ontological and epistemological assumptions adopted. To the extent that a RS adopts the same assumptions, it is also open to the same criticisms. For example, the criticisms that have been made of Positivism and Critical Rationalism also apply, respectively, to the Inductive and Deductive RSs – that is, the original versions as described in chapter 3.

It should be evident by now that there is no perfect way to conduct research. Even the modified versions of the RSs cannot escape entirely the dilemmas that were raised in chapter 2 and have been further elaborated in this chapter. Hence, all four RSs will continue to have some limitations. The researcher's task is to choose the RS(s) that best fit(s) the investigation of the research problem at hand, and the RQs that express it, while at the same time recognizing these limitations.

Whereas researchers may prefer to work with only one set of ontological and epistemological assumptions, a dogmatic adherence to a single point of view can place severe restrictions on how a researcher approaches research problems. While I also have my preferences, I have found that, given the revisions made to the RSs in chapter 3, particularly to the Inductive and Deductive RSs, it is possible to be flexible and make use of all four RSs. This will involve moving between ontological and epistemological assumptions.

Further Reading

Adorno, T. W. et al. 1976. *The Positivist Dispute in German Sociology.*
Atkinson, P. 1988. 'Ethnomethodology: a critical review'.
Bernstein, R. J. 1976. *Restructuring Social and Political Theory.*
——1983. *Beyond Objectivism and Relativism.*
Bryant, C. G. A. 1985. *Positivism in Social Theory and Research.*
——and D. J. Jary. 1991. *Giddens' Theory of Structuration.*
Chalmers, A. F. 1982. *What is this Thing Called Science?*
Fay, B. 1987. *Critical Social Science.*
Giddens, A. 1977a. 'Positivism and its critics'.
Grünbaum, A. and W. C. Salmon (eds). 1988. *The Limits of Deductivism.*
Held, D. 1980. *Introduction to Critical Theory.*
Kuhn, T. 1970a. *The Structure of Scientific Revolutions,* 2nd edn.
Lakatos, I. and A. Musgrave (eds). 1970. *Criticism and the Growth of Knowledge.*
McCarthy, T. 1984. *The Critical Theory of Jürgen Habermas,* 2nd edn.
Smith, M. J. 1998. *Social Science in Question.*
Stockman, N. 1983. *Antipositivist Theories of the Sciences.*

Postscript: The Complexity Turn

Introduction

Since the publication of the first edition of this book in 1993, a major development in the social sciences has been the advent of *complexity theory*. The ideas behind *complexity theory* can be traced back to early last century, in attempts to apply systems thinking to the understanding of living systems. Systems thinking is about relationships, patterns, processes and context (Capra 2005: 33). Of course, such ideas are not new in the social sciences, but *complexity theory* has given them a radically new twist. In the process, it 'now offers the exciting possibility of developing a unified view of life by integrating life's biological, cognitive and social dimensions' (Capra 2005: 33). In fact, *complexity theory* is seen as providing a way of transcending the outdated divisions between the physical and the social sciences (Urry 2003: 18).

It seems that the idea of complexity is now everywhere in the field of knowledge; perhaps it is an idea whose time has come (Byrne 2005: 97, 98). *Complexity theory* has found its way into a wide range of academic subjects, such as economics, town planning, architecture, literary theory, history, anthropology and sociology (Thrift 1999: 39). The term 'complexity' is doing 'metaphorical, theoretical and empirical work within many social and intellectual discourses and practices besides "science" ' (Urry 2005a: 2). It refocuses our attention on system analysis, something that much of social science has either rejected or ignored since the demise of Parsonian structural functionalism in the 1970s, and it does this by overcoming earlier deficiencies and, at the same time, taking account of developments in the philosophies of science and social science over the last fifty or so years.

While *complexity theory* is primarily concerned with presenting a new scientific ontology, it also rejects the epistemology of traditional science based on notions of universal knowledge, experimental control, determinism and a linear logic of causal explanation. It offers instead explanatory accounts based on limited and contextual knowledge, open and unpredictable systems, and complex, non-linear interaction between elements that leads to emergent properties and self-organizing structures and processes. *Complexity theory* has been defined as 'the interdisciplinary understanding of reality as composed of complex open systems with emergent properties and transformational potential' (Byrne 2005: 97). We shall return to these ideas shortly.

Origins

It is a commonly held view that the precursor to *complexity theory* was chaos theory. The popular view of chaos is that it is concerned with randomness and lack of order, something to be feared for its possible consequences. However, the scientific usage 'sees chaos as containing and/or preceding order' (Byrne 1998: 16). Byrne uses 'and/or' here to reflect the point made by Hayles (1991) that there are two dominant views on this: one that order is hidden within chaos (mainly US-based) and the other that order emerges from chaos (a European view).

While *complexity theory* may have had its origins in chaos theory, there are disagreements as to how the two are now related. Lee (1997: 21), for example, has asserted that complexity is a more important theoretical concept than chaos. Cillers (1998: p. ix) has argued that while there is a widespread perception that chaos theory has played an important role in the study of complex systems, its contribution is extremely limited. Chaos theory is sensitive to the initial conditions of a system, and claims that small changes in these conditions can produce massive outcomes. This is known as 'deterministic chaos', and is captured in the classic metaphor of a butterfly's flapping its wings causing a major weather disturbance on the other side of the globe. Cillers has argued that *complexity theory* is less concerned with initial conditions, focusing instead on the huge number of interacting components and their unpredictable outcomes. Thrift (1999) appears to have accepted the view that chaos and complexity are distinctly different concepts, as evidenced by the fact that chaos theory has provided no great insights in fields such as economics, while *complexity theory* has been much more useful. He has also supported the idea that *complexity theory* subsumes the idea of chaos and gives it a second chance (1999: 61). Hence, chaos and complexity are regarded as distinctly different concepts. Chaos is seen to be totally determined by non-linear laws that amplify small changes in the initial conditions of a system into unpredictable outcomes. Complexity, on the other hand, is concerned with order that emerges from complex interactions among the components of a system based on one or more simple guiding principles. The components organize themselves without external control (Sherden 1997: 69). Sokal and Bricmont (1998: 135) see the difference between chaos and complexity theories as the former being well developed mathematically, while the latter is much more speculative.

By contrast, Byrne (1998) has used the concepts of chaos and complexity in tandem, frequently as 'chaos/complexity'. Similarly, Urry (2003) has regarded chaos and complexity as being part of one paradigm. Many writers appear to move comfortably back and forth between ideas in chaos theory and *complexity theory*. It is clear from the literature that some ideas in chaos theory are present in many of the formulations of *complexity theory*.

The complexity turn in the social sciences took off in the late 1990s, stimulated by the report of the Gulbenkian Commission on the Restructuring of the Social Sciences (Wallerstein 1996). This Commission included the Russian-born chemist and Nobel Laureate Ilya Prigogine, who, in the 1960s, developed many of the ideas that are now part of *complexity theory*. He realized that systems that are far from a state of equilibrium need to be understood in non-linear terms rather than the linear, causal logic that has dominated scientific thinking. In the 1970s, Prigogine launched his theory of 'dissipative structures' to identify open, dynamic systems that develop and evolve from states of disequilibrium. In these systems there is a close interplay between structure and flow and change (or dissipation). The dynamics of these systems are such that if they become unstable, they may reach a point where they branch off into a new form of order with new structures. These systems are able to maintain a considerable degree of order, even when they are far from a state of equilibrium.

This idea of spontaneous creation of a new order at critical points of instability, known now as *emergence*, is, according to Prigogine, a key concept for understanding all life.

> The theory of dissipative structures explains not only the spontaneous emergence of order, but also helps us to define complexity. Whereas traditionally the study of complexity has been a study of complex structures, the focus is now shifting from the structures to the processes of their emergence. (Capra 2005: 37)

It would be misleading to give the impression that social theory has been devoid of all the ideas now contained in *complexity theory*. For example, Mihata (1997) has argued that the notions of emergence and complexity were discussed by G. H. Mead (1938) in the early part of last century. And Marx 'prefigured some elements of complexity analysis, although he struggled to characterize his argument without the terminology now available' (Urry 2005b: 243).

Characteristics of Complex Systems

Complexity theory is a scientific amalgam. The chief impulse behind it is anti-reductionist; that is, it rejects the idea that explanations can be achieved by examining the elements of a system, if necessary down to the most fundamental. Instead, it argues for an understanding of the properties of a system based on the idea that they are more than the sum of the parts. Complex systems have the potential to produce unpredictable and novel outcomes from the interaction between their parts.

Various writers have discussed the characteristics of complex systems. The following are drawn mainly from Cillers (1998, 2005). They represent an ideal-typical picture that appears to be as much a set of ontological assumptions as the result of detailed investigation.

1 Complex systems are open systems; they interact with their environment.
2 They operate under conditions far from equilibrium; they require a constant flow of activity to maintain their structure and ensure their survival.
3 Complex systems have a history; they not only evolve through time, but their past has an influence on their present behaviour.

4 They consist of a large number of components, many of which may be quite simple.

5 Components can interact with many others; that is, they can influence and be influenced.

6 Interactions usually have a fairly short range, but, given the richness of the interactions, influence can be wide-ranging.

7 Some sequences of interaction will involve feedback loops, long and short as well as positive and negative; positive feedback enhances or stimulates the activity, whereas negative feedback inhibits or restricts the activity.

8 System behaviour is the result of interactions between the components, not the characteristics of the components themselves.

9 Structure is maintained, even though the components may be replaced.

10 Each element in the system is ignorant of the behaviour of the whole system; it can only act locally, and only knows what goes on there.

Cillers has illustrated these characteristics with reference to the economic system (1998: 6).

It is important to distinguish between complex and complicated systems. Some systems, such as large modern aircraft, consist of a huge number of components. If a complete description can be given of these components, the system is merely complicated. However, in complex systems, it is not possible to understand fully the interaction among the components, and the interaction between the system and its environment, by analysing its components. In addition, these relationships shift and change, often as the result of self-organization, leading to the emergence of novel features (Cillers 1998: pp. viii–ix).

Key Ideas

Complexity theory combines the ideas of system and process. These are understood by means of an array of concepts, the two most important being *emergence* and *self-organization*. The notion of *emergence* has been a persistent theme in social thought, but now it has a place in an elaborate theoretical framework.

> The concept of emergence is now most often used today to refer to the process by which patterns or global-level structures arise from interactive local-level processes. This 'structure' or 'pattern' cannot be understood or predicted from the behaviour or properties of the component units alone. (Mihata 1997: 31)

Cillers has argued that a complex system has to develop and adapt its structure in order to cope with changes in the environment. This is achieved by *self-organization*, not some kind of central control mechanism. Self-organization is responsible for the emergence of new structures and patterns of relationship between components. It is 'a process whereby a system can develop a complex structure from fairly unstructured beginnings. This process changes the relationships between the distributed elements of the system under influence of both the external environment and the history of the system' (Cillers 1998: 12).

LIVERPOOL JOHN MOORES UNIVERSITY
LEARNING & INFORMATION SERVICES

Whereas a complex system needs to respond to influences in its environment, self-organization implies internal processes. 'Components, their relationships, and change in these relationships over time are, by definition, self-organizing if no "external" factors are needed to model the change in component relationships over time' (Lee 1997: 21).

Complex systems can move forward with limited change if there are neither internal nor external disturbances. However, at some point this stable behaviour can give way to random fluctuations and the system abandons its original trajectory. 'That is, once destabilized, the system begins to fluctuate between two or more new points. The oscillation continues until it abandons its original path and takes one or more of the alternative points as its path of development' (Harvey and Reed 1994: 385). These points of change are referred to as *tipping points*, or bifurcations. Major disturbances in world climate at present, no doubt as a result of global warming, are a good example of a system experiencing increasing fluctuations. Left to follow its present path, we can but wait for the tipping point and a new trajectory.

Champions of *complexity theory* reject the use of linear logics of explanation for complex systems in favour of non-linear analysis. Traditional scientific explanations have been based on linear, causal sequences or chains. While one sequence may be connected to others, and conditions may enter into the ways in which causes produce effects, the flow is from cause to effect, with the possibility that this effect will become the cause of another effect, and so on until the phenomenon in question has been explained. Such sequences have been represented by linear equations.

While linear logic may still have limited use, most systems are not based on linear processes (Byrne 1998: 19). The recognition that systems far from equilibrium have to be described by *non-linear* equations was a crucial breakthrough in the establishment of *complexity theory*. The greater the degree to which a system deviates from equilibrium, the greater is its complexity and the need to deal with it in non-linear terms (Capra 2005: 37). A complex system is characterized not only by a high level of interaction between its components, but also by the way in which it generates outcomes that are not linearly related to the initial conditions of the system (Mihata 1997: 31).

In non-linear explanatory models, the emphasis is on interaction and feedback loops. The influence between components in a system can go in both directions at different times, and feedback iterations can change the whole system over time.[1] Feedback and feed-forward are essential features of self-organization (Lee 1997: 23). Repeated feedback or iteration enables a system 'to exhibit its emergent properties and new forms of organization' (Turner 1997: p. xv).

The Reality of the Complex

Starting with the work of Reed and Harvey (1992), a number of writers have argued that Bhaskar's *critical realism* provides an ideal philosophical ontology for the scientific ontology developed by Prigogine.

Each endorses an approach that treats both nature and society as if they were open, historically delineated systems; both assume that the particular province of reality they study is hierarchically structured and nested, yet interactively and stochastically complex. As for their respective methodologies, both are committed to non-reductive perspectives. Both assume that the real world has a built-in indeterminacy, yet each strives to achieve a rational scientific explanation which will fit the peculiar nature of its respective object. Finally, each sees nature as a self-organizing enterprise without succumbing to anthropomorphism and reification. (Reed and Harvey 1992: 369)

Reed and Harvey believe that this combination will not only 'form a powerful basis for grasping the dynamics of both physical and social systems', but will also 'offer social scientists a new way of looking at society, one that promises to profoundly alter how we think of social structure and social process' (1992: 354).

Byrne has thoroughly endorsed this view. He has asserted that the marrying of these two versions of ontology allows *complexity theory* to make very firm statements about the nature of reality (1998: 47). In addition, he has argued that this paradigm can deal convincingly with the three critical issues by which any social theory must be judged: the relation of the individual (micro level) and society (macro level); conceptualizing the relationship between agency and structure; and explaining social and structural change (1998: 46). The capacity of *complexity theory* to deal with these critical issues lies in its central concern with emergent order (1998: 48).

Complexity and Postmodernism

It is a common misconception that *complexity theory* represents some kind of post-modern science. However, Price (1997: 3–4) considers this notion a contradiction in terms. As *postmodernism* is against traditional notions of science, the complexity paradigm is incompatible with the postmodern project. He argued that while modifications are required to the classical reductionist model of science, *complexity theory* remains within some kind of scientific tradition. The complexity view is that by 'correcting inadequacies in our scientific paradigm, we may appropriately and fruitfully continue to do "science". . . . [C]omplexity is a reconstruction rather than a deconstruction of the classical science model' (Price 1997: 4).

Complexity theory is seen as steering a course between modernism and *postmodernism* by 'rejecting the former's rigid formalism and determinism and the latter's reaction and irrationalism' (Reed and Harvey 1992: 351). Perhaps most importantly for social scientists who wish to understand the social world, *complexity theory* 'confronts the subjective relativism of *postmodernism* with an assertion that explanation is possible' (Byrne 2005: 97). Byrne goes further when he argues that the linking of the philosophical ontology of *critical realism* with the scientific ontology of *complexity theory* 'should be fatal for *postmodernism* as an intellectual project' (1998: 8). However, in contrast to these views, Cillers (2005) sees *complexity theory* as having a close affinity with *postmodernism* and poststructuralism.

Cillers has insisted 'on the fruitfulness of combining *complexity theory* with post-structuralism' (1998: 136). Drawing on the work of Lyotard and Derrida, he has claimed that *postmodernism* is inherently sensitive to complexity and to the importance of self-organization, and does not imply that 'anything goes' (1998: 112–13).

Following Lyotard (1984), Cillers has contrasted the traditional view of scientific knowledge with a more general kind of knowledge, which he called 'narrative knowledge'. Traditional scientific knowledge is the property of experts and professionals who maintain an exclusive language-game. It is dependent on the competence of the researcher, not the competence of research participants or its receivers. This knowledge is cumulative, and its validity is not increased by being reported or being popular. Against this view, Cillers has argued that the criteria for useful knowledge must be more flexible; such knowledge is part of an open system, and 'cannot depend solely on the authority of either history, or the expert, to legitimate it' (1998: 130). Only those narratives that make real differences will survive. He used the following argument to claim not only that narrative knowledge is also scientific knowledge, but that scientific knowledge can be viewed as a complex system.

> The world we live in is complex. This complexity is diverse but organised, not chaotic. Descriptions of it cannot be reduced to simple, coherent and universally valid discourses. If we model complexity in terms of a network, any given narrative will form a path, or trajectory, through the network. There are [*sic*] a great diversity of such paths. The network is not only complex, but also dynamic. As we trace various narrative paths through it, it changes. However, all paths are constrained by the local structure of the network. In some places these constraints can be fairly loose, in others they can be quite tight. The fact that there are many narrative paths to follow, even between two specific points, does not imply that anything goes. All narratives are subject to some form of constraint, and some paths are ruled out. All paths share the characteristics of contingency and provisionality. For strategic reasons, certain parts of the network can be closed off and fixed. This process of 'framing' is a necessary part of scientific inquiry, but the knowledge hereby produced remains relative to that specific frame and cannot be generalised in either a temporal or spatial sense. (Cillers 1998: 130)

Cillers supported his argument by examining the work of a number of writers whose views are similar to those derived from Lyotard (1984), Blackwell (1976), Churchland (1984, 1989), Rouse (1990) and Hesse (1992). In later work, the conclusion he has drawn from the relationship between *postmodernism* and *complexity theory* is that even though we cannot know complex things completely (Cillers 2002), we can still make strong knowledge claims. However, since these claims are limited, we need to be modest about them. 'In order to open up the possibility of a better future we need to resist the arrogance of certainty and self-sufficient knowledge. Modesty should not be a capitulation, it should serve as a challenge – but always first as a challenge to ourselves' (Cillers 2005: 265).

Complexity and Research

In the social sciences, *complexity theory* has remained largely a metaphorical device, a set of ontological assumptions. A major exception has been the work of Byrne, especially his book *Complexity Theory and the Social Sciences* (1998). He has argued that 'complexity must become more than a metaphorical apparatus in social science and this can only happen if the complexity frame of reference shapes the actual tools of investigative social science themselves' (Byrne 2005: 96). Initially, Byrne (1998) turned to conventional quantitative tools, such as the contingency table, and more sophisticated tools, such as cluster analysis and correspondence analysis. He has applied *complexity theory* to substantive areas, such as hierarchical spaces, health and illness, education, and urban governance. More recently (Byrne 2005), he has advocated the use of case-based methods and a reconfigured version of comparative analysis. He accepted that knowledge gained by the use of these methods must be regarded as local, though not relative; socially constructed, but not reified – all of which is consistent with *critical realism*. He now has a preference for methods that engage research participants in dialogue 'rather than the decomposition of the complex social through analysis based on the reification of variables' (Byrne 2005: 99). I cannot agree more, having argued against the latter many years ago (Blaikie 1977, 1978).

Byrne regards cases as complex systems that are themselves 'nested in, have nested within them, and intersect with other complex systems. So, for example, a city-region is nested within global and national systems and has nested within it neighbourhoods, households and individuals' (Byrne 2005: 105). Different methods of research and analysis may be required for each level in such a set of complex systems.

Byrne has also been a major advocate of the use of *complexity theory* in applied social research, particularly as an accompaniment to reflexive participatory social research (2005: 98). A special issue of the e-journal *Journal of Social Issues* (2001) was devoted to the topic, 'Complexity Science and Social Policy'. The contributions have relevance to the conduct of social research from a complexity perspective.[2]

Conclusion

Is *complexity theory* the way forward out of the morass of competing research paradigms in the social sciences? Some writers argue that it is (see, e.g., Byrne 1998; Cillers 1998; Urry 2003). As we have seen, some disciples of *critical realism* have rejoiced in the way their paradigm can be elaborated through its integration with *complexity theory* (Reed and Harvey 1992; Byrne 1998; Harvey 2002). Some of these writers, and others, see in *complexity theory* an answer to what they regard as the troubling anti-scientific doctrines of *postmodernism*. Certainly, *complexity theory* is far more revolutionary than *postmodernism*. This confidence in the future of social science, perhaps all sciences, based on *complexity theory* was clearly stated ten years ago.

> Probably not since victory was seized in the bloody and hard-won battle to displace the Earth from the center of the physical solar system (and even the universe) has a set of ideas and the accompanying mathematics been so likely to change the nature of how we see everything in the cosmos, and every individual in the cosmos. (Eve, Horsfall and Lee 1997: p. xxxii)

If there were to be a further edition of this book in another ten years or so, I wonder what Research Paradigm would be advocated as the answer to all our methodological problems then. The eminent Cambridge scientist Stephen Hawking is reputed to have said: 'I think the next century [meaning the twenty-first] will be the century of complexity.' Perhaps *complexity theory* will be with us for some time to come, at least for analysis where the notion of social system is relevant.

Further Reading

Byrne, D. 1988. *Complexity Theory and the Social Sciences.*
——2005. 'Complexity, configurations and cases'.
Capra, F. 2002. *The Hidden Connections.*
——2005. 'Complexity and life'.
Cillers, P. 1988. *Complexity and Postmodernism.*
——2005. 'Complexity, deconstruction and relativism'.
Eve, R. A., S. Horsfall and M. E. Lee (eds). 1977. *Chaos, Complexity and Sociology.*
Harvey, D. and M. H. Reed. 1994. 'The evolution of dissipative social systems'.
Reed, M. H. and D. Harvey. 1992. 'The new science and the old: complexity and realism in the social sciences'.
Thrift, N. 1999. 'The place of complexity'.
Urry, J. 2003. *Global Complexity.*
——2005a. 'The complexity turn'.
——2005b. 'The complexities of the global'.

Notes

Chapter 1 Major Choices in Social Enquiry

1 For a more elaborate discussion of RQs, and their association with research objectives, see Blaikie (2000: ch. 3).
2 Some readers will no doubt be able to add to this list and may be concerned that their favourite paradigm is missing. I have chosen to review these ones on the ground that, in my view, they have had the greatest relevance to the majority of social science researchers.
3 To help to identify the ontological and epistemological categories, note that the former end with 'ist', the latter with 'ism'.
4 As we shall see, this concept, and its companions 'objective' and 'objectivity', are extremely contentious. For the proponents of *empiricism*, objective observations and measurements are essential for the production of true knowledge. Other epistemologies regard objectivity as either problematic or unachievable.

Chapter 2 Major Dilemmas in Social Enquiry

1 There is another use of the term *naturalism* that is quite distinct from the one discussed here. It refers to social research that takes place in real-world settings where the researcher attempts to discover and understand a social world without imposing social scientific concepts and theories on it (see Lincoln and Guba 1985).
2 For similar reviews see Nagel (1961) and Runciman (1969).
3 This view will be challenged in the Postscript.
4 See, e.g., Winch (1958), Friedrichs (1970),Douglas (1971), Gouldner (1971), Filmer et al. (1972), Giddens (1974), (1976a), Fay (1975), Keat and Urry (1975, 1982), Ritzer (1975), Bernstein (1976, 1983), Benton (1977), Hindess (1977), Bhaskar (1979), Stockman (1983), Johnson et al. (1984) and Habermas (1987).
5 See Williams and May (1996: ch. 5) for a useful overview of some of the positions in the debate, and Williams (2005) for a more detailed discussion.

Chapter 3 Advancing Knowledge Using Four Research Strategies

1 'Observation' or 'experience' is not restricted to what can be perceived directly by the human senses. It includes the use of machines and other instruments that extend the senses, the readings from which can be inspected and interpreted.

2   There is some dispute amongst philosophers as to whether Bacon's method is strictly inductive. See, e.g., Harré (1972: 38) and O'Hear (1989: 12).
3   The following discussion of Bacon's ideas is drawn mainly from Quinton (1980) and O'Hear (1989).
4   See Giddens (1976a: 132) for a useful summary of Durkheim's position.
5   See Blaikie (2003: chs 3 and 4), for an elaboration of these levels of analysis.
6   What follows is based mainly on Wallace's earlier work (1971). However, a more elaborate scheme, which distinguishes between the processes involved in both 'pure' and 'applied' science, can be found in his later work (Wallace 1983).
7   For an example of this, see Research Design 2 in Blaikie (2000: ch. 8).
8   For such a discussion, see the 1993 edition of this book, pp. 170–2.
9   For more recent expositions of the method, see B. A. Turner (1981), Strauss (1987), Strauss and Corbin (1990, 1998).
10   I have been involved, directly or indirectly, in the supervision of all this research.
11   Chapters 4 and 7 of Blaikie (2000) include a parable about what it might be like for social scientists from outer space using the four RSs to make sense of life on Earth, and in chapter 8 there are four sample research designs each of which uses one of the RSs.

Chapter 4 Classical Research Paradigms

1   The division between classical and contemporary RPs is based on writings that roughly precede and follow the middle of last century.
2   In much of the literature, the concept of 'positivism' is used to refer to any natural science methods that have been adopted in the social sciences, with the result that Positivism and Critical Rationalism are usually grouped together. A major exception is Guba (1990a), who distinguished between positivism and post-positivism.
3   For a detailed discussion of Whewell's work see Butts (1968, 1973).
4   The outline of the hermeneutic tradition given here is based mainly on Palmer (1969), Outhwaite (1975), Makkreel (1975), Linge (1976), Rickman (1976, 1979, 1988), Bauman (1978), Thompson (1981a, 1981b), Betanzos (1988) and Gadamer (1989).
5   It is important to recognize that Weber's concept of *action* is not a new term for behaviour. Action is behaviour and motives brought together: behaviour is observed, and motives are inferred.
6   This association between occupation and religion now appears to be much less evident in most societies.
7   See S. P. Turner (1980 for a useful review and critique of Winch's position.

Chapter 5 Contemporary Research Paradigms

1   For summaries of Habermas's theory of cognitive interests, see Keat and Urry (1975: 223–4), Giddens (1977b: 137–41), Held (1980: 255–6), Thompson (1981a: 82–4), Thompson and Held (1982), Bubner (1982: 46), and Outhwaite (1987: 81. For critical reviews, see Bernstein (1976: 173–225) and McCarthy (1984: 53–91).
2   This is only one of Garfinkel's definitions of Ethnomethodology. Filmer (1972) has discussed four of them.
3   Garfinkel used the notion of 'member', rather than 'individual' or 'social actor', to emphasize the collective nature of the work that goes into producing social facts and making social life orderly and meaningful. He was interested in the competencies of bona fide 'collectivity members'.
4   For another recent review, see Baert (2005: ch. 4).

5   Critical realism is not Bhaskar's label. It combines two of his own: 'transcendental realism' for his philosophy of science, and 'critical naturalism' for his natural science of society.

6   This is clearly evident in their debate on 'Critical realism and ethnomethodology' in Bhaskar (2002).

7   It is important to note that Giddens's view of social structure is very different from Bhaskar's and more like Harré's (Varela and Harré 1996).

8   Keat and Urry (1975, 1982) and Giddens (1977a) have argued that the natural sciences are also concerned with 'understanding' or 'interpretation' in so far as communication occurs between members of natural scientific communities. However, this use of 'understanding' is misleading, as the relationship between the members of these communities and their objects of study is monologic, not dialogic. These objects cannot participate in the relationship that scientists have with them (Stockman 1983: 210–11).

9   For a detailed critique of androcentricism in psychology, see Sherif (1987).

10 The methodological debates in the social sciences in recent decades, particularly those initiated by feminist methodologists, have gone some way to ameliorating these deficiencies. The fact that women are now very well represented, if not over-represented, in academic sociology in many countries has no doubt also contributed. Nevertheless, many of these criticisms still have relevance.

11 As we shall see, Harding (1993) later subdivided feminist empiricism into two versions: 'spontaneous' and 'philosophical'.

12 Harding (1986) has reviewed the work of these four contributors to the feminist standpoint.

13 D. E. Smith (1997), however, claimed that there has been no decline of interest and use in sociology.

Chapter 6 Review and Critique of the Research Paradigms

1   For discussions with a social science orientation, see, e.g., Keat and Urry (1975, 1982), Hindess (1977), Bhaskar (1979, 1986), and Stockman (1983).

2   See Hesse (1974) for an alternative discussion of this issue.

3   For a review of the 'theory dependence of observations', see Chalmers (1982).

4   See Keat and Urry (1975: 46–54) for an elaboration of these and other points of criticism.

5   It is important to note that Giddens and Rex have quite different notions of 'social structure'. In this regard, Rex adopts a realist or materialist position and regards them as external to social actors. Giddens defines 'structure' as having a virtual existence in the practices and memory traces of social actors; it consists of the semantic and moral rules, and the material and non-material resources, that social actors have at their disposal.

6   In the context of the positivist dispute in German sociology, Adorno et al. (1976) and Albert (1976a, 1976b) have offered a critique of Habermas's Critical Theory from the point of view of Critical Rationalism.

7   As van Fraassen directed his attack at J. J. C. Smart's (1963) formulation of scientific realism, and did not refer to either Harré or Bhaskar, his critique must be viewed in the light of their precursors.

8   This notion of 'emergence' is central in 'complexity theory', which we will encounter in the Postscript.

9   For critical discussions of Bhaskar's more recent work, see Dean, Joseph and Norrie (2005).

10 See comments on this topic in ch. 5.

11 The comments in the first three paragraphs here are based on an overall familiarity with the literature and personal experience in six academic social science departments in five countries over the past forty or so years.

12 For a critical discussion of Giddens's position, see Bauman (1989: 47–8).

Postscript: The Complexity Turn

1 Feedback is important in chaos theory, and complex interaction in *complexity theory*.
2 See particularly the contributions of Medd (2001), Byrne (2001), Williams (2001) and Harvey (2001). For example, Williams has applied complexity ideas to policy research on homelessness, and came to the conclusion that a rethinking of traditional methods of explanation and prediction, particularly in this kind of research, is required. This special issue concludes with a set of challenging discussion questions.

References

Abbagano, N. 1967. 'Positivism', in P. Edwards (ed.), *The Encyclopedia of Philosophy*, Vol. 6, pp. 414–19. New York: Macmillan.

Adorno, T. W., H. Albert, R. Dahrendorf, J. Habermas, H. Pilot and K. R. Popper. 1976. *The Positivist Dispute in German Sociology*. Translated by G. Adey and D. Frisby. London: Heinemann.

Albert, H. 1976a. 'The myth of total reason: dialectical claims in the light of undialectical criticism', in T. W. Adorno et al., *The Positivist Dispute in German Sociology*, pp. 163–97. London: Heinemann.

——1976b. 'Behind positivism's back? A critical illumination of dialectical digression', in T. W. Adorno et al., *The Positivist Dispute in German Sociology*, pp. 226–57. London: Heinemann.

Alcoff, L. and E. Potter (eds). 1993. *Feminist Epistemologies*. New York: Routledge.

Alvesson, M. 2002. *Postmodernism and Social Research*. Buckingham: Open University Press.

——2004. 'Postmodernism', in M. S. Lewis-Beck, A. Bryman and T. F. Liao (eds), *The SAGE Encyclopedia of Social Science Research Methods*, pp. 842–6. Thousand Oaks, Calif.: Sage.

——and K. Sköldberg. 2000. *Reflexive Methodology: New Vistas for Qualitative Research*. London: Sage.

Anderson, R. J., J. A. Hughes and W. W. Sharrock. 1986. *Philosophy and the Human Sciences*. London: Croom Helm.

Antonio, R. J. and D. Kellner. 1994. 'The future of social theory and the limits of post-modern critique', in D. R. Dickens and A. Fontana (eds), *Postmodernism and Social Inquiry*, pp. 127–52. London: UCL Press.

Archer, M. S. 2003. *Structure, Agency and the Internal Conversation*. Cambridge: Cambridge University Press.

——R. Bhaskar, A. Collier, T. Lawson and A. Norrie (eds). 1998. *Critical Realism: Essential Readings*. London: Routledge.

Atkinson, J. M. 1978. *Discovering Suicide*. London: Macmillan.

Atkinson, P. 1988. 'Ethnomethodology: a critical review', *Annual Review of Sociology* 14: 441–65.

Babbie, E. 1992. *The Practice of Social Research*, 6th edn. Belmont, Calif.: Wadsworth.

Bacon, F. 1889. *Novum Organon*. Translated by G. W. Kitchin. Oxford: Clarendon Press. (First published in 1620.)

Baert, P. 2005. *Philosophy of the Social Sciences: Towards Pragmatism*. Cambridge: Polity.

Balnaves, M. 1990. Communication and Information: An Analysis of Concepts. Ph.D. thesis, Royal Melbourne Institute of Technology.

Bauman, Z. 1978. *Hermeneutics and Social Science*. London: Hutchinson.

——1989. 'Hermeneutics and modern social theory', in D. Held and J. B. Thompson (eds), *Social Theory of Modern Societies: Anthony Giddens and his Critics*, pp. 34–55. Cambridge: Cambridge University Press.

——1990. 'Philosophical affinities of postmodern sociology', *Sociological Review* 38: 411–44.

Benson, D. and J. A. Hughes. 1983. *The Perspective of Ethnomethodology*. London: Longman.

Benton, T. 1977. *Philosophical Foundations of the Three Sociologies*. London: Routledge & Kegan Paul.

——1981. 'Realism and social science: some comments on Roy Bhaskar's "The Possibility of Naturalism"', *Radical Philosophy* 27: 13–21.

——and I. Craib. 2001. *Philosophy of Social Science: The Philosophical Foundations of Social Thought*. Basingstoke: Palgrave.

Berger, P. L. 1963. *Invitation to Sociology*. New York: Doubleday.

——and T. Luckmann. 1967. *The Social Construction of Reality*. Garden City, NY: Anchor Books.

Bergmann, J. R. 2004. 'Ethnomethodology', in U. Flick, E. von Kardorff and I. Steinke (eds), *A Companion to Qualitative Research*, pp. 72–80. London: Sage.

Bernard, J. 1973. 'My four revolutions: an autobiographical history of the ASA', *American Journal of Sociology* 78: 773–91.

Bernstein, R. J. 1976. *Restructuring Social and Political Theory*. Oxford: Blackwell.

——1983. *Beyond Objectivism and Relativism: Science, Hermeneutics and Praxis*. Oxford: Blackwell.

——1989. 'Social theory as critique', in D. Held and J. B. Thompson (eds), *Social Theory of Modern Societies: Anthony Giddens and his Critics*, pp. 19–33. Cambridge: Cambridge University Press.

Best, S. and D. Kellner. 1997. *The Postmodern Turn*. New York: Guilford.

Betanzos, R. J. 1988. 'Introduction', in *Wilhelm Dilthey, Introduction to the Human Sciences*, pp. 9–63. Detroit: Wayne State University Press.

Betti, E. 1962. *Die Hermeneutik als Allgemeine Methodik der Geisteswissenschaften*. Tübingen: Mohr.

Bhaskar, R. 1978. *A Realist Theory of Science*, 2nd edn. Hassocks: Harvester Press.

——1979. *The Possibility of Naturalism: A Philosophical Critique of the Contemporary Human Sciences*. Brighton: Harvester.

——1983. *Dialectical Materialism and Human Emancipation*. London: New Left Books.

——1986. *Scientific Realism and Human Emancipation*. London: Verso.

——1989. *Reclaiming Reality: A Critical Introduction to Contemporary Philosophy*. London: Verso.

——1998. *A Realist Theory of Science*, 3rd edn. London: Routledge.

—— (ed.). 2002. *From Science to Emancipation: Alienation and the Actuality of Enlightenment*. London: Sage.

Blackwell, R. J. 1976. 'A structuralist account of scientific theories', *International Philosophical Quarterly* 16: 263–74.

Blaikie, N. 1977. 'The meaning and measurement of occupational prestige', *Australian and New Zealand Journal of Sociology* 13: 102–15.

——1978. 'Towards an alternative methodology for the study of occupational prestige: a reply to my reviewers', *Australian and New Zealand Journal of Sociology* 14: 87–95.

——1981. 'Occupational prestige and social reality', in P. Hiller (ed.), *Class and Inequality in Australia: Sociological Perspective and Research*, pp. 111–30. Sydney: Harcourt Brace Jovanovich.

——1993. *Approaches to Social Enquiry*. Cambridge: Polity.

——2000. *Designing Social Research*. Cambridge: Polity.

——2003. *Analyzing Quantitative Data*. London: Sage.

—— and S. J. G. Stacy. 1982. 'The dialogical generation of typologies in the study of the care of the aged.' Paper presented at the X World Congress of Sociology, Mexico City.

——1984. 'The generation of grounded concepts: a critical appraisal of the literature and a case study.' Paper presented at the European Symposium on Concept and Theory Formation, Rome.

Blau, P. M. and O. D. Duncan. 1967. *The American Occupational Structure*. New York: Wiley.

Blishen, B. R. 1967. 'A socio-economic index for occupations in Canada', *Canadian Review of Sociology and Anthropology* 4: 41–53.

Bottomore, T. 1984. *The Frankfurt School*. London: Tavistock.

Braithwaite, R. B. 1953. *Scientific Explanation*. Cambridge: Cambridge University Press.

Brentano, F. 1972. *Psychology from an Empirical Standpoint*. London: Routledge & Kegan Paul. (First published in German in 1874.)

Brody, B. A. and N. Capaldi (eds). 1968. *Science: Men, Methods, Goals*. New York: W. A. Benjamin.

Broom, L., F. L. Jones and J. Zubrzski. 1968. 'Social stratification in Australia', in J. A. Jackson (ed.), *Social Stratification*, pp. 212–33. Cambridge: Cambridge University Press.

Brown, R. H. 1994. 'Rhetoric, textuality, and the postmodern turn in sociological theory', in S. Seidman (ed.), *The Postmodern Turn: New Perspectives in Social Theory*, pp. 229–41. Cambridge: Cambridge University Press.

Bryant, C. G. A. 1985. *Positivism in Social Theory and Research*. London: Macmillan.

——1991. 'The dialogical model of applied sociology', in C. G. A. Bryant and D. Jary (eds), *Giddens' Theory of Structuration: A Critical Appreciation*, pp. 176–200. London: Routledge.

——and D. Jary. 1991. *Giddens' Theory of Structuration: A Critical Appreciation*. London: Routledge.

Bubner, R. 1982. 'Habermas's concept of critical theory', in J. B. Thompson and D. Held (eds), *Habermas: Critical Debates*, pp. 42–56. London: Macmillan.

Butts, R. E. (ed.). 1968. *William Whewell's Theory of Scientific Method*. Pittsburgh: University of Pittsburgh Press.

——1973. 'Whewell's logic of induction', in R. N. Giere and R. S. Westfall (eds), *Foundations of Scientific Method: The Nineteenth Century*, pp. 53–85. Bloomington: Indiana University Press.

Byrne, D. 1998. *Complexity Theory and the Social Sciences: An Introduction*. London: Routledge.

——2001. 'Complexity science and the transformations in social policy', e-journal *Journal of Social Issues* 1(2) at <http://whb.co.uk/socialissues/db.htm>

——2005. 'Complexity, configurations and cases', *Theory, Culture and Society* 22: 95–111.

Capra, F. 2002. *The Hidden Connections*. London: HarperCollins.

——2005. 'Complexity and life', *Theory, Culture and Society* 22: 33–44.

Carter, B. 2002. 'People power: Harré and the myth of social structure', *European Journal of Social Theory* 5: 134–42.

——and C. New (eds). 2004. *Making Realism Work: Realist Social Theory and Empirical Research*. London: Routledge.

Chalmers, A. F. 1982. *What is this Thing Called Science?* 2nd edn. St Lucia: University of Queensland Press.

Churchland, P. M. 1985. 'The ontological status of observables: in praise of the super-empirical virtues', in P. M. Churchland and C. A. Hooker (eds), *Images of Science*, pp. 35–47. Chicago: University of Chicago Press.

——1984. *Matter and Conscience*. Cambridge, Mass.: MIT Press.

Churchland, P. M. 1989. *A Neurocomputational Perspective: The Nature of Mind and the*

Structure of Science. Cambridge, Mass.: MIT Press.

——and C. Hooker (eds). 1985. *Images of Science.* Chicago: University of Chicago Press.

Cicourel, A. V. 1973. *Cognitive Sociology: Language and Meaning in Social Interaction.* Harmondsworth: Penguin.

Cillers, P. 1998. *Complexity and Postmodernism: Understanding Complex Systems.* London: Routledge.

——2002. 'Why we cannot know complex things completely', *Emergence* 4: 77–84.

——2005. 'Complexity, deconstruction and relativism', *Theory, Culture and Society* 22: 255–67.

Clark, J., C. Modgil and F. Modgil (eds). 1990. *Anthony Giddens: Consensus and Controversy.* Brighton: Falmer Press.

Clegg, S. 1979. *The Theory of Power and Organization.* London: Routledge & Kegan Paul.

Cohen, I. J. 1989. *Structuration Theory: Anthony Giddens and the Constitution of Social Life.* London: Macmillan.

Cohen, P. S. 1968. *Modern Social Theory.* London: Heinemann.

Collier, A. 1994. *Critical Realism: An Introduction to Roy Bhaskar's Philosophy.* London: Verso.

Collins, P. H. 1997. 'Comment on Hekman's "Truth and method: feminist standpoint theory revisited": Where's the power?', *Signs* 22: 375–81.

Comte, A. 1970. *Introduction to Positive Philosophy.* Indianapolis: Bobbs-Merrill. (First published in 1830.)

Congalton, A. A. 1969. *Status and Prestige in Australia.* Melbourne: Cheshire.

Coulter, J. 1983a. *Rethinking Cognitive Theory.* London: Macmillan.

——1983b. 'Contingent and a priori structures in sequential analysis', *Human Studies* 6: 361–76.

Craib, I. 1992. *Anthony Giddens.* London: Routledge.

Crotty, M. 1998. *The Foundations of Social Research.* London: Sage.

Cuff, E. C., W. W. Sharrock and D. W. Francis. 1998. *Perspectives in Sociology*, 4th edn. London: Routledge.

Dallmayr, F. R. 1982. 'The theory of structuration: a critique', in A. Giddens, *Profiles and Critiques in Social Theory*, pp. 18–27. London: Macmillan.

Daniel, A. 1983. *Power, Privilege and Prestige: Occupations in Australia.* Melbourne: Longman Cheshire.

Dean, K., J. Joseph and A. Norrie (eds). 2005. 'Editorial: New Essays in Critical Realism', *New Formations* 56: 7–26.

Denzin, N. K. and Y. S. Lincoln (eds). 2000. *Handbook of Qualitative Research*, 2nd edn. Thousand Oaks, Calif.: Sage.

de Vaus, D. A. 1995. *Surveys in Social Research*, 4th edn. London: Routledge.

——2001. *Research Design in Social Research.* London: Sage.

Dickens, D. R. and A. Fontana (eds). 1994. *Postmodernism and Social Inquiry.* London: UCL Press.

Douglas, J. D. 1967. *The Social Meanings of Suicide.* Princeton: Princeton University Press.

——1971. *Understanding Everyday Life.* London: Routledge & Kegan Paul.

Doyal, L. and R. Harris. 1986. *Empiricism, Explanation and Rationality: An Introduction to the Philosophy of the Social Sciences.* London: Routledge & Kegan Paul.

Drysdale, M. 1985. Beliefs and Behaviours of the Community with Regard to Social Justice: An Application of the Dialogical Method. M.A. thesis, Royal Melbourne Institute of Technology.

——1996. Environment, Culture and the Experience of Nature among Australian Visual Artists. Ph.D. thesis, Royal Melbourne Institute of Technology.

Dugdale, A. 1990. 'Beyond relativism: moving on – feminist struggles with scientific/ medical knowledge', *Australian Feminist Studies* 12: 51–63.

Duncan, O. D. 1961. 'A socio-economic index for all occupations', in A. J. Reiss, O. D. Duncan, P. K. Hatt and C. C. North, *Occupations and Social Status*. New York: Free Press.

Durkheim, E. 1964. *The Rules of Sociological Method*. Glencoe, Ill.: Free Press. (First published in 1895.)

——1970. *Suicide*. Translated by J. A. Spaulding and G. Simpson. London: Routledge & Kegan Paul. (First published in 1897.)

Eve, R. A., S. Horsfall and M. E. Lee (eds). 1997. *Chaos, Complexity, and Sociology: Myths, Models, and Theories*. Thousand Oaks, Calif.: Sage.

Farganis, S. 1994. 'Postmodernism and feminism', in D. R. Dickens and A. Fontana (eds), *Postmodernism and Social Inquiry*, pp. 101–26. London: UCL Press.

Fay, B. 1975. *Social Theory and Political Practice*. London: Allen & Unwin.

——1987. *Critical Social Science: Liberation and its Limits*. Ithaca, NY: Cornell University Press.

——1990. 'Critical realism?', *Journal for the Theory of Social Behaviour* 20: 33–41.

Featherman, D. L., F. L. Jones and R. M. Hauser. 1975. 'Assumptions of social mobility research in the U.S.: the case of occupational status', *Social Science Research* 4: 329–60.

Fee, E. 1986. 'Critiques of modern science: the relationship of feminism to other radical epistemologies', in R. Bleier (ed.), *Feminist Approaches to Science*, pp. 42–56. New York: Pergamon.

Feyerabend, P. K. 1978. *Against Method: Outline of an Anarchistic Theory of Knowledge*. London: Verso.

Feynman, R. 1967. *The Character of Physical Law*. Cambridge, Mass.: MIT Press.

Filmer, P. 1972. 'On Harold Garfinkel's ethnomethodology', in Filmer et al., *New Directions in Sociological Theory*, pp. 203–34. London: Macmillan.

——M. Phillipson, D. Silverman and D. Walsh. 1972. *New Directions in Sociological Theory*. London: Collier-Macmillan.

Flax, J. 1983. 'Political philosophy and the patriarchal unconscious: a psychoanalytic perspective', in S. Harding and M. B. Hintikka (eds), *Discovering Reality*, pp. 245–81. Dordrecht: Reidel.

Friedrichs, R. W. 1970. *A Sociology of Sociology*. New York: Free Press.

Gadamer, H.-G. 1989. *Truth and Method*, rev. 2nd edn. New York: Crossroad.

Garfinkel, H. 1952. The Perception of the Other: A Study in Social Order. Ph.D. dissertation, Harvard University.

——1967. *Studies in ethnomethodology*. Englewood Cliffs, NJ: Prentice-Hall.

——1974. 'The origins of the term "ethnomethodology"', in R. Turner (ed.), *Ethnomethodology*, pp. 15–18. Harmondsworth: Penguin.

Gergen, K. J. 1994. *Realities and Relationships: Soundings in Social Construction*. Cambridge, Mass.: Harvard University Press.

Giddens, A. 1974. *Positivism and Sociology*. London: Heinemann.

——1976a. *New Rules of Sociological Method*. London: Hutchinson.

——1976b. 'Hermeneutics, ethnomethodology, and the problem of interpretive analysis', in L. A. Coser and O. Larsen (eds), *The Uses of Controversy in Sociology*, pp. 315–28. New York: Basic Books. Also published in A. Giddens, *Studies in Social and Political Theory*, pp. 165–78. London: Hutchinson, 1977.

——1977a. 'Positivism and its critics', in A. Giddens, *Studies in Social and Political Theory*, pp. 29–89. London: Hutchinson.

——1977b. 'Habermas's critique of hermeneutics', in A. Giddens, *Studies in Social and Political Theory*, pp. 135–64. London: Hutchinson.

——1979. *Central Problems in Social Theory: Action, Structure and Contradiction in Social Analysis*. London: Macmillan.

——1981. *A Contemporary Critique of Historical Materialism*. London: Macmillan.

——1982. *Profiles and Critiques in Social Theory*. London: Macmillan.

Giddens, A. 1984. *The Constitution of Society: Outline of the Theory of Structuration.* Cambridge: Polity.

——1987. *Social Theory and Modern Sociology.* Cambridge: Polity.

——1989. 'A reply to my critics', in D. Held and J. B. Thompson (eds), *Social Theory of Modern Societies: Anthony Giddens and his Critics*, pp. 249–301. Cambridge: Cambridge University Press.

——1991. 'Structuration theory: past, present and future', in C. G. A. Bryant and D. Jary (eds), *Giddens' Theory of Structuration: A Critical Appraisal*, pp. 201–21. London: Routledge.

Giedymin, J. 1975. 'Antipositivism in contemporary philosophy of social science and humanities', *British Journal for the Philosophy of Science* 26: 275–301.

Glaser, B. G. and A. L. Strauss. 1965. *Awareness of Dying.* Chicago: Aldine.

——1968. *The Discovery of Grounded Theory.* London: Weidenfeld & Nicolson.

Goldthorpe, J. H. and K. Hope. 1974. *The Social Gradings of Occupations: A New Approach and Scale.* Oxford: Clarendon Press.

Gouldner, A. W. 1971. *The Coming Crisis in Western Sociology.* London: Heinemann.

Grbich, C. 2004. *New Approaches in Social Research.* London: Sage.

Gregory, D. 1989. 'Presences and absences: time–space relations and structuration theory', in D. Held and J. B. Thompson (eds), *Social Theory of Modern Societies: Anthony Giddens and his Critics*, pp. 185–214. Cambridge: Cambridge University Press.

Gregson, N. 1989. 'On the irrelevance of structuration theory to empirical research', in D. Held and J. B. Thompson (eds), *Social Theory of Modern Societies: Anthony Giddens and his Critics*, pp. 235–48. Cambridge: Cambridge University Press.

Grünbaum, A. and W. C. Salmon (eds). 1988. *The Limitations of Deductivism.* Berkeley: University of California Press.

Guba, E. G. (ed.). 1990a. *The Paradigm Dialog.* Newbury Park, Calif.: Sage.

——1990b. 'The alternative paradigm dialog', in E. G. Guba (ed.), *The Paradigm Dialog*, pp. 17–27. Newbury Park, Calif.: Sage.

Habermas, J. 1970. 'Knowledge and interest', in D. Emmet and A. MacIntyre (eds), *Sociological Theory and Philosophical Analysis*, pp. 36–54. London: Macmillan.

——1971. *Towards a Rational Society.* Translated by J. J. Shapiro. London: Heinemann.

——1972. *Knowledge and Human Interests.* Translated by J. J. Shapiro. London: Heinemann.

——1976. 'A positivistically bisected rationalism: a reply to a pamphlet', in T. W. Adorno et al., *The Positivist Dispute in German Sociology*, pp. 198–225. London: Heinemann.

——1987. *The Theory of Communicative Action*, Vol. 2: *Lifeworld and System: The Critique of Functionalist Reason.* Translated by T. McCarthy. Cambridge: Polity.

Hacking, I. 1983. *Representing and Intervening: Introductory Topics in the Philosophy of Natural Science.* Cambridge: Cambridge University Press.

Halfpenny, P. 1982. *Positivism and Sociology: Explaining Social Life.* London: Allen & Unwin.

Hall, J. and D. C. Jones. 1950. 'The social grading of occupations', *British Journal of Sociology* 1: 31–55.

Hammersley, M. 1992. *What's Wrong with Ethnography?* London: Routledge.

Hanson, N. R. 1958. *Patterns of Discovery.* Cambridge: Cambridge University Press.

Haraway, D. 1986. 'Primatology is politics by other means', in R. Bleier (ed.), *Feminist Approaches to Science*, pp. 77–118. New York: Pergamon.

Harding, S. 1986. *The Science Question in Feminism.* Milton Keynes: Open University Press.

——(ed.). 1987a. *Feminism and Methodology.* Milton Keynes: Open University Press.

——1987b. 'Introduction: is there a feminist method?', in S. Harding (ed.), *Feminism and Methodology*, pp. 1–14. Milton Keynes: Open University Press.

——1987c. 'Conclusion: epistemological questions', in S. Harding (ed.), *Feminism and Methodology*, pp. 181–90. Milton Keynes: Open University Press.

——1990. 'Feminism, science, and the anti-enlightenment critiques', in L. J. Nicholson (ed.), *Feminism/Postmodernism*, pp. 83–106. New York: Routledge.

——1991. *Whose Science? Whose Knowledge? Thinking from Women's Lives*. Ithaca, NY: Cornell University Press.

——1993. 'Rethinking standpoint epistemology: what is "strong objectivity"?', in L. Alcoff and E. Potter (eds), *Feminist Epistemologies*, pp. 49–82. New York: Routledge. Reprinted in Harding 2004: 127–40.

——1997. 'Comment on Hekman's "Truth and method: feminist standpoint theory revisited": whose standpoint needs the regimes of truth and reality?', *Signs* 22: 382–91.

—— (ed.). 2004. *The Feminist Standpoint Theory Reader: Intellectual and Political Controversies*. New York: Routledge.

——and M. B. Hintikka (eds). 1983a. *Discovering Reality: Feminist Perspectives on Epistemology, Metaphysics, Methodology and Philosophy*. Dordrecht: Reidel.

——1983b. 'Introduction', in S. Harding and M. B. Hintikka (eds), *Discovering Reality*, pp. ix–xix. Dordrecht: Reidel.

Harré, R. 1961. *Theories and Things*. London: Sheed & Ward.

——1970. *The Principles of Scientific Thinking*. London: Macmillan.

——1972. *The Philosophy of Science: An Introductory Survey*. London: Oxford University Press.

——1974. 'Blueprint for a new science', in N. Armistead (ed.), *Restructuring Social Psychology*, pp. 240–9. Harmondsworth: Penguin.

——1976. 'The constructive role of models', in L. Collins (ed.), *The Use of Models in the Social Sciences*, pp. 16–43. London: Tavistock.

——1977. 'The ethogenic approach: theory and practice', *Advances in Experimental Social Psychology* 10: 283–314.

——1979. *Social Being: A Theory for Social Psychology*. Oxford: Blackwell.

——1983. *Personal Being*. Oxford: Blackwell.

——1986. *Varieties of Realism: A Rationale for the Natural Sciences*. Oxford: Blackwell.

——1991. *Physical Being*. Oxford: Blackwell.

——1998. 'When the knower is also the known', in T. May and M. Williams (eds), *Knowing the Social World*, pp. 37–49. Buckingham: Open University Press.

——2002a. 'Social reality and the myth of social structure', *European Journal of Social Theory* 5: 111–23.

——2002b. 'Tilting at windmills: sociological commonplaces and miscellaneous ontological fallacies', *European Journal of Social Theory* 5: 143–8.

——and P. F. Secord. 1972. *The Explanation of Social Behaviour*. Oxford: Blackwell.

Hartsock, N. C. M. 1983a. *Money, Sex, and Power*. New York: Longman.

——1983b. 'The feminist standpoint: developing the ground for a specifically feminist historical materialism', in S. Harding and M. B. Hintikka (eds), *Discovering Reality*, pp. 283–310. Dordrecht: Reidel.

——1987. 'Rethinking modernism: minority vs. majority theories', *Cultural Critique* 7: 187–206.

——1997. 'Comment on Hekman's "Truth and method: feminist standpoint theory revisited": truth or justice?' *Signs* 22: 367–73.

Harvey, D. L. 2001. 'Chaos and complexity: their bearing on social policy research', e-journal *Journal of Social Issues* 1(2) at <http://whb.co.uk/socialissues/harvey.htm>

——2002. 'Agency and community: a critical realist paradigm', *Journal for the Theory of Social Behaviour* 32: 163–94.

——and M. H. Reed. 1994. 'The evolution of dissipative social systems', *Journal of Social and Evolutionary Systems* 17: 371–411.

Hayles, N. K. 1991. *Chaos and Order*. Chicago: University of Chicago Press.

Hedström, P. 2005. *Dissecting the Social: On the Principles of Analytic Sociology*. Cambridge: Cambridge University Press.

Hekman, S. 1983. *Weber, the Ideal Type, and Contemporary Social Theory*. Notre Dame, Ind.: University of Notre Dame Press.

——1992. *Gender and Knowledge: Elements of a Postmodern Feminism*. Cambridge: Polity.

——1997. 'Truth and method: feminist standpoint theory revisited', *Signs* 22: 341–65.

Held, D. 1980. *Introduction to Critical Theory*. London: Hutchinson.

——and J. B. Thompson (eds). 1989. *Habermas: Critical Debates*. Cambridge: Cambridge University Press.

Hempel, C. E. 1966. *Philosophy of Natural Science*. Englewood Cliffs, NJ: Prentice-Hall.

Heritage, J. 1984. *Garfinkel and Ethnomethodology*. Cambridge: Polity.

Hesse, M. B. 1953. 'Models in physics', *British Journal for the Philosophy of Science* 4: 198–214.

——1974. *The Structure of Scientific Inference*. London: Macmillan.

——1992. 'Models, metaphors and truth', in F. R. Akkersmit and J. J. A. Mooij (eds), *Knowledge and Language III*, pp. 49–66. Dordrecht: Kluwer Academic Press.

Hindess, B. 1977. *Philosophy and Methodology in the Social Sciences*. Hassocks: Harvester.

Hodge, R. W., P. M. Siegel and P. H. Rossi. 1966. 'Occupational prestige in the United States: 1925–1963', in R. Bendix and S. M. Lipset (eds), *Class, Status, and Power*, 2nd edn, pp. 322–34. New York: Free Press.

——D. J. Treiman and P. H. Rossi. 1966. 'A comparative study of occupational prestige', in R. Bendix and S. M. Lipset (eds), *Class, Status, and Power*, 2nd edn, pp. 309–21. New York: Free Press.

Hollinger, R. 1994. *Postmodernism and the Social Sciences: A Thematic Approach*. Thousand Oaks, Calif.: Sage.

Homans, G. C. 1964. 'Contemporary theory in sociology', in R. E. L. Faris (ed.), *Handbook of Modern Sociology*, pp. 951–77. Chicago: Rand McNally.

Hughes, J. 1991. *The Philosophy of Social Research*, 2nd edn. London: Longman.

Husserl, E. 1964. *The Idea of Phenomenology*. The Hague: Nijhoff.

——1967. *Ideas: General Introduction to Pure Phenomenology*. London: Allen & Unwin. (First published in English in 1931.)

Inkeles, A. 1964. *What is Sociology?* Englewood Cliffs, NJ: Prentice-Hall.

Jevons, W. S. 1958. *The Principles of Science*. New York: Dover. (First published in 1874.)

Johnson, J. M. 1977. 'Ethnomethodology and existential sociology', in J. D. Douglas and J. M. Johnson (eds), *Existential Sociology*, pp. 153–73. Cambridge: Cambridge University Press.

Johnson, T., C. Dandeker and C. Ashworth. 1984. *The Structure of Social Theory: Dilemmas and Strategies*. London: Macmillan.

Jones, F. E. and F. L. Jones. 1972. 'Occupational prestige in Australia and Canada: a comparison and validation of some occupational scales', *Australian and New Zealand Journal of Sociology* 8: 75–82.

Kaplan, A. 1964. *The Conduct of Inquiry: Methodology for Behavioural Science*. San Francisco: Chandler.

Keat, R. 1971. 'Positivism, naturalism and anti-naturalism in the social sciences', *Journal for the Theory of Social Behaviour* 1: 3–17.

——and J. Urry. 1975. *Social Theory as Science*. London: Routledge & Kegan Paul.

——1982. *Social Theory as Science*, 2nd edn. London: Routledge & Kegan Paul.

Keller, E. F. 1978. 'Gender and science', *Psychoanalysis and Contemporary Thought* 1: 409–33.

——1985. *Reflections on Gender and Science*. New Haven: Yale University Press.

——1987. 'Feminism and science', in S. Harding and J. F. O'Barr (eds), *Sex and Scientific Inquiry*, pp. 233–46. Chicago: University of Chicago Press.

Kilminster, R. 1991. 'Structuration theory as world-view', in C. G. A. Bryant and D. Jary (eds), *Giddens' Theory of Structuration: A Critical Appreciation*, pp. 74–115. London: Routledge.

King, A. 1999. 'The impossibility of naturalism: the antinomies of Bhaskar's realism', *Journal for the Theory of Social Behaviour* 29: 267–88.

Kivinen, O. and T. Piiroinen. 2004. 'The relevance of ontological commitments in social sciences: realist and pragmatist viewpoints', *Journal for the Theory of Social Behaviour* 34: 231–48.

Kolakowski, L. 1972. *Positivist Philosophy: From Hume to the Vienna Circle*. Harmondsworth: Penguin.

Kuhn, T. S. 1970a. *The Structure of Scientific Revolutions*, 2nd edn. Chicago: University of Chicago Press.

——1970b. 'Logic of discovery or psychology of research?', in I. Lakatos and A. Musgrave (eds), *Criticism and the Growth of Knowledge*, pp. 1–23. Cambridge: Cambridge University Press.

——1970c. 'Reflections on my critics', in I. Lakatos and A. Musgrave (eds), *Criticism and the Growth of Knowledge*, pp. 231–78. Cambridge: Cambridge University Press.

Lakatos, I. 1970. 'Falsification and the methodology of scientific research programmes', in I. Lakatos and A. Musgrave (eds), *Criticism and the Growth of Knowledge*, pp. 91–230. Cambridge: Cambridge University Press.

——and A. Musgrave (eds). 1970. *Criticism and the Growth of Knowledge*. Cambridge: Cambridge University Press.

Lasswell, T. E. 1965. *Class and Stratum*. New York: Houghton Mifflin.

Laudan, L. 1977. *Progress and its Problems: Towards a Theory of Scientific Growth*. London: Routledge & Kegan Paul.

Layder, D. 1981. *Structure, Interaction and Social Theory*. London: Routledge & Kegan Paul.

——1985a. 'Power, structure and agency', *Journal for the Theory of Social Behaviour* 15: 131–49.

——1985b. 'Beyond empiricism? The promise of realism', *Philosophy of the Social Sciences* 15: 255–74.

Lee, M. E. 1997. 'From enlightenment to chaos: toward nonmodern social theory', in R. A. Eve, S. Horsfall and M. E. Lee (eds), *Chaos, Complexity, and Sociology: Myths, Models, and Theories*, pp. 15–29. Thousand Oaks, Calif.: Sage.

Letherby, G. 2004. 'Quoting and counting: an autobiographical response to Oakley', *Sociology* 38: 175–89.

Lewis, P. 2000. 'Realism, causality and the problem of social structure', *Journal for the Theory of Social Behaviour* 30: 249–68.

Lincoln, Y. S. and E. G. Guba. 1985. *Naturalistic Inquiry*. Beverly Hills, Calif.: Sage.

——2000. 'Paradigmatic controversies, contradictions, and emerging confluences', in N. K. Denzin and Y. S. Lincoln (eds), *Handbook of Qualitative Research*, 2nd edn, pp. 163–88. Thousand Oaks, Calif.: Sage.

Linge, D. E. 1976. 'Editor's introduction', in H.-G. Gadamer, *Philosophical Hermeneutics*, pp. xi–lviii. Berkeley: University of California Press.

Longino, H. 1990. *Science as Social Knowledge*. Princeton: Princeton University Press.

Lyotard, J.-F. 1984. *The Postmodern Condition: A Report on Knowledge*. Minneapolis: University of Minnesota Press.

Makkreel, R. A. 1975. *Dilthey: Philosopher of the Human Studies*. Princeton: Princeton University Press.

Marsh, R. M. 1971. 'The explanation of occupational prestige hierarchies', *Social Forces* 50: 214–22.

Marshall, G., H. Newby, D. Rose and C. Vogler. 1988. *Social Class in Modern Britain*. London: Hutchinson.

McCarthy, T. 1984. *The Critical Theory of Jürgen Habermas*, 2nd edn. Cambridge: Polity.

Mead, G. H. 1938. *The Philosophy of the Act*. Edited by C. W. Morris. Chicago: University of Chicago Press.

Medawar, P. B. 1969a. *Induction and Intuition in Scientific Thought*. London: Methuen.

——1969b. *The Art of the Soluble: Creativity and Originality in Science*. Harmondsworth: Penguin.

Medd, W. 2001. 'Critical emergence: complexity science and social policy', e-journal *Journal of Social Issues* 1(2) at <http://whb.co.uk/socialissues/2ed.htm>

Mehan, H. and H. Wood. 1975. *The Reality of Ethnomethodology*. New York: Wiley.

Merleau-Ponty, M. 1962. *Phenomenology of Perception*. London: Routledge & Kegan Paul.

——1964. *The Primacy of Perception: And Other Essays*. Evanston, Ill.: Northwestern University Press.

Merton, R. K. 1957. *Social Theory and Social Structure*. Glencoe, Ill.: Free Press.

Meštrović, S. G. 1998. *Anthony Giddens: The Last Modernist*. London: Routledge.

Mies, M. 1983. 'Towards a methodology for feminist research', in G. Bowles and R. D. Klein (eds), *Theories of Women's Studies*, pp. 117–39. London: Routledge & Kegan Paul.

Mihata, K. 1997. 'The persistence of "emergence"', in R. A. Eve, S. Horsfall and M. E. Lee (eds), *Chaos, Complexity, and Sociology: Myths, Models, and Theories*, pp. 30–8. Thousand Oaks, Calif.: Sage.

Mill, J. S. 1947. *A System of Logic*. London: Longman Green & Co. (First published in 1843.)

Millman, M. and R. M. Kanter (eds). 1975. *Another Voice: Feminist Perspectives on Social Life and Social Science*. New York: Anchor Books.

Moser, C. A. and J. R. Hall. 1954. 'The social grading of occupations', in D. V. Glass (ed.), *Social Mobility in Britain*, pp. 29–50. London: Routledge & Kegan Paul.

Musgrave, A. 1985. 'Realism versus constructive empiricism', in P. Churchland and C. A. Hooker (eds), *Images of Science: Essays on Realism and Empiricism*, pp. 197–221. Chicago: University of Chicago Press.

Nagel, E. 1961. *The Structure of Science: Problems in the Logic of Scientific Explanation*. London: Routledge & Kegan Paul.

Nelson, L. H. 1990. *Who Knows?: From Quine to Feminist Empiricism*. Philadelphia: Temple University Press.

Neuman, W. L. 2000. *Social Research Methods: Qualitative and Quantitative Approaches*, 4th edn. Boston: Allyn & Bacon.

Nicholson, L. J. (ed.). 1990. *Feminism/Postmodernism*. New York: Routledge.

Oakley, A. 1974. *The Sociology of Housework*. Oxford: Martin Robertson.

——1981. 'Interviewing women: a contradiction in terms?', in H. Roberts (ed.), *Doing Feminist Research*, pp. 30–61. London: Routledge.

——1998. 'Gender, methodology and people's ways of knowing: some problems with feminism and the paradigm debate in social science', *Sociology* 32: 707–31.

——2000. *Experiments in Knowing: Gender and Methods in the Social Sciences*. Cambridge: Polity.

O'Hear, A. 1989. *An Introduction to the Philosophy of Science*. Oxford: Clarendon Press.

Ong, Beng Kok. 2005. The Experience of Work: A Case Study of Chinese Sales Workers in an Electronics Company and a Life Insurance Company. Ph.D. thesis, University of Science, Malaysia.

Outhwaite, W. 1975. *Understanding Social Life: The Method Called* Verstehen. London: Allen & Unwin.

——1983. 'Towards a realist perspective', in G. Morgan (ed.), *Beyond Method*, pp. 321–30. Beverly Hills, Calif.: Sage.

——1987. *New Philosophies of Social Science: Realism, Hermeneutics and Critical Theory*. London: Macmillan.

Palmer, R. E. 1969. *Hermeneutics: Interpretation Theory in Schleiermacher, Dilthey, Heidegger, and Gadamer*. Evanston, Ill.: Northwestern University Press.

Pawson, R. 1989. *A Measure for Measures: A Manifesto for Empirical Sociology*. London: Routledge.

——2000. 'Middle-range realism', *Archives Européennes de Sociologie* 41: 283–325.

——and N. Tilley. 1997. *Realistic Evaluation*. London: Sage.

Peirce, C. S. 1934. *Collected Papers*, Vol. 5. Edited by Charles Hartshorne and Paul Weiss. Cambridge, Mass.: Harvard University Press.

Phillipson, M. 1972. 'Phenomenological philosophy and sociology', in P. Filmer, M. Phillipson, D. Silverman and D. Walsh (eds), *New Directions in Sociological Theory*, pp. 119–63. London: Collier-Macmillan.

Pineo, P. C. and J. Porter. 1967. 'Occupational prestige in Canada', *Canadian Review of Sociology and Anthropology* 4: 24–40.

Polanyi, M. 1958. *Personal Knowledge: Towards a Post-Critical Philosophy*. Chicago: University of Chicago Press.

Pollner, M. 1991. 'Left of ethnomethodology: the rise and decline of radical reflexivity', *American Sociological Review* 56: 370–80.

——and R. M. Emerson. 2001. 'Ethnomethodology and ethnography', in P. Atkinson, A. Coffey, S. Delmont, J. Lofland and L. Lofland (eds), *Handbook of Ethnography*, pp. 118–35. London: Sage.

Popper, K. R. 1959. *The Logic of Scientific Discovery*. London: Hutchinson.

——1961. *The Poverty of Historicism*. London: Routledge & Kegan Paul.

——1970. 'Normal science and its dangers', in I. Lakatos and A. Musgrave (eds), *Criticism and the Growth of Knowledge*, pp. 51–8. Cambridge: Cambridge University Press.

——1972. *Conjectures and Refutations*. London: Routledge & Kegan Paul.

——1976. 'The logic of the social sciences', in T. W. Adorno et al., *The Positivist Dispute in German Sociology*, pp. 87–104. London: Heinemann.

——1979. *Objective Knowledge: An Evolutionary Approach*, rev. edn. Oxford: Clarendon Press.

Potter, J. 1996. *Representing Reality: Discourse, Rhetoric and Social Construction*. London: Sage.

Price, B. 1997. 'The myth of modern science', in R. A. Eve, S. Horsfall and M. E. Lee (eds), *Chaos, Complexity, and Sociology: Myths, Models, and Theories*, pp. 3–14. Thousand Oaks, Calif.: Sage.

Priest, J. G. 1997. A Framework to Manage Delivery of Information Systems. M. Eng. thesis, Melbourne: RMIT University.

——2000. Managing Investments in Information Systems: Exploring Effective Practice. DBA thesis, Melbourne: RMIT University.

Quinton, A. 1980. *Francis Bacon*. Oxford: Oxford University Press.

Ramazanoğlu, C. and J. Holland. 2002. *Feminist Methodology: Challenges and Critiques*. London: Sage.

Reed, M. and D. L. Harvey. 1992. 'The new science and the old: complexity and realism in the social sciences', *Journal for the Theory of Social Behaviour* 22: 351–80.

Reichenbach, H. 1948. *Experience and Prediction*. Chicago: University of Chicago Press.

Reinharz, S. 1983. 'Experiential analysis: a contribution to feminist theory', in G. Bowles and R. D. Klein (eds), *Theories of Women's Studies*, pp. 162–91. London: Routledge.

Rex, J. 1971. 'Typology and objectivity: a comment on Weber's four sociological methods', in A. Sahay (ed.), *Max Weber and Modern Sociology*, pp. 17–36. London: Routledge & Kegan Paul.

——1974. *Sociology and the Demystification of the Modern World*. London: Routledge & Kegan Paul.

Richards, S. 1983. *Philosophy and Sociology of Science: An Introduction*. Oxford: Blackwell.

Rickman, H. P. (ed.). 1976. *Wilhelm Dilthey – Selected Writings*. Cambridge: Cambridge University Press.

——1979. *Wilhelm Dilthey: Pioneer of the Human Sciences*. Berkeley: University of California Press.

——1988. *Dilthey Today: A Critical Appraisal of the Contemporary Relevance of his Work*. New York: Greenwood.

Ricoeur, P. 1981. 'What is a text? Explanation and understanding', in J. B. Thompson (ed.), *Paul Ricoeur, Hermeneutics and the Human Sciences*, pp. 145–64. Cambridge: Cambridge University Press.

Riggs, P. L. 1992. *Whys and Ways of Science: Introducing Philosophical and Sociological Theories of Science*. Melbourne: Melbourne University Press.

Ritzer, G. 1975. *Sociology: A Multiple Paradigm Science*. Boston: Allyn & Bacon.

——1996. *Modern Sociological Theory*, 4th edn. New York: McGraw-Hill.

Roche, M. 1973. *Phenomenology, Language and the Social Sciences*. London: Routledge & Kegan Paul.

Rorty, R. 1989. *Contingency, Irony and Solidarity*. Cambridge: Cambridge University Press.

Rose, H. 1983. 'Hand, brain and heart: towards a feminist epistemology for the natural sciences', *Signs* 9: 73–90.

——1986. 'Beyond masculinist realities: a feminist epistemology for the sciences', in R. Bleier (ed.), *Feminist Approaches to Science*, pp. 57–76. New York: Pergamon.

Rosenau, P. M. 1992. *Post-modernism and the Social Sciences: Insights, Inroads and Intrusions*. Princeton: Princeton University Press.

Rossi, P., R. Berk and K. Lenihan. 1980. *Money, Work and Crime*. New York: Academic Press.

Rouse, J. 1990. 'The narrative reconstruction of science', *Inquiry* 33: 179–96.

Rubinstein, R. A., C. D. Laughlin and J. McMannis. 1984. *Science as Cognitive Process: Towards an Empirical Philosophy of Science*. Philadelphia: University of Pennsylvania Press.

Runciman, W. G. 1969. *Social Science and Political Theory*, 2nd edn. Cambridge: Cambridge University Press.

——(ed.). 1977. *Max Weber: Selections in Translation*. Translated by E. Matthews. Cambridge: Cambridge University Press.

Sahay, A. 1971. 'The importance of Weber's methodology in sociological explanation', in A. Sahay (ed.), *Max Weber and Modern Sociology*, pp. 67–81. London: Routledge & Kegan Paul.

Sartre, J.-P. 1968. *Search for Method*. New York: Vintage Books.

——1969. *Being and Nothingness: An Essay in Phenomenological Ontology*. New York: Washington Square Press.

Sayer, A. 2000. *Realism and Social Science*. London: Sage.

Schütz, A. 1963a. 'Concept and theory formation in the social sciences', in M. A. Natanson (ed.), *Philosophy of the Social Sciences*, pp. 231–49. New York: Random House.

——1963b. 'Common-sense and scientific interpretation of human action', in M. A. Natanson (ed.), *Philosophy of the Social Sciences*, pp. 302–46. New York: Random House.

——1970. 'Interpretive sociology', in H. R. Wagner (ed.), *Alfred Schütz on Phenomenology and Social Relations*, pp. 265–93. Chicago: University of Chicago Press.

——1976. *The Phenomenology of the Social World*. London: Heinemann.

Schwandt, T. R. 1990. 'Paths to inquiry in the social disciplines: scientific, constructive, and critical theory methodologies', in E. G. Guba (ed.), *The Paradigm Dialog*, pp. 258–76. Newbury Park, Calif.: Sage.

——1994. 'Constructivist, interpretivist approaches to human inquiry', in N. K. Denzin and Y. S. Lincoln (eds), *Handbook of Qualitative Research*, 1st edn, pp. 118–37. Thousand Oaks, Calif.: Sage.

——2000. 'Three epistemological stances for qualitative inquiry', in N. K. Denzin and Y. S. Lincoln (eds), *Handbook of Qualitative Research*, 2nd edn, pp. 189–213. Thousand Oaks, Calif.: Sage.

Schwartz, H. and J. Jacobs. 1979. *Qualitative Sociology: A Method to the Madness*. New York: Free Press.

Seale, C. 1999. *The Quality of Qualitative Research*. London: Sage.

Seidman, S. (ed.). 1994. *The Postmodern Turn: New Perspectives in Social Theory*. Cambridge: Cambridge University Press.

Sherden, W. A. 1997. *The Fortune Sellers: The Big Business of Buying and Selling Predictions*. New York: Wiley.

Sherif, C. W. 1987. 'Bias in psychology', in S. Harding (ed.), *Feminism and Methodology*, pp. 37–55. Milton Keynes: Open University Press.

Smart, B. 1996. 'Postmodern social theory', in B. S. Turner (ed.), *The Blackwell Companion to Social Theory*, pp. 396–428. Oxford: Blackwell.

Smart, C. 1976. *Women, Crime and Criminology*. London: Routledge & Kegan Paul.

Smart, J. J. C. 1963. *Philosophy and Scientific Realism*. London: Routledge & Kegan Paul.

Smith, D. E. 1974. 'Women's perspective as a radical critique of sociology', *Sociological Inquiry* 44: 7–13.

——1979. 'A sociology for women', in J. A. Sherman and E. T. Beck (eds), *The Prism of Sex: Essays in the Sociology of Knowledge*, pp. 135–87. Madison: University of Wisconsin Press.

——1997. 'Comment on Hekman's "Truth and method: feminist standpoint theory revisited"', *Signs* 22: 392–7.

Smith, M. J. 1998. *Social Science in Question*. London: Sage.

Sokal, A. and J. Bricmont. 1998. *Intellectual Postures*. London: Profile.

Stacy, S. J. G. 1977. Parents and Children Growing Old. M.A. (prelim.) thesis, Monash University, Melbourne.

——1983. Limitations of Ageing: Old People and Caring Professions. Ph.D. thesis, Monash University, Melbourne.

Stanley, L. and S. Wise. 1983. *Breaking Out: Feminist Consciousness and Feminist Research*. London: Routledge & Kegan Paul.

Stewart, A., K. Prandy and R. M. Blackburn. 1980. *Social Stratification and Occupations*. London: Macmillan.

Stockman, N. 1983. *Antipositivist Theories of the Sciences*. Dordrecht: Reidel.

Strauss, A. 1987. *Qualitative Analysis for Social Scientists*. New York: Cambridge University Press.

——and J. Corbin. 1990. *Basics of Qualitative Research: Grounded Theory Procedures and Techniques*. Newbury Park, Calif.: Sage.

——and——1998. *Basics of Qualitative Research: Techniques and Procedures for Developing Grounded Theory*, 2nd edn. Thousand Oaks, Calif.: Sage.

Taylor, S. 1982. *Durkheim and the Study of Suicide*. London: Macmillan.

ten Have, P. 2004a. *Understanding Qualitative Research and Ethnomethodology*. London: Sage.

——2004b. 'Ethnomethodology', in C. Seale, G. Gobo, J. F. Gubrium and D. Silverman (eds), *Qualitative Research Practice*, pp. 151–64. London: Sage.

Thomas, W. I. 1928. *The Child in America*. New York: Alfred A. Knopf.

Thompson, J. B. 1981a. *Critical Hermeneutics: A Study in the Thought of Paul Ricoeur and Jürgen Habermas*. Cambridge: Cambridge University Press.

——1981b. *Paul Ricoeur: Hermeneutics and the Human Sciences*. Cambridge: Cambridge University Press.

——1984. *Studies in the Theory of Ideology*. Cambridge: Polity.

Thomas, J. B. 1989. 'The theory of structuration', in D. Held and J. B. Thompson (eds),

Social Theory of Modern Societies: Anthony Giddens and his Critics, pp. 56–76. Cambridge: Cambridge University Press.

——and D. Held (eds). 1982. *Habermas: Critical Debates*. London: Macmillan.

Thrift, N. 1985. 'Bear and mouse or bear and tree? Anthony Giddens's reconstruction of social theory', *Sociology* 19: 609–23.

——1999. 'The place of complexity', *Theory, Culture and Society* 16: 31–69.

Treiman, D. J. 1977. *Occupational Prestige in Comparative Perspective*. New York: Academic Press.

Trigg, R. 1985. *Understanding Social Science: A Philosophical Introduction to the Social Sciences*. Oxford: Blackwell.

Turner, B. A. 1981. 'Some practical aspects of qualitative data analysis: one way of organizing the cognitive process associated with the generation of grounded theory', *Quality and Quantity* 15: 225–47.

Turner, F. 1997. 'Foreword: chaos and social science', in R. A. Eve, S. Horsfall and M. E. Lee (eds), *Chaos, Complexity, and Sociology: Myths, Models, and Theories*, pp. xi–xxvii. Thousand Oaks, Calif.: Sage.

Turner, S. P. 1980. *Sociological Explanation as Translation*. New York: Cambridge University Press.

Urry, J. 2003. *Global Complexity*. Cambridge: Polity.

——2005a. 'The complexity turn', *Theory, Culture and Society* 22: 1–14.

——2005b. 'The complexities of the global', *Theory, Culture and Society* 22: 235–54.

van Fraassen, B. C. 1980. *The Scientific Image*. Oxford: Clarendon Press.

Varela, C. R. 2002. 'The impossibility of which naturalism? A response and a reply', *Journal for the Theory of Social Behaviour* 32: 105–11.

——and R. Harré. 1996. 'Conflicting varieties of realism: causal powers and the problems of social structure', *Journal for the Theory of Social Behaviour* 26: 313–25.

——2001. *Research Design in Social Research*. London: Sage.

von Wright, G. H. 1971. *Explanation and Understanding*. London: Routledge & Kegan Paul.

Wallace, W. L. 1971. *The Logic of Science in Sociology*. Chicago: Aldine-Atherton.

——1983. *Principles of Scientific Sociology*. Chicago: Aldine.

Wallerstein, I. 1996. *Open the Social Sciences: Report of the Gulbenkian Commission on the Restructuring of the Social Sciences*. Stanford, Calif.: Stanford University Press.

Weber, M. 1949. *The Methodology of the Social Sciences*. Translated and edited by E. A. Shils and H. A. Finch. Glencoe, Ill.: Free Press.

——1958. *The Protestant Ethic and the Spirit of Capitalism*. New York: Scribners.

——1962. *Basic Concepts in Sociology*. New York: The Citadel Press.

——1964. *The Theory of Social and Economic Organization*. Translated by A. M. Henderson and T. Parsons. New York: Free Press.

Whewell, W. 1847. *The Philosophy of the Inductive Sciences*, 2 vols. London: Parker.

Whyte, W. F. (ed.). 1991. *Participatory Action Research*. Newbury Park, Calif.: Sage.

Willer, D. 1967. *Scientific Sociology: Theory and Method*. Englewood Cliffs, NJ: Prentice-Hall.

Williams, M. 2000. *Science and Social Science: An Introduction*. London: Routledge.

——2001. 'Complexity, probability and causation: implications for homelessness research', e-journal *Journal of Social Issues* 1(2) at <http://whb.co.uk/socialissues/mw.htm>

——2005. 'Situated objectivity', *Journal for the Theory of Social Behaviour* 35: 99–120.

——and T. May. 1996. *Introduction to the Philosophy of Social Research*. London: UCL Press.

Winch, P. 1958. *The Idea of Social Science and its Relation to Philosophy*. London: Routledge & Kegan Paul.

——1964. 'Understanding a primitive society', *American Philosophical Quarterly* 1: 307–24.

Wylie, A. 2004. 'Why standpoint matters', in S. G. Harding (ed.), *Feminist Standpoint Theory Reader: Intellectual and Political Controversies*, pp. 339–51. New York: Routledge.

Zimmerman, D. H. and M. Pollner. 1971. 'The everyday world as a phenomenon', in J. D. Douglas (ed.), *Understanding Everyday Life*, pp. 80–103. London: Routledge & Kegan Paul.

Zimmerman, D. H. and D. L. Wieder. 1971. 'Ethnomethodology and the problem of order: comment on Denzin', in J. D. Douglas (ed.), *Understanding Everyday Life*, pp. 285–98. London: Routledge & Kegan Paul.

Index